THE AUSTRALIAN CITIZENS' PARLIAMENT AND THE
FUTURE OF DELIBERATIVE DEMOCRACY

RDD

RHETORIC AND **DEMOCRATIC** DELIBERATION

EDITED BY CHERYL GLENN AND J. MICHAEL HOGAN
THE PENNSYLVANIA STATE UNIVERSITY

Editorial Board:

Robert Asen (University of Wisconsin–Madison)
Debra Hawhee (The Pennsylvania State University)
Peter Levine (Tufts University)
Steven J. Mailloux (University of California, Irvine)
Krista Ratcliffe (Marquette University)
Karen Tracy (University of Colorado, Boulder)
Kirt Wilson (The Pennsylvania State University)
David Zarefsky (Northwestern University)

Rhetoric and Democratic Deliberation is a series of
groundbreaking monographs and edited volumes focusing
on the character and quality of public discourse in American
politics and culture. It is sponsored by the Center for Democratic
Deliberation, an interdisciplinary center for research, teaching,
and outreach on issues of rhetoric, civic engagement,
and public deliberation.

A complete list of books in this series is located in the back of this volume.

THE AUSTRALIAN CITIZENS' PARLIAMENT AND THE FUTURE OF DELIBERATIVE DEMOCRACY

Edited by

LYN CARSON

JOHN GASTIL

JANETTE HARTZ-KARP

RON LUBENSKY

The Pennsylvania State University Press | University Park, Pennsylvania

Library of Congress Cataloging-in-Publication Data

The Australian Citizens' Parliament and the
future of deliberative democracy / edited by
Lyn Carson . . . [et al.].
   p.   cm. — (Rhetoric and democratic deliberation)
Summary: "A collection of essays examining
the Australian Citizens' Parliament, a project in
deliberative democracy held in 2009. Explores its
organization, the deliberation, the flow of beliefs and
ideas, facilitator and organizer effects, and its impacts
from a variety of theoretical, empirical, and practice
perspectives"—Provided by publisher.
ISBN 978-0-271-06012-5 (cloth : alk. paper)
ISBN 978-0-271-06013-2 (pbk : alk. paper)
   1. Political participation—Australia.
   2. Deliberative democracy—Australia.
   3. Australian Citizens' Parliament (2009 :
Canberra, A.C.T.).
   I. Carson, Lyn, 1949– .

JQ4081.A88 2013
323'.0420994—dc23
2013005063

The Pennsylvania State University Press is a member
of the Association of American University Presses.

It is the policy of The Pennsylvania State University
Press to use acid-free paper. Publications on uncoated
stock satisfy the minimum requirements of American
National Standard for Information Sciences—
Permanence of Paper for Printed Library Material,
ANSI Z39.48–1992.

CONTENTS

ILLUSTRATIONS

TABLES

ACKNOWLEDGMENTS

Our heartfelt appreciation goes to the 150 Citizen Parliamentarians (CPs), without whom there would have been no Citizens' Parliament and no book. We can't name them because that was a condition of our research grant, but they know who they are, and so do we. We thank, in particular, those CPs who continued to act beyond the lifespan of the Australian Citizens' Parliament (ACP). They wrote letters to the editor and articles, and they responded to a follow-up survey a year later. Each provides an impressive example of active citizenship.

Financial support for the research presented herein came from the Australian Research Council (a generous ARC-Linkage grant—No. LP0882714), as well as from the U.S. National Science Foundation (NSF) Directorate for Social, Behavioral & Economic Sciences (Political Science and Decision, Risk and Management Sciences Programs, Grant No. 0908554). Any opinions, findings, and conclusions or recommendations expressed in this material are those of the authors and do not necessarily reflect the views of ARC or NSF.

The Australian Citizens' Parliament itself would not have been possible without considerable financial assistance from the newDemocracy Foundation, itself the recipient of funds from the Anita and Luca Belgiorno-Nettis Foundation. The newDemocracy Foundation also supported this book project by providing an online space for sharing additional materials and supplemental chapters on the ACP. In addition, Campus Living made possible the accommodation of hundreds of people.

Often forgotten in an event as massive as a Citizens' Parliament are the professionals working behind the scenes, the ones in the "engine room," doing all the logistical work: organizing flights and accommodation, venues, catering, handling honorariums and accomplishing many often-tedious but nevertheless essential organizational feats. Vickianne Lane and Joan Donohue did everything so well that we often forgot there was an engine room. That is surely a measure of their combined talents. As one tiny example, because of the extraordinary heat wave that hung over the face-to-face ACP, they were given yet another challenge, which involved assembling dozens of upright electrical fans. Vickianne and Joan, we bow down to your competence and indefatigability throughout the whole process.

Other support team members taking over diverse tasks included (because we know we have missed some): Angela Arvanitakis, Selen Ayirtman, Carmel Anderson, Catherine Baldwin, Heba Batainah, Therese Chiu, Rhys Dryzek, Gerry O'Brien, Wendy Mildren, Craig Sheedy, Kevin White, and Darren Wilkins. Volunteers were coordinated through the tireless efforts of Elizabeth Cage, and a big thank you to all. We have not forgotten, though not named, the myriad of volunteers from all over Australia and even overseas who supported this project; many of these assisted us at the early stage when we undertook regional meetings and convened World Cafés throughout Australia. Nameless here but recalled with gratitude.

We also acknowledge the efforts of Kathryn Kelly, PhD candidate and Research Associate at Australia National University (ANU), for managing the initial invitation procedure and organizing selected participants and their replacements. Thanks also go to Brian Sullivan, who customized the online platform for the ACP and provided around the clock administrative support for the online deliberators.

Throughout this book, mention will be made of the original research team: Luca Belgiorno-Nettis, Lyn Carson, John Dryzek, Janette Hartz-Karp, Ron Lubensky, Ian Marsh and Simon Niemeyer. Later this research team expanded to include John Gastil from the US. Later still, Luisa Batalha, Nicole Curato, and Andrea Felicetti joined the project at ANU.

The co-chairs Fred Chaney and Lowitja O'Donoghue provided exemplary oversight of the ACP's activities, whereas Janette Hartz-Karp and Max Hardy were its energetic co-lead-facilitators. They were ably supported by a team of table facilitators and scribes: Kath Fisher (their coordinator), Isabella Allen, Lindy Amos, Catherine Atoms, Mark Barnier, Maria Barredo, Meg Bishop, Annie Bolitho, Chad Foulkes, Graeme Gibson, Carolyn Hendriks, Rodger Hills, Leighton Jay, Dare Kavanagh, Helen Lawrence, Crystal Legacy, Maria Maguire, Siobhan Marrer, Anne Murphy, Peter Nolan, Chiara Pacifica, Rosemary Shapiro-Liu, Tom Schwarz, Stuart Waters, Ron West, Kimbra White, and Melanie White.

Data input and analysis in real time was an integral part of the process, and to this end, the theme team did a sterling job: Rachel Armstrong (coordinator), Rob Weymouth, Ed Oldmeadow, Erin Kreeger, Lindy Edwards, David Litvak and Nicci Whitehouse. Thanks to Dora Marinova for her calm competence and efficiency coordinating the daily participant reports, supported by Lyn Carson and John Dryzek, who continually updated and summarized the ever-increasing list of CP proposals. Also thanks to Eric and Kim Ling who provided the IT support for the 21st Century Dialogue, and to Les Buchanan, who orchestrated the seamless technological support for the deliberations as well as overall event management.

Research was an integral part of the ACP. Ron Lubensky coordinated the recording of conversations at every table. John Gastil headed up a vigilant team of researchers who assisted with data collection and participant observation during the ACP, so thanks go to Abigail Jeffs, Brian Sullivan, Dinny Laurence, Patrick Anderson and Gabby Higgins. For help with data preparation, thanks go to Jason Gilmore. The Opinion Charting, coordinated by Simon Niemeyer, was made possible through a team of volunteers: Katie Curchin, Lindy Edwards, Melissa Lovell, Penelope Marshall, André Bächtiger, Ben Moody, Bora Kanra, Carina Wyborn and Karolina Milewicz. Thanks also to the reporters, Leah Flint, Maria Maguire, Richard Maguire and Kate Lawrence.

The diligence of the Ombudsmen, Phillip Hart and Fiona Hollier, was greatly appreciated; fortunately, they were under-utilized. Thanks, too, for the wise counsel of the Reference Panel, which included Fred Chaney, Geoff Gallop, Kath Fisher, David Hammil, David Yencken, James Button, Simon Sheikh, Campbell Newman, Warwick Smith, Martin Krygier and Alannah MacTiernan. New ideas and discussion came from our Panel Experts, which Ian Marsh coordinated; the panel included Martin Krygier, Anthony Green, John Warhurst, Mark Yettica-Paulson, Alannah MacTiernan, and David Hammil. Thanks also to Simon Sheikh (GetUp!) for his enthusiastic blogs.

Kathy Jones was a determined media director (also a director of NewDemocracy Foundation) before, during, and after the ACP—valiantly attracting media against considerable odds (not the least of which was Australia's worst bush fires ever). Our oldest Citizen Parliamentarian was accompanied by a caregiver (her daughter, Wendy), who not only attended to her mother's needs but also kept track of the dreadful bushfires that were raging in Victoria and reported daily to the ACP. This was appreciated by all.

Kaye Shumack (University of Western Sydney), along with John Pacitto, Gerry O'Brien and Rob Leggo, tracked participants with their cameras and compiled a wonderful DVD that does credit to the ACP participants and organizers. Jesse Blackadder helped us produce a very readable handbook for others who might wish to convene a similar process. Tara Stobart (Digital & Audio Transcription Services) and her team were most capable transcribers of many, many hours of table conversations.

The ACP was endowed with a sense of gravitas: Lewis Langdon 'Knucku' heralded the arrival of the CPs into the Assembly with his didgeridoo; Shane Mortimer gave the Welcome to Country. Old Parliament House in Canberra was an extraordinary venue, and we are grateful that areas normally closed to the public (because of their heritage value) were opened because of the national and democratic nature of this event. This sense of importance was reaffirmed by the Government representatives—Senator the Hon. John Faulkner, who opened the proceedings, and Anthony Byrne, who received the ACP Report and closed the Citizens' Parliament, as well as other members of the federal parliament who came to witness the opening and closing ceremonies. We thank you all.

Finally, we thank this book's many authors and, especially, Robert Richards and the staff at the Pennsylvania State University Press for their assistance with editing, copyediting, and referencing.

Could we do this all again? With friends like these, anything is possible!

Lyn Carson, Sydney, Australia
John Gastil, State College, Pennsylvania
Janette Hartz-Karp, Perth, Australia
Ron Lubensky, Melbourne, Australia

INTRODUCTION

Lyn Carson, John Gastil, Janette Hartz-Karp, and Ron Lubensky

Democracy remains the aspiration held by governments the world over. Newly minted nations typically build popular sovereignty into their constitutions, and those nations with long-standing traditions of self-governance continue to amend their own distinct methods of assembling, informing, and aggregating their many publics.

At the same time, many critics have decried the emergence of a "democratic deficit," wherein representative government resists more direct forms of public involvement. Though representative institutions have endured for decades or even centuries in some countries, they have tended to concentrate power, particularly in those groups with particular vested interests. Citizens have been relegated to voters, responsible only for choosing decision makers, whom voters may hold accountable if a sufficiently strong opposition can form.[1]

Fortunately, with dozens of nations and thousands of municipalities experimenting with democratic reforms, there exist many opportunities to glimpse the brightest possible future for democracy. One such vision comes from Australia, a country with a proud history of political innovation. Australia led the world in the use of the secret ballot, which was known simply as the "Australian ballot" for many years. It also led the way in developing preferential voting, and women gained the vote in Australia long before women's suffrage arrived in the United States and other countries.[2] In the twenty-first century, Australia has helped lead a global movement toward a *deliberative* form of democracy.[3]

The Deliberative-Democratic Vision

As defined by scholars and refined by civic reformers, deliberative democracy is a theory of a different form of democracy. In simple terms, this conception of self-government emphasizes the need for informed, reflective, and inclusive public discussion, debate, and dialogue, with the judgments yielded from such exchanges holding sway over public policy in particular, but broader public opinion as well.

This vision shares the participatory-democratic commitment to inclusion and civic engagement and the direct-democratic demand for empowered citizens, but it balances this with representative democracy's aspiration for the sober judgment that comes most readily when a body forms to study and weigh the complexities of public issues. Though championed, at times, as an *alternative* to adversarial representative government, more often the deliberative turn shows the way to a more robust adaptation of existing government practices.[4] Whatever its inflection, deliberative-democratic reform is a normative project premised on the belief that developing a deeply considered public judgment among a diverse group of citizens can strengthen government decision making, as well as create a more politically efficacious citizenry.[5]

For some it is an ideal towards which we might aspire, for others it can be and is enacted every day. It is more a preoccupation (in philosophical thought and practice) of developed rather than developing countries, though there is evidence of deliberative democracy being practiced in some unlikely locations.[6] Deliberative democracy can be seen as both a theoretical framework within which the practice resides as well as an umbrella term which includes processes such as citizens' juries, consensus conferences, planning cells, deliberative opinion polls, and large-scale citizens' assemblies and town meetings.[7]

How this deliberative intellectual and civic-reform movement will reshape the nation-state remains to be seen. In particular, researchers and reformers face the challenge of designing an inclusive process that meets a high standard for deliberation and yields meaningful long-term changes in the participants, the government, or even the wider society.[8]

It is the contention of the editors of this volume that we can only understand the likely trajectory of deliberative reform if we first take stock of the work already undertaken in its name. Thus, we turn to Australia—that curious incubator of new democratic procedures—and focus on its grandest and most recent creation, a special parliament of citizens.[9]

Citizens' Parliament

Chaps. 1, 3	Chap. 1	Chaps. 1–2	Chaps. 3–4	Chap 3	Intro	Chaps. 4, 7, 11	Chaps. 5–18	
British Columbia's Citizens' Assembly	First discussion of the ACP between Lyn Carson and Luca Belgiorno-Nettis	newDemocracy Foundation commits to funding ACP; World Cafés held to frame ACP's topic	One-third (2,762) of randomly selected invitees ask to participate in the ACP	Random selection of 150 ACP participants	Selected participants attend regional meetings around country	Online Parliament held to generate initial proposals for ACP	One hundred fifty citizens participate in ACP at Old Parliament House in Canberra	ACP Handbook and final results sent to all participants and elected officials
Jan–Nov 2004	July 2005	May 2007	Aug–Sept 2008	Sept 2008	Oct–Dec 2008	Oct 2008– Jan 2009	Feb 6–9 2009	Jan 2010

Timeline: **2004 2005 → 2008 → 2009 → 2010**

Research Project

Sept 2007	Nov 2007	Sept 2008	Oct 2008	Feb 6–9 2009	Sept 2009	Feb 2010
Australian Research Council funding approved to study ACP	First research team meeting held in Sydney	National Science Foundation funding approved to study ACP	First survey of ACP participants' views of politics/government	Multiple surveys over course of ACP; event audio-recorded	Transcripts completed; analysis begins	Longitudinal follow-up survey conducted
			Chap. 10		Chaps. 5– 9, 11—16, 18	Chap. 17

Australian Context

Nov 2005	Dec 2007	April 2008	Feb 7 2009	April 2009	June 2010	July 2010
Belgiorno-Nettis forms New Republic; later incorporated as newDemocracy Foundation	Kevin Rudd sworn in as Prime Minister	Rudd convenes Australia 2020 Summit at Parliament House in Canberra	Victoria bushfires ignite	John Dryzek gives speech on the ACP to Australian Senate	Australian Labor Party replaces Prime Minister Kevin Rudd with Julia Gillard	Gillard proposes convening a Citizens' Assembly on Climate Change
		Chap. 2	Chap. 19	Chap. 10		Chap. 20

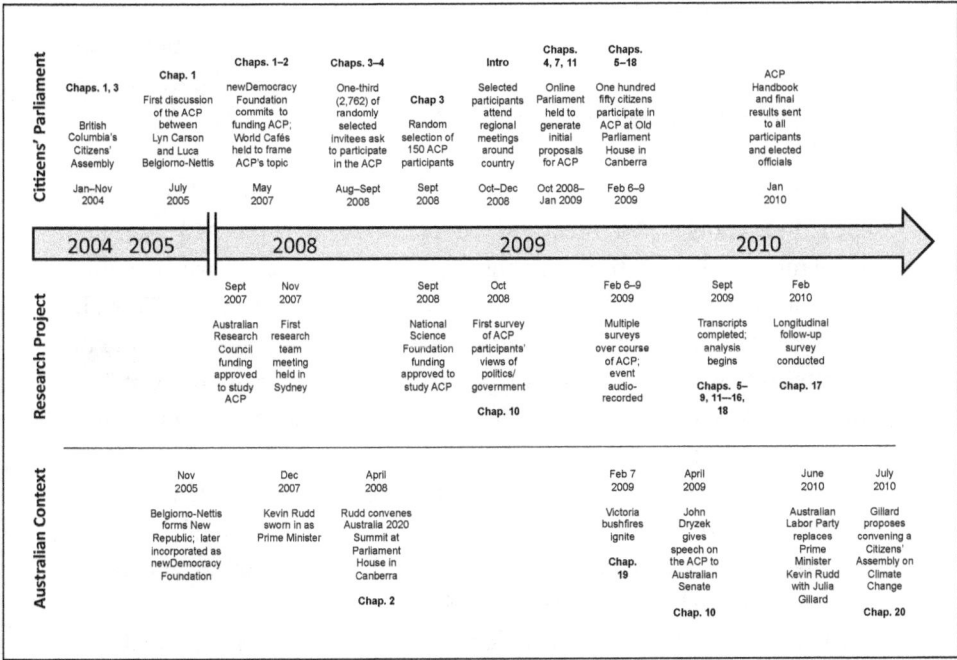

FIGURE I.I Timeline of the Australian Citizens' Parliament, the research program associated with it, and the larger Australian context

The Design of the Australian Citizens' Parliament

In grasping the design of the Australian Citizens' Parliament (ACP), it is important to understand that the four-day assembly in Canberra constituted the pinnacle of the process, but important preliminary events preceded that. Figure I.I gives a complete overview of the ACP process, its research components, and how they dovetailed with contemporary events in Australia.

The ACP deliberative assembly took place in Old Parliament House in Canberra on February 6–9, 2009. This forum was the final event of a deliberative process that began years before (see chapter 2) with a series of public World Cafés which determined the question to be answered by the ACP, often referred to as a "charge" as for trial jury deliberation. The ACP began in earnest in October 2008 and involved introductory regional meetings, online deliberations, and a four-day face-to-face event by 150 randomly selected "Citizen Parliamentarians" (CPs). The ACP addressed the question

"How can Australia's political system be strengthened to serve us better?"[10] The CPs ultimately made a series of prioritized recommendations that were included in the ACP's final document and delivered to the Australian prime minister and members of Parliament. [11]

Unlike many deliberative forums, the ACP was not a "top-down" affair convened by decision makers and drawing citizens into "invited spaces" to solicit their counsel.[12] Rather, a key organizer behind the ACP was the newDemocracy Foundation, a non-government organization whose *raison d'être* is to instigate the search for alternatives to the current system. Though the ACP's recommendations ultimately were handed *over* to government, the latter was not the host. This is an example of an "insisted space," in which citizens self-organize or are facilitated by civil society (including universities) to influence the government.[13]

The ACP structure and design aimed to maximize "representativeness," "deliberativeness," and "influence."[14] Representativeness and influence are de-scribed in the chapters that follow; however, the story of how deliberation was generated needs more elaboration.

The structure of the ACP included the daily random seating of CPs in small facilitated groups and the assistance of networked computers and a theme team to collect and synthesize information from each table. Process design features included sharing the role of lead facilitator to reflect a separate focus on dialogue and deliberation, the selection of facilitators, prior training and information, and daily debriefs. The agenda design was the deliberation engine room. Known and innovative deliberative techniques were integrated, each building on the prior and preparing the ground for the next, often with adaptations or innovations to push the boundaries of usual practice. The following description highlights why various techniques were used and where they fit into the overall story of the ACP. The detailed agendas are also available.[15]

The ACP began with a series of regional meetings, which focused on welcoming, informing, building confidence skills, and teamwork. Techniques used to achieve this included speed introductions, World Café, brainstorming, and an adaptation of Open Space. In effect, these meetings were a highly unusual opportunity for citizen deliberators to help frame their question and shape the process they would later use to examine it. The Online Parliament deliberation that followed was an innovative platform pioneering self-managed, deliberative teams. It aimed to spark deliberation using a different mode and to produce proposals that could frame the initial agenda of the face-to-face assembly in Canberra.

Given the breadth of the ACP charge, it was a challenge to reach an outcome from the four-day ACP that all involved would deem satisfactory, rather than dismissing it as "yet another talkfest." The technique connecting the different pieces of the agenda puzzle, helping to produce a coherent outcome acceptable to participants, was a 21st Century Dialogue system.[16] The networked computers enabled the inputs from the small-group deliberation to be rapidly themed, prioritized, and displayed to the whole group, culminating in daily preliminary reports and the final report.

Each day, the ACP agenda was bookended with a welcome/icebreaker and a closing activity at the end. This was interspersed with plenary sessions, usually in the formal House of Representatives chamber, and small-group deliberation, usually in the parliamentary dining room. CPs were asked (though not compelled) to fill out a reflections card daily. When they had left the parliament, each of the support teams conducted its own briefing session. Social events in the evenings encouraged informal discourse and fraternity.

The stated aim of Day 1 of the ACP was "Understanding what we want to achieve together at the ACP." It began with traditional pomp and ceremony to welcome CPs, attending members of Parliament, the support team, and others, with the representatives of the top five prioritized online deliberation teams then formally presenting their proposals. The remaining agenda focused on improving CPs' understanding of dialogue and deliberation and how they would work together. This began with small-group dialogue to visualize what success might look like and how this deliberation might be different, followed by deliberation using the 21st Century Dialogue system to comment on, add to, and amend the online proposals.

The aim of Day 2 was "Broadening our perspectives." This included both content issues and understanding of dialogue and deliberation. Throughout the day, new proposals and ideas for them were generated. Techniques used included a World Café using Appreciative Inquiry to explore the positive aspects of our political system; deliberation to develop table questions and ideas for expert panelists representing different viewpoints on the pros and cons of existing and new proposals; a reflective conversation, with "experts" being interviewed; and an Open Space so CPs could delve into the particular issues they wanted to pursue.

The Day 3 aim was "Determining what is most important to us." This was a pivotal day, when the large number of generated proposals (fifty-two) needed to be understood and potentially challenged and the criteria for assessing them determined and weighted, and then preferenced accordingly using a prioritization facility in the 21st Century Dialogue system. The day began with a focus on further understanding the proposals, amending them, and adding new proposals, with expert panelists commenting and responding to questions. Next, small groups deliberated the characteristics of a healthy political system that would reflect the legacy they would like to leave to future generations. Using the prioritization facility, the CPs determined the top five characteristics and then honed down the list of proposals to the top thirteen. To promote further reflection and critique, a Fishbowl technique was applied, whereby nominated CPs deliberated on stage about proposals they favored in light of the dominant characteristic. Then using the same prioritization facility the thirteen proposals were assessed by all CPs against each of the top five characteristics. Final prioritizations included which proposals were the easiest to implement, the most innovative, and the most important in the long term. The day concluded with CPs being nominated to present the ACP findings to the assembly and the Government representative in attendance on the final day.

The aim of Day 4 was "Consolidating and delivering our recommendations." A draft of the final report was distributed to CPs for their consideration and amendment. Following this there was a dialogue on the lowlights, highlights, and insights of the ACP. In parallel, the nominated CP presenters prepared what they would say, with some coaching and a practice session to the ACP plenary. After their formal presentation in the House of Representatives, and the Government response, the ACP concluded with small-group dialogue (about next steps, impacts, and learning), followed by lighthearted performances by CPs reflecting their experiences and then the viewing of a final short video of ACP highlights.

A Plurality of Research Methods

A primary reason this book exists is that its organizers always conceived it as both a public-engagement process and a research exercise—one that ultimately secured funding from both the Australian Research Council and the U.S. National Science Foundation. Completing a stream of surveys and having their every word recorded, the CPs themselves became acutely aware of the project's dual mission, and, at one point during the Canberra assembly, they collectively demanded that the researchers better explain themselves and their purposes. It was through the patience and commitment of the CPs that the ACP became an ideal site for detailed scholarly examination.

Above all else, the ACP's Canberra assembly was the first large-scale, face-to-face deliberative project to be completely audio-recorded and transcribed. This makes possible an unprecedented level of qualitative and quantitative assessment of the *actual spoken discourse* of the participants. These transcripts are coupled with comprehensive participant-survey data and electronic records of the 21st Century Dialogue system. This amounts to hundreds of data points that can be organized around each person, group, or activity.

How should research about a large-scale deliberative process be conducted? The contributors to this volume work in a range of disciplines both inside and outside of academia. Each reports on different research questions for different purposes to benefit different audiences. Most methodologists would identify three broad modes of research in this volume, which can be distinguished as social-scientific, interpretive, and critical modes of inquiry.

The *social-scientific* mode includes studies that attempt to make claims about how and why aspects of deliberative processes really occur. The studies might identify categories that would apply to cases beyond the ACP, and even provide evidence for theories that can predict the activity and outcomes of similar deliberative processes in the future. These studies are usually organized scientifically, with hypotheses that lead to an unambiguous assessment of the truth of them through rigorous methods. Some studies invert that approach, generating theory that is grounded in observation and logical analysis. Unfortunately, for research about human activity rather than the natural world, the findings are rarely unequivocal, so statistical methods are often used to uncover probabilities, trends, and clustering. Usually, the researcher seeks to remain objective and detached from the subjects of the study.

In the *interpretive* mode of studies, the main aim is to gain an understanding of the activity and its aspects through interpretive analytic methods. In some of these studies the researcher, as with the social-scientific studies, takes an authoritative stance, which may involve direct contact with participants through nonparticipant observation or structured interview, or persuasive deductive analysis on secondary sources. In other studies the researcher takes a more reflexive stance with participants to investigate subjectivity and particularity and is more tolerant to multiple interpretations and understandings. These latter "postmodern" studies often explore the range of meanings and experiences of participants from their perspectives and relate these using social, cultural, and other frameworks by well-respected scholars. In this volume we also include pragmatic practitioner reporting in the interpretive mode.

Finally, the *critical* mode of studies can draw methods from either of the first two, but is differentiated by a critical researcher stance that not only takes sides with the participants, but may actively advocate for change and improvement in the situation under study. Often the researcher is a practitioner who becomes the central participant in the study. At the heart of most of these studies is an effort to bring taken-for-granted aspects of the study context into focus, especially when those aspects are found to hinder progress towards an idealized situation.

The authors of this volume have traversed broadly across this research landscape. Some chapters are firmly positioned in a particular approach, whereas others develop lines of argument using multiple modes. To help appreciate these differences, we note the predominant modes as we introduce each of the chapters.

Organization of the Book

To study this unique process, we took what may be an equally novel editorial approach. We began with our team of four editors, each of whom was intensively involved in the creation, design, implementation, and/or study of the ACP. For Lyn Carson and Janette Hartz-Karp, the ACP represented a continuation of a multiyear collaboration in which they have experimented with combining different methods of deliberation and dialogue in Australia.[17] Ron Lubensky has devoted his postgraduate career to understanding and advancing the practice of public deliberation, and he helped design many key features of the ACP, as well as its online components. Though John Gastil attended the ACP, he did so as a researcher rather than a designer or organizer, and he brings to this project two decades of experience studying and writing on deliberative processes large and small.[18]

Rather than playing a relatively passive editorial role, however, we took on authorial roles in nearly all of the chapters in this book. This gave the book a stronger narrative continuity and ensured that every chapter drew not only on outside knowledge but also on the direct experience of event organizers and researchers. That said, we released the ACP data into the wider scholarly community and successfully solicited a large team of chapter authors from coast to coast in Australia and the United States, plus investigators from Germany, Italy, Switzerland, and the United Kingdom.

The chapters of this book are organized into five parts, each prefaced by a brief introduction to the chapters that are included. Part I provides detail about the inception and design of the ACP, providing context for the rest of the book and informing discussion about large-scale process improvement. Through a range of study approaches, part II contains chapters that explore the nature of the deliberation by ACP participants. The authors in part III present their analyses of the content of the ACP deliberations to show how beliefs and ideas shifted and flowed during the process. Part IV presents several chapters about facilitation and the organizers' effects on participants. The chapters in part V reflect on the exercise and take a wider look at its impacts. Additional material deriving from our research is available online at http://www.newdemocracy.com.au/index.php/library/research-papers. That website will also provide periodic updates, links to related activities, and archival documents from the ACP.

We cannot say whether, after reading this book, one will come away more sanguine or more glum about the prospects for deliberative democracy. All the authors herein share what might be called a cautious optimism. We have seen in the ACP great potential for robust and influential deliberation, but we have also glimpsed some of the same pathologies that plague contemporary politics and government. It is our greatest hope that by sharing our diverse perspectives, we will have enriched the reader's own understanding of the potential and limitations of deliberative-democratic reform.

NOTES

1. This view is informed by our earlier writings on this subject. See Lyn Carson and Brian Martin, *Random Selection in Politics* (Westport, Conn.: Praeger, 1999); John Gastil, *By Popular Demand: Revitalizing Representative Democracy Through Deliberative Elections* (Berkeley: University of California Press, 2000). See also Matt Leighninger, *The Next Form of Democracy: How Expert Rule Is Giving Way to Shared Governance—and Why Politics Will Never Be the Same* (Nashville: Vanderbilt University Press, 2006).

2. Lyn Carson and Janette Hartz-Karp, "Adapting and Combining Deliberative Designs: Juries, Polls, and Forums," in *The Deliberative Democracy Handbook: Strategies for Effective Civic Engagement in the Twenty-First Century*, ed. John Gastil and Peter Levine (San Francisco: Jossey-Bass, 2005), 120–38.

3. Key writings on the subject include Amy Gutmann and Dennis Thompson, *Why Deliberative Democracy?* (Princeton: Princeton University Press, 2004); John S. Dryzek with Simon Niemeyer, *Foundations and Frontiers of Deliberative Governance* (Oxford: Oxford University Press, 2010); James A. Fishkin, *When the People Speak: Deliberative Democracy and Public Consultation* (Oxford: Oxford University Press, 2009). This now constitutes a vast body of

literature. The *Journal of Public Deliberation* (http://services.bepress.com/jpd/) is the repository for the most recent writing on both the theory and practice of deliberative democracy.

4. On radical reform, see John Burnheim, *Is Democracy Possible? The Alternative to Electoral Politics* (Berkeley: University of California Press, 1985). On incremental reform, see Lyn Carson and Rodolfo Lewanski, "Fostering Citizen Participation Top-Down," *International Journal of Public Participation* 2, no. 1 (2008): 72–83, accessed January 8, 2012, http://www.iap2 .org/displaycommon.cfm?an=1&subarticlenbr=277. On the interplay of deliberation at different levels of society and government, see John Parkinson and Jane Mansbridge, *Deliberative Systems: Deliberative Democracy at the Large Scale* (New York: Cambridge University Press, 2012).

5. Archon Fung and Erik Olin Wright, eds., *Deepening Democracy: Institutional Innovations in Empowered Participatory Governance* (New York: Verso, 2003); John Gastil, *Political Communication and Deliberation* (Thousand Oaks, Calif.: Sage, 2008).

6. See the 2010 IAP2 online publications accessed January 8, 2012, "Painting the Landscape," http://www.iap2.org/associations/4748/files/Research percent20Project percent202010 _usFINAL_Nov_v2.pdf, and "A Cross-Cultural Exploration of Public-Government Decision Making: A Joint Research Project of IAP2 and the Charles F. Kettering Foundation," http://www .iap2.org/associations/4748/files/Research %20Project %202010_FINAL_Nov_v2.pdf. On deliberation in China, see James S. Fishkin, Baogang He, Robert C. Luskin, and Alice Siu, "Deliberative Democracy in an Unlikely Place: Deliberative Polling in China," *British Journal of Political Science* 40 (2010): 435–48.

7. A good overview can be found in Gastil and Levine, *Deliberative Democracy Handbook*.

8. Carson and Hartz-Karp, "Adapting and Combining Deliberative Designs."

9. Deliberative-democratic beliefs underpinned the willingness of the many volunteers who supported this project, even though many would have been unfamiliar with the term *deliberative democracy*. Public participation or community engagement is a growing field of practice in Australia, and it was from these ranks that many volunteers emerged. Many were members of the International Association of Public Participation (IAP2) or the Australian Facilitators Network—both professional associations that have arisen to support this work. In recognition of the IAP2's contributions, the royalties from this book will go to that organization's Australasian chapter.

10. On the condition of Australian government, see "Democratic Audit of Australia," Australian National University Swinburne Institute for Social Research, accessed January 7, 2012, http://arts.anu.edu.au/democraticaudit.

11. Complete details are available online through the Library at newDemocracy Foundation, accessed January 7, 2012, http://www.newdemocracy.com.au.

12. Andrea Cornwall, "Spaces for Transformation? Reflections on Issues of Power and Difference in Participation and Development," in *Participation: From Tyranny to Transformation? Exploring New Approaches to Participation in Development,* ed. Samuel Hickey and Giles Mohan (London: Zed Books, 2004), 75–91.

13. Lyn Carson, "Creating Democratic Surplus Through Citizens' Assemblies," *Journal of Public Deliberation* 4, no. 1 (2008): art. 5, accessed January 7, 2012, http://services.bepress. com/jpd/vol4/iss1/art5/.

14. Carson and Hartz-Karp, "Adapting and Combining Deliberative Designs."

15. See the Handbook, "Putting People Back into Politics, Australia's 2009 Citizens Parliament," http://www.newdemocracy.com.au.

16. Janette Hartz-Karp and associates developed this proprietary system and brought it to the ACP.

17. Carson and Hartz-Karp, "Adapting and Combining Deliberative Designs."

18. Gastil, *Political Communication and Deliberation*.

PART I

DELIBERATIVE DESIGN AND INNOVATION

The introduction to the book provided a brief overview of the Australia Citizens' Parliament. The chapters in part I go further to describe the context, preparation, and procedures of the participatory process. In "Origins of the First Citizens' Parliament" (chapter 1), Lyn Carson and Luca Belgiorno-Nettis look back on how the ACP came about. Written as a conversation between the two authors, this chapter shows the serendipitous quality of the ACP's initial conception and development. Janette Hartz-Karp and Carson compare the ACP's design with an earlier government initiative in "Putting Citizens in Charge: Comparing the Australian Citizens' Parliament and the Australia 2020 Summit" (chapter 2). Lubensky and Carson provide details and analysis about the randomized recruitment of ACP participants in "Choose Me: The Challenges of National Random Selection" (chapter 3). Software expert Brian Sullivan and Hartz-Karp explain how the ACP's online component developed in "Grafting an Online Parliament onto a Face-to-Face Process" (chapter 4).

I

ORIGINS OF THE FIRST CITIZENS' PARLIAMENT

Lyn Carson and Luca Belgiorno-Nettis

In this chapter we take a look at the origins of the Australian Citizens' Parliament (ACP) in the same way it began, with a casual conversation. This happened years before the ACP itself. The two people involved, Lyn Carson and Luca Belgiorno-Nettis, recall both their first meetings, the fateful conversation, and the events which followed. In the spirit of deliberative democracy, the chapter takes the form of a conversation, recorded at the office of the newDemocracy Foundation (nDF) with the assistance of nDF's executive director, Iain Walker. In the spirit of conversation, the transcript below lists both persons by their most familiar names.

LUCA: The catalyst for my interest in deliberative democracy? I think it was one particular luncheon I had on the "rubber chicken circuit" with an Australian politician. I call it the "rubber chicken circuit" because of the awful food that was served. At these functions, the political host (no matter from which political party) would talk about the same subjects and answer the challenges in similar ways. There was no difference really between the two political parties. It was nothing more than puerile debate. I thought that there had to be a better way to do politics.

CARSON: Did you have a background in political science?

LUCA: Politics was not my strong suit or my major at university. I began inquiring and I ended up doing a course, it was only a couple of days, in Melbourne, sponsored by the Myer Foundation. It brought together a number of people interested in politics and political reform, and that sparked my ongoing interest. At that forum Martin Krygier [an Australian political philosopher, later a member of nDF's Research Committee] spoke, and he suggested I speak with Ian Marsh [an Australian political scientist and later a fellow director of nDF]. I read some of Ian's works first, but somehow I got onto you. I was looking for other ways of talking about the subject of politics, and you offered that to me.

CARSON: I'd be interested to have you check my memory about what happened at that first meeting. I went back through my diary to find the exact date so I know it was 6th July 2004. I remember your phone call and your request to come and see me. You said you were from Transfield, and when you came into my office I was trying to work out, "What's this guy doing here? Is he trying to democratize his organization?" I couldn't quite work out where you were coming from. I'd stereotyped you: businessman, profit motive, and so on. You asked me about different democratic methods, and this thing called deliberative democracy. It felt like we were having a little "Oxbridge" tutorial. We discussed what you would need to know in order to really understand deliberative democracy, and I sent you off with some readings, as I would a grad student. I thought, "Well, that will be the end of that character."

LUCA: Well, you were wrong about that!

CARSON: Yes. A couple of weeks later you rang and said, "I've done the readings, now I need to talk to you again," and I thought, "Wow, he's tenacious." At the end of the second "tutorial" we had another discussion, and then you asked a fantastic strategic question, which was, "If money was no object, what would be the thing that you consider would best further this cause of deliberative democracy in Australia?" I didn't have any hesitation and suggested a citizens' assembly like British Columbia. I wanted to do it in Australia because I think we have distinctive differences based on our geography. You asked how much it would cost and didn't flinch when I said hundreds of thousands of dollars. You simply said, "Oh well, I reckon we should do it." I almost fell off my chair thinking, "Wow, does he think he could attract that kind of money?" Then we just started plotting it.

LUCA: Yes, we started doing this even before the idea for an Australian Research Council-Linkage proposal entered our minds.

CARSON: Do you remember it as I do?

LUCA: Yes, I do, but I've just remembered how I ended up getting through to you. It was because of Kathy Jones [fellow director of nDF]. Kathy had met Janette Hartz-Karp [coeditor of this book and based in Western Australia] and pointed out a paper she had written that cited your work at the University of Sydney. But it was also because of what happened at another university, where I was rebuffed. A lovely woman from the University of Southern California who'd moved from the U.S. tried to introduce me to the department of politics at another university, thinking this could be a partnership between the private sector and academia. But the reaction from that politics department was that there was no way they were going to meet with me, let alone partner with me.

CARSON: Why was that?

LUCA: I was told quite clearly that they didn't want to have anything to do with private enterprise. And I'm not talking so many years ago. We're talking only six years ago, and this is indicative of how academia was then. This would not happen now, I suspect. There's been quite a radical transformation when it comes to universities and corporate partnerships.

CARSON: How did the idea of a citizens' assembly develop? I can hardly recall.

LUCA: You are testing my memory, but I think everyone who had come across the British Columbia (BC) Citizens' Assembly (CA) at the time was inspired by it. We met during its life [BC's CA met from January to November 2004] and before it went to the vote, to the referendum [which happened in May 2005]. It was all very inspirational, and there was always perhaps a flicker in my mind that this could be used here in Australia as well. I know we talked about the Canadian experience.

CARSON: Perhaps I gave you a reading about it at that first meeting and said, "Well, look at this, this is interesting." Therefore, when you came back and said, if I could do anything, what would it be, it was easy for me to refer to BC's CA because you were familiar with it. It was an easy sell because you knew about the BC experiment.

LUCA: You know, it was nearly five years from the time we talked about it until the time it actually happened. A long time. A few things happened in between that first conversation and the ACP.

CARSON: Yes, there were many lunches and an organization to establish.

LUCA: Ah, yes, newRepublic, as we were originally. I didn't quite understand (although others did) how people would simply focus on the republic question, i.e., the monarchy, as opposed to the broader question of how one establishes a democratic state. So we changed the name to newDemocracy, but that was later in the piece. [nDF was incorporated in 2007.] It just seemed right to create an organization, some sort of grouping, that could focus on these matters.

CARSON: We couldn't do it as individuals. You couldn't do it as an individual. It made sense to create a non-government organization of some sort.

LUCA: Yes, of like-minded people and among them some impressive former politicians: the late senator John Button and former senator Fred Chaney. John's health was deteriorating after the launch of newRepublic [November 17, 2005] and he died in 2008, so it was really Fred who took the carriage of the ACP as the statesman. I felt it was important, and still do, that people who had a certain profile in politics could be seen to be relating to us, and I had the great fortune to have known Fred and John in previous business dealings, so it was reasonably easy to approach them. I had great respect for them both. They weren't just figureheads. They had great track records in their own right of being independently minded thinkers and well respected in many ways.

CARSON: I think there's something else that I'd like to say about that. When I first met you, you started immediately inviting me to lunch. I remember thinking that this was a curious relationship. You would invite me to lunch and you would invite journalists or politicians, usually very well-known. You would do it as an advocate for these processes, and you would say to me, "Come along to lunch." I had this sense that you'd push a button and say, "All right, Carson, now speak." I would do my little "blather, blather, blather" around whatever it was, random selection or deliberation, and you'd sit back proudly like you'd discovered a new audio toy. That this person could say the things that you really believed in, but she was an academic, which gave it added legitimacy.

LUCA [laughing]: I'm sorry you took it that way.

CARSON [laughing]: Oh, no, in the nicest possible way, I loved it. It was a neat partnership: you had the contacts and I had the intellectual arguments. Back then, we thought we could attract government sponsorship and that, like British Columbia, the government would support the experiment. More naïveté?! Instead, we encountered indifference or fiery arguments. I recall one heated argument with a former federal Opposition leader (though he was not at the time) about Athenian democracy. But I met some interesting political elites, some fabulous journalists. Most of them were quite resistant, virtually all of them, but at least it gave us an opportunity to state our case and test our beliefs.

LUCA: All of the existing politicians, the incumbents, were very resistant. There was very little openness. We met only about six of them, I think. I didn't bother to entertain any more of them; it became rather frustrating.

CARSON: Yes, it can lead to frustration and cynicism, encountering that degree of indifference to alternatives, especially when *we* considered the options to be so exciting.

LUCA: They'd be courteous enough at the lunch, but there would be no follow-up and no real interest. So it was plain in my mind that they believed themselves to be the legitimate representatives and saw no other system that was worthwhile. Clearly they had full agendas and didn't have time to occupy themselves with changing the system per se.

CARSON: There were two parallel processes going on, weren't there? You were endeavoring to attract support from key people and establishing an NGO in the form of newRepublic and later the newDemocracy Foundation, you had a whole creative strategy—eventually a music video, a website, and more. You did some extraordinary things that had a more generic appeal than the proposed Citizens' Assembly. Meanwhile my strategy was the Australian Research Council (ARC)-Linkage proposal. We needed to find more funds, beyond your generous support, and therefore we had to have other researchers on board. A key researcher from my point of view was John Dryzek because of his tremendous reputation in the field of deliberative democracy. I was thrilled when John came on board. Is that how you remember it?

LUCA: I think that's quite right. And thankfully, of course. I'd launched the project independently from this ARC potential. Fortunately, the ARC funds were granted, which gave us further legitimacy and obviously contributed half the funds. That was really a fantastic outcome, but it's safe to say that we were proceeding down this track irrespective of the ARC and really I was determined it was going to happen anyway, but frankly I'm not sure it would have happened so easily without the ARC, because it did bring all of the other research capacity to the table.

CARSON: You've contributed an awful lot of money to this venture. You know, not just the Citizens' Parliament but this idea of the newDemocracy Foundation. And clearly you could be spending that money on other things. Why do you keep doing it?

LUCA: People have their passions and lots of philanthropists (if that's the word) spend money on medical research, poverty alleviation. It's not an either/or. I mean I do a bit of that as well. I just find that this is an area of need.

CARSON: No one else in Australia is doing it, though.

LUCA: Well, there's the Lowy family, and they do international policy development, but there seems to be a need. There aren't similar organizations. There aren't people that have rallied around this notion of trying to find a way through this high school debating that passes for politics.

CARSON: When we pictured success in 2004 I know what mine was: it was to prove that the process was possible, that we could do a large-scale Citizens'

Assembly. Australia is much bigger in many ways than British Columbia, with different challenges and constraints. I just wanted to prove that it could be done, in the hope that a precedent was established, that it was a workable model for a country the size of Australia. I wanted to stimulate discussion about its usability, but we just couldn't have factored in the dreadful Victoria bushfire weekend coinciding with it. That was definitely my picture of success. Do you recall the hopes of others?

LUCA: Ian [Marsh] had hopes for a Private Member's Bill, I seem to recall.

CARSON: John [Dryzek] and Simon [Niemeyer] were interested in finding a site for further experimentation with their Q-sort method. Ron [Lubensky] was able to do his PhD as a result of ARC funding—a scholarship. Janette [Hartz-Karp], though swamped with other projects, could not resist another large-scale deliberative event. We had different expectations depending upon our respective backgrounds, academic researcher or practitioner, or a combination of both. What were *your* hopes, Luca?

LUCA: I was focused on the outcomes, and I didn't quite recognize that citizens wouldn't have enough time to deliberate as fully as I would have wished. I wasn't really prepared for that. Once again it's my naïveté for these things, and yet it should have been so obvious. We had done it in the past with other deliberative events. However, the level of goodwill of this deliberation and how people for a whole lot of reasons . . . perhaps they were excited by the event. They saw it as a unique opportunity. There was such a synthesis of goodwill and enthusiasm to do the right thing by this event, by virtually all the participants.

CARSON: And now we're getting into some after-the-event territory which will be taken up in later chapters. But it seems to me that the way you just described that could have described some of the World Cafés that we did which preceded the ACP. So the forerunner for the face-to-face event in Old Parliament House, Canberra, was a series of World Cafés, and the most spectacular of those was the one in Paddington. You influenced the way that was run, and I don't think I've ever facilitated a World Café quite like that one. Your Italian background meant that there was good food, there was wine. World Cafés don't normally pay that much attention to catering. But yours did. We had live music, and the music video was screened with the song you wrote. People were really excited by that event, and there was that same experience of people going away saying, "Well, I don't normally come along to this sort of thing and have these kinds of conversations." The Citizens' Parliament was an expanded, extended version of what was begun there.

LUCA: That's true, Carson. Thanks for reminding me of that. Paddington Town Hall, then later, Old Parliament House.

CARSON: It had to be in Canberra, didn't it, because it was a national event, and where else would we want it to happen? We tenaciously went with the place that we thought was the right place. Thankfully it's now a museum and available for hire (albeit with all sorts of restrictions to protect its heritage). I had participated in Deliberative Polls in the same venue, so we knew it was possible. It was the perfect location for our Citizens' Parliament. We were lucky to have two excellent co-chairs as well that matched the venue's political reputation.

LUCA: Having a recognizable person at the head of it such as Fred Chaney was crucial to its success. Then to have a co-chair such as Lowitja O'Donoghue was similarly important, and that brought so much credibility to our invitation.

CARSON: Yes, it was a fantastic choice. You know, all of these ideas about the ACP process emerged out of many group discussions. The whole project team was often involved. The proposed venue was a terrific suggestion, and Fred and Lowitja were just the best people to have as chairs. I think we all felt really fortunate to have them both.

LUCA: Everyone involved had great energy for the ACP project. Most of the areas where there was conflict were resolved quite civilly and amicably through good process. I mean there was an enormous logistics exercise that had to be attended to, and not just organizing all the citizens but organizing all the team, the volunteers, speakers, the ICT for the actual event itself, and more.

CARSON: Yes. We had a series of project meetings, and people would have to be flown in, like Janette [Hartz-Karp] from Western Australia and John [Dryzek] and Simon [Niemeyer] would come up from Canberra and Ron [Lubensky] from Melbourne.

LUCA: Just getting together as a team to plan all of this was challenging logistically, let alone the parliament itself.

CARSON: Luca, it's clear from the chapter on organizer bias [chapter 16] that you have strong feelings against political parties. Is there something prior to your "rubber chicken" experience that makes you interested in different forms of democracy?

LUCA: I did live in Malaysia for seven years, and I saw how corrupt government (let's not put any niceties around it) does make for very bad social outcomes. I recognized how important good government is. I also recognized at the same time how as an architect interested in urbanism that so much of our town planning was being compromised by bad government decision making. There was absolutely no reason why, from a technical perspective, you could not have good town planning. It was as much as anything compromised by bad political decision making, by political point scoring and short-term political thinking.

CARSON: Do you think the Malaysian experience threw that into sharp relief for you? Did the local, urban experience of it precede Malaysia or did it come after Malaysia?

LUCA: There was my training in architecture first, and any good urbanism requires long-term planning. They kind of combined. Of course, coming back into Australia, I was back into the "rubber chicken circuit." It was a standard practice, you would go into these political fund-raising events and you would make your donation and I would be asking, "Well, why this group rather than the other group, and they all sound the same to me, they're all sprouting their own fictions, they all profess to be great economists, and yet it seemed all so shallow."

CARSON: They were very formative experiences by the sound of it. Both watching corruption in Malaysia and an absence of long-term planning in your urban environment, and then those rubber chickens!

LUCA: Rubber chicken only because the quality of the food, definitely not the best chicken, the chicken would bounce!

CARSON: That's very significant, then, in terms of how you got to where you are now. Because you've watched both the impact of short-term political thinking on citizens but also closely observed the other side of politics. Now we understand how political parties keep going, maintaining their own destinies, and, amazingly, it's through rubber chickens!

2

PUTTING CITIZENS IN CHARGE: COMPARING THE AUSTRALIAN
CITIZENS' PARLIAMENT AND THE AUSTRALIA 2020 SUMMIT

Janette Hartz-Karp and Lyn Carson

Australia is one of the world's stable liberal democracies. It has a history of democratic innovation.[1] But the "Democratic Audit of Australia" and other studies tell a story of falling confidence in our political system.[2] Symptoms include low levels of citizen engagement, apathy and cynicism toward politics, declining membership in and public support for political parties, and growing numbers of young Australians seeking to avoid mandatory voter registration.[3] Some observers trace the malaise to a "democratic deficit"—institutional arrangements and conduct that appear at odds with the normative ideals of democracy, including factionalism within parties, the intentional polarization of issues by political partisans, the oversimplification of issues in the news media, and the short time horizon of the policy-making process.[4]

Some civic reformers hope to address this deficit by creating new opportunities for meaningful citizen engagement with government officials and each other on issues of public concern.[5] In this chapter, we show how the Australian Citizens' Parliament (ACP) can play this role effectively, and we contrast the ACP's approach with the Australia 2020 Summit, which was initiated and led by the prime minister in April 2008.

The comparison is useful because both initiatives addressed the same issue—public participation in the policy-making process. Both aimed to provide government officials with information to which officials otherwise would not have access, including firsthand knowledge of the public's needs, beliefs, priorities, and readiness to accept trade-offs, and both promised an opportunity to exert genuine influence on substantive policy decisions.

But the contrast between them is what merits the comparison. The Summit is an instance of processes in which government officials *consult* with persons they identify as experts and stakeholders. Questions are formulated in advance by officials for the purpose of eliciting information relevant to the task of formulating sound policy. By contrast, the ACP emphasized the primacy of the general public in the policy-making process, and hence the importance of enabling citizens themselves to set the agenda for discussion. Participants are selected at random in order to achieve a demographically representative cross-section of the population as a whole, sometimes known as a mini-public,[6] and instead of privileging the views of experts, the ACP sought to validate the knowledge participants have acquired through lived experience.

In the discussion that follows, we compare the 2020 Summit and the ACP with a view to assessing their potential to revitalize democracy and to enhance the policy-making process through citizen participation. The comparison centers on differences in design and on the approaches taken to ensure that participation is inclusive and potentially useful to policy makers. The ACP and the Summit did succeed in providing officials with valuable ideas, but in our judgment the ACP delivered ideas that were more deeply and collectively considered as a consequence of differences in process design.

The Australia 2020 Summit

Soon after gaining election in November 2007, the Australian prime minister, Kevin Rudd, decided to convene an Australia 2020 Summit at Parliament House in Canberra on April 19–20, 2008. The rationale for this undertaking was "to tackle the long-term challenges confronting Australia's future—challenges which require long-term responses from the nation beyond the usual three-year electoral cycle."[7] Accordingly, the broad purpose of the Summit was to harvest "big ideas" for the federal government to implement by the year 2020.

The Summit plan called for inviting one thousand of the "best and brightest" minds from across the country to address the challenges facing it and to produce a set of recommendations for action.[8] Challenges were sorted into ten policy discussion "streams."[9] Each stream was co-chaired by a federal cabinet minister and a prominent person selected by the government. The co-chairs in turn constituted the steering committee, headed by the vice-chancellor of the University of Melbourne.[10]

For each stream, organizers sought a hundred participants. The co-chairs extended personal invitations to prominent Australians within each stream. In addition, self-nomination forms were available on the Summit website. Participants were required to cover the costs of their travel and accommodation.[11] More than eight thousand people applied, including the authors. Applicants were allowed to request authorization to participate in up to three streams. The authors applied successfully for admission to their first choice, the governance stream. The application form asked candidates to list notable achievements and to provide a statement explaining how they would contribute to the discussion. Significantly, the co-chairs did not reveal publicly how they made their selections.

A background paper was prepared for the participants in each stream, raising the main issues of concern, providing some related data, and asking a series of open-ended questions.[12] These were "not intended to be definitive or comprehensive, but were put together to stimulate discussion on the main challenges and opportunities facing the country and the choices to be made in addressing them."

The Summit itself was the culmination of a broader "national conversation" that included the Youth Summit held at Parliament House the previous weekend and over five hundred community and school summits across the country. There was also an African Summit, and a Jewish Symposium was convened when it was realized the Summit was being held during Passover. Altogether, before the main event some twenty-six hundred individuals and groups presented eighty-eight hundred public submissions that were published subsequently on the Summit website in both full-length and summary form for the benefit of participants.

At the outset of the Summit, it was evident that most participants were experts in the subject matter of their stream. For example, the governance stream attracted several senior academics, legal experts, and public servants who demonstrated their knowledge of constitutional law and legislated regulations.[13]

Four volunteers from well-known consulting organizations were available to each stream to assist in facilitating discussion sessions. Volunteers were selected from among persons who had offered advice and support to the organizing team. In some streams volunteers facilitated actively, while in others they were relegated by co-chairs or participants to supporting roles.[14] In all streams they served as recorders who took notes and assisted in writing reports.

The two-day agenda included plenary sessions involving all participants at the beginning and end of both days. Stream sessions were conducted in between. The news media maintained a highly visible presence throughout. All participants had signed a release permitting the media to record their images and remarks. Journalists moved freely through the discussion rooms. Roving television, radio, and documentary reporters conducted interviews during session breaks, some of which were shown during plenary sessions. On the government-funded channel ABC2 (available only to the third of the population at the time who subscribed to cable television service or who received digital free-to-air broadcasts), coverage was continuous but dominated in content by the plenary sessions, speeches, celebrity interviews, and studio commentary. Only brief glimpses of participants engaged in stream discussions were available to viewers.

Stream co-chairs conducted their proceedings in styles of their choosing. They could follow or ignore the guidance given to them by the volunteer facilitators. Some controlled the agenda and discussion tightly, while others allowed participants more freedom to determine what was discussed and how. Some streams used an aggregative approach to ascertaining group views (e.g., using dot stickers to set priorities or requesting a show of hands). In others, the approach was more deliberative in the sense of encouraging participants to collaboratively weigh pros and cons and to work toward consensus with regard to recommendations.

At the close of the Summit, each participant received a hurriedly prepared *Initial Report* listing the top ambitions, goals, themes, and "big ideas" from each discussion stream, most captured on the first day.[15] This report was prepared by stream co-chairs and facilitators. Many participants (including the authors of this chapter) were disappointed to discover that items they believed had been assigned priority during the final stream session had been omitted.

A month after the Summit, the Department of the Prime Minister and Cabinet released the somewhat more satisfying *Australia 2020 Summit Final Report,*[16] presented as a comprehensive summary of the discussions and of the items captured by recorders. However, this version of the proceedings was disputed by some, including participants in the governance stream, and dismissed as a "whitewash." The *Final Report* stated explicitly that the ideas that it contained represented the views of participants alone and had not been endorsed by the government.

At the Summit and in the final report, it was stated that the discussions to which participants had contributed would not be the end of this process. The recommendations of each stream were referred by the prime minister to the corresponding government department for consideration. Moreover, the Summit website continued to attract new ideas and commentary some time after the event. The government reputedly followed this commentary and in other channels such as radio talkback, newspaper forums, and online. The prime minister committed to responding to the ideas by the end of 2008; however, this response was delayed until April 2009, when the government officially endorsed nine ideas.[17] In his closing remarks at the Summit, Prime Minister Rudd did make particular note of the "innovative" idea of "collaborative governance." Although those supporting this idea saw this as a hopeful sign at the time, it was not taken up during Rudd's term as prime minister.

The Australian Citizens' Parliament Comparison

The ACP was designed very differently than the Summit. We focus on two key points of contrast—whom the process engaged and how it encouraged collaborative participation in the public interest.

Whom the Process Engaged

The Summit and the ACP were designed to involve two distinct sets of participants. At the opening ceremony, Mr. Rudd stated that he was "opening the windows of democracy" and "turning to you, the people of Australia, to help solve the issues facing us."[18] However, given the background of most participants, it became clear that the process was based on the assumption that *experts and stakeholders* were most likely to contribute "big ideas" that would improve the nation's prospects for the future. Attention from the media increased the probability that people confident in their abilities and knowledge would seek the opportunity to share their views. Thus, the Summit was hardly a "people's convention." It was closer to a meritocratic conclave of the "best and brightest"—as one commentator noted, "a gathering of people selected on indeterminate grounds of general outstandingness."[19] There were also parallels with "Confucian" democracy—Bell's proposal that political representation be determined through public examination.[20]

In fairness to the prime minister, Mr. Rudd did urge subsequently (in the introduction to the 2020 Summit's preliminary report) that the question of reform be made a matter for widespread public consideration: "The challenges facing Australia are great, and *all* Australians need to think about how they will be met."[21]

The ACP was consciously designed to be more public-oriented than the Summit. Its stated goal was to assemble a group of citizens who were representative of the population as a whole. By definition, a statistically representative group includes the full range within the population of demographic characteristics such as age, gender, education, level of political interest, and other factors. Although no subset of a population can mirror precisely all its characteristics, random selection eliminates most of the skewing that is introduced by permitting participants to self-select (see chapter 3).

The public-administration literature about facilitating democratic discussion deals mainly with stakeholders, the people who have a direct interest in how an issue is resolved. Because of their "stake" in the outcome, the knowledge they bring to the issue is considerably greater (though usually more selective) than that possessed by "ordinary citizens." Yet despite the understandably narrow perspective of stakeholders, both the public and government officials assume that they are better able to provide decision makers with useful information and advice than are members of the ostensibly ill-informed, inattentive, and conflicted general public. Even in academia, participation by "ordinary citizens"—beyond actions such as voting and perhaps contacting their representatives—has received only scant attention. Most political "elites" fail to see how citizens' involvement might add value to the policy-making process. The ACP put to the test all the commonly held assumptions about the ability and willingness of "ordinary citizens" to demonstrate their fitness for democratic self-rule.

Collaborative Participation in the Public Interest

Both the Summit and the ACP aimed to achieve collaborative participation in the public interest, but to which extent did they achieve it? The features underlying such processes have been elucidated in numerous publications describing initiatives throughout the world that have revitalized democracy through public participation.[22]

First, priority is given to participant discussions, enhanced by information and mutual learning. Although the conveners of the Summit sent information to participants in advance, and although there was an opportunity for participants to discuss issues through a weblog, only a few (at least in the governance stream) took advantage of these measures. In contrast, 99 of the 150 Citizen Parliamentarians (CPs) contributed to the online deliberations that aimed to encourage active learning by developing ideas into proposals through group deliberation.[23] Importantly, at the Summit almost half the time available was devoted to plenary sessions that were substantially scripted for media consumption rather than to meet the deliberative needs of the participants. On Day 1, for example, of the seven and a quarter hours allocated for work, around four and a half hours were available for participant interaction in the governance stream. In contrast, well over two-thirds of the time at the ACP was devoted to interactive sessions, and most of the plenary sessions were devoted to responding to the deliberation needs of the CPs.

Second, there should be time and opportunity for participants to develop carefully considered, reasoned views. Participants in the Summit met over a shortened weekend. In contrast, the ACP process ran over three months, including the regional meetings, online deliberation, and three full days (over four days) of final deliberation and reporting. Thus, the ACP offered participants more time to explore issues through dialogue and deliberation. This translated into recommendations and a final report, developed and reviewed over the course of the ACP. By the end of the ACP, there was a clustering of preferred options. This was documented through computer technology (using a 21st Century Town Meeting) and was open for CPs to audit.[24] In contrast, the quick count of hands supporting proposals at the Summit was done in rushed sessions with rarely a proper count to indicate the degree of unanimity achieved. There was also little effort made to publicize the criteria participants applied when voting. In contrast, the CPs discussed the criteria for prioritizing, and in each instance the criterion being applied was clarified and discussed before the prioritization.

The Summit's stream discussions only minimally allowed for intensive small-group deliberation. In the governance stream, for example, the program opened with speeches followed by a large-group session during which participants promoted their "big ideas." Individual participants were encouraged in a short space of time to advocate for these ideas, in the hope that others would support them. Another plenary followed, in which the key ideas of four subgroups were reviewed. It finished with the co-chair delivering a plea to "think bigger." On the second day, the governance stream started with a plenary to review the work done the previous evening by the facilitators, who had produced a summary of the stream's work from the day before (the accuracy of which was substantially disputed by participants). The stream's work concluded with a plenary involving a chaotic, high-pressure session to prioritize the items that would be submitted to the concluding multistream plenary. The recording was performed manually by facilitators on flip charts. Too little time was left for the smaller-group sessions to do the real work of developing key themes, ideas, and actions.

In contrast, at the ACP the intention was to generate the ideas through deliberation. The ACP commenced with the ideas developed by the online teams, which were deliberated during Day 1. The danger to deliberation of personal investment in ideas became evident when some online parliamentarians saw it as their role to champion their online proposals at the ACP. This was not ideal when the focus was on investigating possibilities rather than advocating for one. By the end of the ACP, however, a number of these online parliamentarians had changed their viewpoints. At the ACP, in contrast to the Summit, most of the available time was used to broaden and deepen the discussion. Of course, time was still limited, so the sessions were not without some pressure. Small-group interactive sessions predominated using a variety of deliberative techniques to maximize participation. The panel discussions were substantially interactive, too. Moreover, using the technology of networked computers meant there was prompt synthesis, theming, and prioritization of team and individual inputs, significantly reducing the time needed for feedback plenary sessions. An additional advantage of this technology was that it enabled the participants' inputs (in their own words) and priorities (accurately documented) to form the preliminary and final reports rather than a post-event analysis by the facilitators.

Third, process integrity is essential. This starts with how the issues are framed and how the agenda is designed to enable all those involved to participate to the best of their ability. The ACP agenda was based on designing a deliberative process that used proven adult-learning principles. For example, more time was made available for participants to collaborate and construct meaning themselves. Rather than being taught by experts, the participants sought guidance from each other and from experts on their own terms. It was expected that participants would gradually gain confidence in contributing to public-policy formation. For example, the youngest participant stated at the final plenary session that she initially knew nothing about politics and was not interested in it, noting that she said little in the first two days of the ACP, but could not be stopped by the end. She concluded: "I can now go home, open the newspaper, and turn to the politics page. . . . I'm going to work for the first woman prime minister."[25]

In the Summit, the prime minister and his support team organized the discussion in terms of various streams, or topic areas. A team consisting of a federal minister and a person well-known in the field convened each stream. The convening teams then framed the issues they wanted stream participants to consider, and subgroups were formed accordingly. Although volunteer facilitators were employed, more often than not it appeared the conveners had determined beforehand how the sessions would proceed. In contrast, the organizers of the ACP avoided preframing the problems, issues, or challenges to be explored. Instead, they employed a bottom-up approach, harvesting ideas for discussion topics from multiple World Cafés and the online deliberations completed beforehand.[26] In Canberra, CPs were encouraged to take or leave these as they deliberated further.

Process integrity should result in participants, believing that they have co-created the outcomes rather than had them managed or pushed through. This was problematic at the Summit since participants, encouraged to think through their "big ideas" prior to the Summit, used their skills in charismatic influence to gain a competitive advantage through debate. This approach was unfettered by the stream facilitators. For many participants, it was simpler and safer to leave this hurly-burly of ideas to the experts. The collaborative development of proposals was the exception rather than the norm. The ACP, on the other hand, was designed to generate "*deep* ideas" through dialogue. This required (among other things) a sincere interest in what others thought and why they thought that way, exploration of different perspectives through mutually respectful dialogue, the desire to find or create common ground, and acceptance of reasons and arguments that were understandable even if ultimately one felt obliged to disagree with them.[27] Whereas the notion of "big ideas" implies intellectuality, analysis, and creativity, the notion of deep ideas adds grounding in values, principles, purposes, and priorities established *through interaction with others*.

At the end of the first day of the Summit, the co-chair of the governance stream expressed disappointment that few "big ideas" had been proposed. In small-group sessions, it was apparent that many of the specialists were less than frank and open, displaying a certain preciousness about their acquired knowledge. They spoke in cautious, tentative tones of incremental and short-term change within existing structures of government. The effect was an absence of imagination, creativity, boldness, and the willingness to think aloud for the benefit of all.[28]

Many Summit participants who were not government experts also behaved in typical political style. Familiar with partisan politics, parliamentary procedure, and bureaucratic infighting, they caucused, lobbied, and strategically bargained to have their ideas adopted. As a consequence, few new ideas arose as a result of participant interaction. Each participant came as an individual and left as an individual. The process provided no impetus to draw people out of their roles (and shells) and to prompt them to remix and redevelop their proposals into more inclusive and more far-reaching inspirations. Instead, it encouraged participants to hold tenaciously to their original views and to advocate for their adoption. As a result, they failed to capitalize on the invaluable asset of diversity. The presence of more nonspecialists might have improved the Summit discussions, if only by asking naïve but humanizing questions to provide some relief from the pedantic, technocratic habit of mind that pervaded the governance stream.

To avoid the pitfalls of the Summit, participants in the ACP were enabled and encouraged to foster the growth of "collective intelligence,"[29] the emergence of knowledge produced from collaboration, where the sum knowledge and intelligence of the small group was likely to be greater than that of the individuals involved. The potential of harnessing such collective intelligence has been shown to far exceed the knowledge, experience, and certainly wisdom of even the "best and brightest."[30]

The designers of the ACP believed that ordinary citizens would be less possessive and protective of their ideas and more willing to allow for changes to be made. While inevitably some CPs held firmly to individual viewpoints, the deliberative nature of the process helped them to let go. By utilizing processes that were nonthreatening—even fun—participants were freed from the sort of inhibition that often deters people from making valuable contributions. As a result, novel ideas and useful suggestions emerged quite unpredictably: for example, creating a "Policy Idol" (possibly a reality TV show based on Parliament); abolishing the name and ideal of an "opposition"; implementing an Indigenous Citizens' Parliament; and innovative ways to keep politicians accountable, as with a three-strikes red card. Despite participants' relative lack of "expertise," the CPs did focus on some of the more predictable, big-picture issues raised by the Summit, including, for example, a Bill or Charter of Rights, modernizing federalism, rigorously accountable government, changing the electoral system, and empowering citizens through community engagement. However, the CPs also brought fresh priorities to the fore, such as empowering citizens to participate in politics through education (done differently—by experientially practicing the sort of deliberative methods used in the ACP), citizens' question time in Parliament, and introducing optional voting for high school students aged fourteen to eighteen.

There was a different intensity to the experience of participants at each event. While participants at the Summit were often heard to say that it was an enjoyable, albeit frustrating, experience, Citizen Parliamentarians said during the ACP and later on Internet that this was "a life-changing experience." Chapter 17 confirms the enduring nature of that change.

In summary, the Summit reflected the premises that underpin "community consultation" in Australia:[31] the indispensability of experts, the tendency to focus on factual information rather than values, a single loop of feedback rather than a protracted dialogue, and the primacy of the government in decision-making responsibility. There was no attempt by the federal government to go beyond consultation to achieve "[a]ctive participation[,] . . . [a] collaboration in which citizens actively shape policy options, but where government retains the responsibility for final decisions."[32] In contrast, the design of the ACP was geared towards "deliberative democracy"—a political practice during which demographically representative participants reason together under conditions that promote mutual respect and understanding, to arrive at a broadly supported, coherent voice, which then influences policy development. Although the policy influence of both processes was moot, the participation, design, and perceived integrity, transparency, and personal transformational capability of the two processes were very different.

Conclusion

Although it was an exhilarating experience for the authors to attend the Summit and to talk with extraordinary people about the future of the nation, it was also disheartening to discover that so little of the learning and innovation that has occurred in recent years in the fields of community engagement and deliberative democracy had been incorporated into the proceedings. We believe that more profound, more dramatic, and more promising ideas would have emerged had this been the case, and that additional time spent deliberating could have developed those ideas into concrete, workable recommendations.

The prime minister's stated aim at the Summit, to "transform our future," did not eventuate. Some proposals were prioritized as issues the government would support. This, after all, is what the government committed to do at the outset of the Summit. However, neither did the grassroots-oriented ACP acquire the power of influence. It was hoped that by gaining more traction and by striking people as more democratically authentic, it could genuinely transform Australian democracy. While the ACP certainly transformed some participants in terms of their sense of efficacy and willingness to change the political system without media or financial support, it was not able to gain the breadth and depth of public exposure to bring about political transformational change. It would appear that mini-publics such as these, while an important first step in achieving more considered, democratic outcomes, may not be capable of achieving transformational change without extensive and impartial media coverage, together with new forms of collaborative governance.

To be clear, we offer the foregoing criticisms in the spirit of constructive critique. Despite the 2020 Summit's shortcomings and limited take-up of the ACP's recommendations, we believe that these two initiatives herald the beginning of a democratic renewal in Australia—and perhaps across the globe. Scrutinizing and comparing such processes help us imagine and design better ones, and it is in that spirit that we join the other authors in this volume in the collective pursuit of better understanding and advancing deliberative democracy.

NOTES

This chapter is a revised version of an article previously published as Janette Hartz-Karp and Lyn Carson, "Putting the People into Politics: The Australian Citizens' Parliament," *International Journal of Public Participation* 3, no. 1 (2009): 9–31.

   1. For example, in 1856 Australia introduced the secret ballot (known initially in the rest of the world as the "Australian Ballot"). Terry Newman, "Tasmania and the Secret Ballot," *Australian Journal of Politics and History* 49 (2003): 93–101. In 1894 the South Australian Parliament gave women the right to stand for Parliament. Australia was the first nation-state to be federated by popular vote (1901). It remains among the few countries that continue a national policy of compulsory voting (resulting in extremely high [> 90 percent] voter-participation rates). Australia was also the first country to introduce preferential voting. David M. Farrell and Ian McAllister, "1902 and the Origins of Preferential Electoral Systems in Australia," *Australian Journal of Politics and History* 51, no. 2 (2005): 155–67.

   2. On the audit, see "Democratic Audit of Australia," March 2009, Swinburne Institute for Social Research, Australian National University, accessed January 14, 2012, http://arts.anu .edu.au/democraticaudit. See also Elim Papadakis, "Constituents of Confidence and Mistrust in Australian Institutions," *Australian Journal of Political Science* 34 (1999): 75–93, and Pippa Norris, "Confidence in Australian Democracy," in *Elections: Full, Free, and Fair,* ed. Marian Sawer (Annandale, NSW: Federation Press, 2001), 202–15.

   3. Australia makes voting compulsory at state and federal levels of government as well as the local-government level in some states.

   4. For example, Lisa Hill, "Democratic Deficit in the ACT: Is the Citizen Initiated Referendum a Solution?" *Australian Journal of Social Issues* 38, no. 4 (2003): 13–19, and Lyn Carson, "Sydney Democracy Forum: The Democratic Deficit and Australia," June 29, 2007, Active

Democracy: Citizen Participation in Decision Making, accessed July 21, 2008, http://www
.activedemocracy.net/, explain this further.

5. Institute on Governance, *Rapporteur's Report: Roundtable on the Democratic Deficit;
Citizen Engagement and Consultation* (Toronto: Institute on Governance, 2005), accessed July
21, 2008, http://www.iog.ca/publications/2005_dem_deficit_roundtable.pdf. The IOG is a
Canadian nonprofit think tank founded in 1990. Its mission is to provide an independent
source of knowledge and advice on good-governance principles, standards, and practices.

6. According to Lyn Carson, "Sydney Democracy Forum," mini-publics are microcosms
of the wider public—a sample (often a random sample) brought together to deliberate to show
what the wider public would decide if given access to the information which a mini-public
receives, and indicating what the wider public would think if given similar opportunities for
deliberation. See James S. Fishkin, *When the People Speak: Deliberative Democracy and Public
Consultation* (Oxford: Oxford University Press, 2009).

7. "Australia 2020—About the Summit," accessed January 14, 2012, http://www.australia
2020.gov.au/about/index.cfm.

8. Perhaps predictably, in view of the cynicism that characterizes contemporary news
reporting, the phrase, first used by the prime minister, became a frequent—and mostly
derisive—shorthand label for the Summit. See, e.g., Malcolm Farr, "Up Close and Personal
at Rudd's Thoughtfest," and Glenn Milne, "The PM's Monster Headache," *Sunday Telegraph*
(Surry Hills, NSW), April 20, 2008, 13 and 15, respectively.

9. These streams included (1) the productivity agenda—education, skills, training, science, and innovation; (2) the future of the Australian economy; (3) population, sustainability,
climate change, water, and the future of our cities; (4) future directions for rural industries and
rural communities; (5) a long-term national health strategy; (6) strengthening communities,
supporting families, and social inclusion; (7) options for the future of Indigenous Australia;
(8) the arts, film, and design; (9) governance—democratic renewal, a more open government
(which included the role of the media), the structure of the federation, and the rights and
responsibilities of citizens; and (10) security and prosperity in a rapidly changing region and
world.

10. The leaders selected were widely respected community members—selected, it would
seem, to gain maximum public buy-in to the process.

11. Whether the need to cover their own costs was a constraining factor for some prospective participants was not made public. However, if it was, it nevertheless did not reduce the
expected number of participants, which was, as expected, one thousand.

12. For the governance stream, see *Australia 2020 Summit: Governance* (n.p.: 2008),
accessed January 14, 2012, http://www.australia2020.gov.au/topics/docs/governance.pdf.

13. There was much discussion in the media about the extent to which the selected participants were of left-leaning/Labor persuasion, despite the many disclaimers from the selec-
tors and the government that the aim and end result was to assemble a broad range of
perspectives.

14. Discussions with several stream facilitators suggest that there was no overall process
discussion about how best to reach the desired outcomes. Each stream functioned as a separate unit, and from all accounts operated with varying degrees of success.

15. *Australia 2020 Summit: Initial Summit Report* (n.p.: 2008), accessed January 14, 2012,
http://www.australia2020.gov.au/initial_report/.

16. *Australia 2020 Summit: Final Report* (Barton, ACT: Department of the Prime Minister
and the Cabinet, 2008), accessed January 14, 2012, http://www.australia2020.gov.au/final_
report/.

17. Australian Government, *Responding to the Australia 2020 Summit* (Barton, ACT:
Department of the Prime Minister and the Cabinet, 2009), accessed January 14, 2012, http://
www.australia2020.gov.au/response/.

18. Kevin Rudd, "Summit Opening and Plenary" (address at the Australia 2020 Summit,
Canberra, ACT, April 19, 2008).

19. David Burchell, *Australian* (Surry Hills, NSW), April 28, 2008.

20. Daniel A. Bell, "From Communism to Confucianism: China's Alternative to Liberal Democracy," *New Perspectives Quarterly* 27, no. 2 (2010): 18–27.

21. *Australia 2020 Summit: Initial Summit Report,* 1.

22. See, e.g., John Gastil and Peter Levine, eds., *The Deliberative Democracy Handbook: Strategies for Effective Civic Engagement in the Twenty-First Century* (San Francisco: Jossey-Bass, 2005), and more recently, the broad array of initiatives to revitalize democracy through participation documented on the Reinhard Mohn Prize 2011 site, "Vitalizing Democracy Through Participation," accessed January 14, 2012, http://www.vitalizing-democracy.org.

23. An innovative platform, CivicEvolution (accessed January 14, 2012, http://civicevolution .org/), provided citizens the opportunity to engage in an unfacilitated sustained dialogue, structured around collaboration to develop a proposal for addressing a problem, not simply creating a louder or better organized complaint or idea.

24. 21st Century Town Hall Meeting as described at America *Speaks,* accessed January 14, 2012, http://www.americaspeaks.org.

25. Julia Gillard earned this accolade when she became Australia's first female prime minister in 2010.

26. World Café as described on their website, The World Café, accessed January 14, 2012, http://www.theworldcafe.com.

27. One of the foremost proponents of dialogue is David Bohm; see David Bohm, *On Dialogue,* ed. Lee Nichol (London: Routledge, 2004).

28. Sustaining creative thought is also problematic in a deliberation, when a coherent voice is sought and often prioritization is used to select the best option.

29. See Anita Williams Woolley et al., "Evidence for a Collective Intelligence Factor in the Performance of Human Groups," *Science* 330, no. 6004 (2010): 686–88.

30. In his book *The Wisdom of Crowds* (New York: Doubleday, 2004), James Surowiecki offers many examples of situations in which input from a wide range of sources has led to better overall decisions. See also Helene Landemore, "Democratic Reason: The Mechanisms of Collective Intelligence in Politics" (paper presented at the International Workshop on Collective Wisdom: Principles and Mechanisms, Collège de France, Paris, May 22–23, 2008), revised version accessed January 14, 2012, http://ssrn.com/abstract=1845709, and chapter 3 of John S. Dryzek with Simon Niemeyer, *Foundations and Frontiers of Deliberative Governance* (Oxford: Oxford University Press, 2010).

31. This is exemplified in government publications, often using the IAP2 Spectrum, *IAP2 Public Participation Spectrum* (n.p.: International Association for Public Participation, 2004), accessed January 14, 2012, http://www.iap2.org.au/resources/spectrum. See, for example, *Consulting Citizens: Planning for Success* (Perth, WA: Citizen and Civics Unit, Department of the Premier and Cabinet, 2003), by the Western Australian government in June 2003.

32. Department of Infrastructure and Planning, *Community Engagement in Queensland Local Government: A Guide* (Brisbane: Department of Infrastructure and Planning, State of Queensland, 2010), accessed January 14, 2012, http://www.dlgp.qld.gov.au/resources/guideline/ local-government/community-engagement-guide.pdf.

3

CHOOSE ME: THE CHALLENGES OF NATIONAL
RANDOM SELECTION

Ron Lubensky and Lyn Carson

A legitimate public-deliberation process must inclusively represent the population that it serves.[1] Logistically, a deliberative process cannot deliver the whole population to the discussion. Instead, a microcosm that mirrors the full diversity and features of the public at large,[2] commonly referred to now as a *mini-public,* accepts the responsibility to deliberate in the common interest. The mini-public should be small enough to be organized into small groups that can deliberate together effectively.[3]

In establishing a mini-public, a public-engagement convener asks not just how many people should be involved, but also how they should be invited. Some conveners prefer to open an event to all comers, in the hope that by sheer force of numbers, the hundreds or thousands of participants will encompass a sufficient diversity of perspectives.[4] Other event conveners prefer using a stratified random-sample approach to create a jury-like body of two dozen participants so that deliberation can be more focused and facilitated.[5] Many eschew the jury method, however, in the belief that inevitable self-selection and abjuration in the absence of conscription compromise the result and undo the hard work of organizing it.

In this chapter, we detail how the Australian Citizens' Parliament (ACP) approached this problem. As the persons directly responsible for inviting and selecting participants, we compare the ACP's experience with one of its strongest influences, the British Columbia Citizens' Assembly for Electoral Reform (BCCAER). We also look beyond logistics to consider how the recruitment method shaped the ACP's proceedings.

Finding the Participants

Stratified random sampling is a randomized selection procedure that ensures that statistical proportionality (also called *descriptive representation*) is achieved across demographic dimensions such as locality, age, education, and ethnicity. These dimensions are divided into categories for which quotas are established from census data and other official sources.

The British Columbia Model

The ACP was largely inspired by the 2004 British Columbia Citizens' Assembly for Electoral Reform, established by the provincial government to recommend the best electoral system for the province.[6] As described by political scientists Mark Warren and Hillary Pearse, the BCCAER design was "intended to approximate a *descriptive representation* of the people of BC, to insulate the process from organized political interests, and to maximize the quality of deliberation and decision-making."[7] Participants were promised that any change from existing electoral arrangements would be presented to the public for a provincial referendum vote.

After a short campaign to encourage voter registration, the government agency responsible for conducting provincial elections (Elections BC) provided the Assembly organizers with a list of 200 citizens from the electoral roll of each of the 79 provincial electoral districts, evenly divided by gender and stratified by age.[8] These 15,800 candidate participants were sent simple letters introducing the BCCAER process and inviting each to register to attend a regional selection meeting. Most electorates yielded insufficient responses in the short time available, causing the organizers to request more randomized names from Elections BC. Of the 23,034 invitations sent, 7 percent (1,715) responded, in varying numbers per electorate.

Elections BC invited 1,441 of these respondents, including a maximum of 10 males and 10 females per electorate based on their random pool sequence number, to attend one of 27 regional selection meetings. The 964 candidates who attended these meetings were provided with further information about their task and asked to confirm their eligibility (i.e., a Canadian citizen, not an elected official) and commitment to participate, leading 50 more candidates to decline at that stage. From the rest, the names of one man and one woman were drawn literally out of hats in each electorate to constitute the assembly of 158 participants.

Three other events altered the final composition of the assembly. First, no Indigenous members were initially selected randomly, so the chair added a man and woman from the Nisga'a Nation who had attended selection meetings but were not chosen (although for statistical representation roughly seven Indigenous members would have been required).[9] Second, there were eight subsequent withdrawals, but replacements were added from a reserve list established at the selection meetings. After the BCCAER began its proceedings, replacements were not permitted. Finally, one member withdrew for personal reasons during the eleven-month journey of the Assembly.

Setting the Size of the ACP

For a national initiative like the ACP that addresses a broad question, a large number of people are required to contribute and consider a full range of ideas and positions. In particular, critical mass must be achieved for minority voices to be heard.[10] Also, the anchoring of national issues in local special interests demands geographic representation at least as granular as the constituencies of elected representatives. Thus, the ACP organizers made an early commitment to draw one participant from each of the 150 federal parliamentary lower-house electorates, to arrive at a forum size comparable to the BCCAER. By mirroring the elected chamber, organizers also hoped to compel interest in the media, politicians, and potential participants.

After deciding on the broad topic of the ACP, the organizers nominated two well-respected and eminent Australians to act as co-chairs. As the public faces of the ACP, they were selected to add gravitas to the event. Fred Chaney was a retired conservative minister in the government, and Lowitja O'Donoghue was a leader in improving Indigenous welfare. This followed the BCCAER model, which was chaired by a respected public intellectual.

In the absence of a conscription law, the organizers only had the option to send out invitations to participate and hope for the best. The decision to send invitations to about 10,000 citizens was made on the presumption that it would—with a conservative 4 percent response rate—produce a sufficiently large participant pool from which to create a stratified random sample of participants. The Australian Electoral Commission is the government agency that maintains the electoral roll, with distinct management for each Australian state and territory. One management group provided randomly selected lists for its electorates (i.e., electoral districts), but the others refused because the ACP was not a government-sanctioned institution.

Thus, the organizers worked with students to extract manually 9,653 citizens' names from recent copies of microfiche rolls for each electorate held by the National Library in Canberra.

An advertising agency accepted the task pro bono of designing the ACP emblem, which resembled an official stamp or letterhead with a stylized outline of Old Parliament House encircled with "Citizens' Parliament." The invitations shown in figure 3.1 were designed to project the prospect of pomp and ceremony, printed on cream-colored heavy card with the emblem embossed on it and an attractive cursive typeface. Again, student helpers proved essential, putting the personal touch of a self-adhesive stamp on each mail-merged envelope. Approximately 1,500 (16 percent) of the invitations returned unopened, with indications of an incorrect address. Many more misdirected invitations were likely tossed into the rubbish, but we estimated that about 8,000 invitations reached their target.

To give credibility and transparency to the endeavor, the first author constructed a public website for the ACP and applied the emblem branding across it.[11] In addition to introducing the ACP to the world, the website contained extensive background and details about how the ACP was organized and would proceed. There was also information about many aspects of Australian democracy. A page was set up for online registration of interest, and it was operational by the time the invitations were posted. A toll-free telephone number was also set up for information and registration.

The organizers were thrilled but completely overwhelmed by the response. In three weeks, 2,762 registrations were lodged—more than a third (34 percent) of the estimated number of invitations sent to correct addresses and seven times the expected result.[12] Not anticipating the huge response, one of the organizers had had a free-call number assigned to her mobile telephone to receive inquiries and registration calls. For three weeks it was constantly in use with an overflowing voicemail queue. About a third of the applicants rang, mainly older citizens in regional centers who were judging the project's legitimacy. Though some were directed to the website, the organizer painstakingly transcribed applicant details from her notepad into the registration entry screen of the website.

One Hundred and Fifty Go Off to Canberra

The online registration included a survey about the key demographic details required for stratification. These included claimed Indigenous status, elec-

It is our privilege to advise that

First / Last Name

has been randomly selected
from the electoral rolls to register for

Australia's first Citizens' Parliament

6 – 9 February 2009,
Old Parliament House, Canberra
RSVP: see over

Fred Chaney AO

Lowitja O'Donoghue AC CBE DSG

This invitation to register has been sent to less than
0.05 per cent of Australians, from the electoral rolls.

One registered citizen will be further randomly
selected, from each of the 150 Federal electorates,
to come to Canberra next February to join the first
Citizens' Parliament.

This is a unique opportunity for everyday Australians
to discuss ways to improve our political system, and make
recommendations to Government.

Travel, meals and accommodation will be provided.

RSVP: Please register by 22 August 2008 at
www.citizensparliament.org.au or call 1800 015 600.

The Citizens' Parliament is independent of any
political donations or funding.

ANU   The University of Sydney   Curtin   democracy

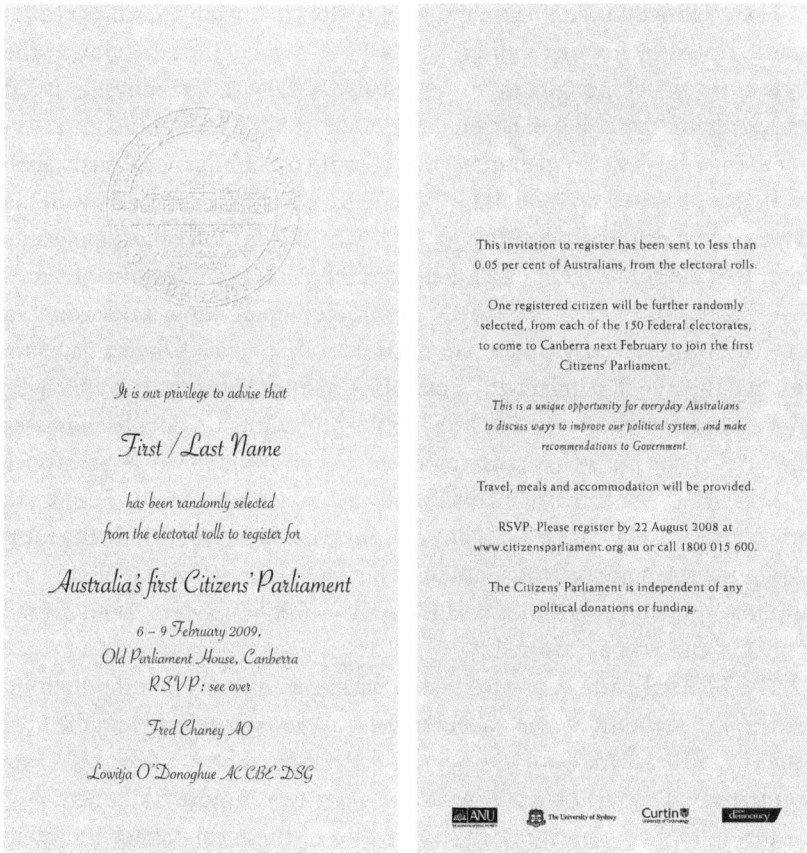

FIGURE 3.1   The invitation to the Australian Citizens' Parliament

torate, gender, age, and education level. Proportional quotas for age and education were derived from census and other data available at the official Australian Bureau of Statistics website.[13] An ideal split of seventy-five men and seventy-five women was sought. Three adult Indigenous participants were also to be found, corresponding to their 1.9 percent ethnic proportion of the adult population of Australia.

Given that the draw was randomized, it would be quite impossible to match the quotas with decimal precision. An arbitrary tolerance (the deviation above and below the quota, as a percentage of the quota) was set on each demographic dimension. The organizers were keen to gain a very precise gender balance (±pm5 percent), but demanded less precision of the categories for age (±10 percent) and education (±25 percent).

The stratified random sampling was performed using a JavaScript program created by the first author. Following is a general description of the algorithm, which sought to strike a balance between randomness and demographic matching. The procedure began with three random selections from the dozen registrations that identified as Indigenous Australian. Participants were then randomly drawn in turn from the electorate with the fewest remaining participants. As each was drawn, the other applicants from that electorate were discarded from the pool. Each demographic category filled up as each new participant incremented the gender count, a particular age category, and a particular education level. When a category reached the top of its tolerated quota, all remaining registrations who were in the same category were discarded. If the procedure ran out of candidates before participants were drawn for all the electorates, the whole procedure was restarted. When participants for all electorates were finally found, the procedure was also restarted if any category had failed to include the minimum tolerated quota. It was not until the tolerances were loosened to the aforementioned ranges that a valid result could be gained. Then a final "official" run was performed.[14]

The selected participants were sent packages formally inviting them to participate, with information about travel to regional meetings and the final trip to Canberra. All were to receive a daily stipend of AU $50, and costs were covered for those traveling more than two hundred kilometers or requiring flights. Unfortunately, twenty-five of these candidates indicated that they had changed their minds and did not want to participate. In telephone calls many cited work commitments, family events, or illness. Some were going overseas, and others indicated unforeseen circumstances or just an inability to attend. A few simply did not respond. Though the organizers expected some attrition, the large number who failed to commit led to a supplementary round of stratified random sampling based on the same algorithm.

The supplementary draw proved futile as only twelve of the twenty-five new candidates committed to participate in the ACP. Worse still, a steady stream of withdrawals occurred over the four months between the supplementary draw and the main assembly in Canberra. Many did not show up to their scheduled regional meetings, while in the ensuing weeks others decided they would rather not continue. In all, fifty-one replacements had to be found after the second draw. For the organizers who had worked so hard on a rigorously stratified randomization, this was a major disappointment.

Unlike BCCAER participants, ACP participants were already selected by the time they attended their regional meetings, because the intent of the meeting was to actually start working on their task. The regional meetings were staggered over six weeks (so that the organizers could attend each one), and this made it possible to send late replacements to later meetings held outside their own regions. This ensured that even late registrants had the same introduction to the ideals and practice of ACP deliberation, as well as an introduction to the Online Parliament (see chapter 4).

Each replacement candidate was chosen arbitrarily and manually from the same electorate as the withdrawn participant, with the closest demographic match to the withdrawn participant in priority order of gender, age, and education. The rationale was that randomness applied not only to the selection of the original person, but also to his or her demographic categorization, which was reapplied to find a similar candidate in the electorate. Each was telephoned directly and asked to participate. Unfortunately, there was often a lack of demographic matches and unwillingness on the part of called respondents to accept the direct invitation. Gradually, the demographic distributions skewed towards higher-educated and older replacements.

In the two weeks after the Christmas holiday break leading up to the assembly in Canberra, there was a flurry of withdrawals that overwhelmed and exasperated the organizers. The problem with recruiting more candidates from the original registration list was that they would not have received the crucial briefing at regional meetings. Also, not many from the original list had participated in the Online Parliament that led into the main event, even though they were invited to do so. These difficulties coincided with evolving design concerns about integrating the Online Parliament, which had been opened to all registrants, with the face-to-face assembly (see chapter 4). In the end, the organizers decided to invite 11 of the most active Online Parliament participants who were not yet part of the final group to join the Canberra meeting. This took the ACP's size up to 152.

Table 3.1 shows the final category distribution of the ACP attendees. The rise and fall in numbers through the age and education dimensions followed the quota for most categories, but there was substantial underrepresentation in the "25–34" and "65+" age categories. Also, the "Year 11 or below" education category was underrepresented, whereas university-educated citizens were overrepresented.

Table 3.1   Demographic analysis of the ACP

Category	Quota	1st Draw ($n = 150$)	Final ($n = 152$)
Male	50%	52.67%	49.3%
Female	50%	47.33%	50.7%
Age 18–24	12.43%	13.33%	12.5%
Age 25–34	17.74%	17.33%	9.9%
Age 35–44	19.47%	18.67%	21.7%
Age 45–54	18.31%	17.33%	23.7%
Age 55–64	14.53%	16.00%	19.7%
Age 65 +	17.52%	17.33%	12.5%
Education Year 11 or below	32.7%	25.33%	17.1%
Education Year 12	20.7%	21.33%	14.5%
Education Trade qualification	25.6%	29.33%	27.6%
Education Bachelor degree	17.5%	19.33%	27.0%
Education Postgraduate degree	3.5%	4.67%	13.8%
Indigenous	1.91%	2.00%	1.97%

Selection Effects on the ACP Process

That the ACP participants were randomly selected had mixed effects on their attitudes and performance. On the plus side, almost all participants reveled in their good fortune to be involved. During proceedings, it was taken in stride that daily table seating and callouts during plenary sessions were randomized. Many participants expressed the view that they felt that randomness had made the process fairer. They felt that they did not have to justify their right to be there.

Many participants thought the ACP was government-sanctioned, even though there was no intent to deceive them. They saw themselves as standing shoulder to shoulder with their elected members of Parliament, and many identified strongly as representatives of their electorates, although this declined during the three days of deliberation. Several gained local newspaper coverage. However, there were many others who accepted the invitation as a lottery chance for an expenses-paid adventure holiday to Canberra. Australia is a large country, and many, especially those who lived in far-flung rural corners, had never visited its political center.

Participants were frequently reminded of the academic research purpose of the ACP. Starting with the completion of research consent forms at the

regional meetings and continuing through a litany of survey, direct observation, and conversation audio recording, the participants were constantly
probed. Each participant wore a name badge that had a number on it
(although it was a number that was familiar to them). The random selection
added to their oft-expressed feeling that they were merely research subjects
and hardly empowered in the full sense that deliberation promises.

Through informal discussions in Canberra, it became apparent to most
participants just how many of them had been replacements. They expressed
surprise at why anybody would choose not to take part or change their
minds afterwards. While many participants wondered whether they would
make a useful contribution, and some had accepted against the advice of
relatives and friends, there is no conversational evidence that participants
who made it to the end ever questioned their involvement. The BCCAER
was more demanding because its process required almost a year of multiple gatherings, whereas the ACP participants needed only to attend one
regional meeting followed quickly by the main event in Canberra. Sociolo-
gist Amy Lang suggests that a protracted public-engagement process can
only retain people who have a tendency to see things through to the end, to
finish what they start.[15] In both the BCCAER and the ACP the lock-in was
complete when the main assembly began. But the BCCAER was able to
gain participant buy-in earlier and avoid the cascade of attrition that befell
the ACP. Participants at the BCCAER were repeatedly asked to commit
themselves, then actually saw themselves being drawn out of a hat. This act
was not technically necessary as the final cohort could simply have been
computer-generated as with the ACP. It complicated the selection process
and resulted in a lower match to the ideal demographic distribution. It had
a powerful symbolic impact on participants who had to make a very public
commitment. With few replacements necessary thereafter, the demographic distribution did not get any worse.

The standout quality of the ACP recruitment procedure was its ability to
attract a massive initial pool of registrations, due primarily to the compelling design of the invitations and the website. The online registration made
it easier for those who chose that method. Candidates signed up to the ACP
even though they admitted to a poor understanding about Australian government.

However, after attracting such a large pool, the commitment of ACP
participants was not sufficiently sustained. Unlike the BCCAER, which
promised to make a real political difference, the ACP was more moderate

in its aspirations. As with most public-engagement processes, including the BCCAER, there are no data available about why people withdraw. It is a difficult research problem, because participation in survey or interview is contradictorily required to gain these data from people who no longer want to participate. Even if these data are gained, as was attempted by the recruiting officer for the ACP, they may not be reliable because people may avoid telling the whole truth, such as when they have lost faith in the process or the ultimate value of their participation.

Lang suggests that the unavoidable self-selection inevitably exaggerates the trait of enjoying learning and consequently being fearless about it.[16] This was certainly evident in the ACP, as the majority of participants arrived open to the unknown possibilities and then spoke often and positively about the opportunity to learn more about how government works from the experts and each other. While this trait may not be as extensive in the broad public, the quality of deliberation would certainly be enhanced by it. The flip side is that the significant proportion of people who would tend to resist challenge to their knowledge or opinions, or who might naïvely dismiss the ACP as a mere "talkfest," would probably not sign up.

The trait evident in the BCCAER of participants tending to be involved in community activities was less evident at the ACP. Surveys of the ACP showed that while most participants enjoyed working in groups, there were many who had a disregard for decision making in groups like committees and caucuses.

The BCCAER selection process applied stratified sampling to draw the initial pool of invitations, and then used simple random sequencing and selection to derive the participants from the self-selected registrations. The BCCAER ended up with overrepresentation by people who were "white, older, university educated, and employed in or retired from professions" and active community volunteers.[17] On the other hand, the ACP started with simple randomization to get the pool of invitations, then applied stratification to the self-selected registrations to derive the participants. Even after the manual replacement procedure, which skewed the distribution, the ACP ended up matching its demographic ideal better than the BCCAER because stratification occurred after self-selection in the ACP. This could have been improved if computer software had been developed to dynamically and randomly select the next best replacement candidate from a subset of participants who would improve the demographic fit at that stage.

Selection Effects on the ACP's Outcomes

But did it matter? To what extent did the demographic dimensions stratified in the ACP cohort impact the process and the outcome?

There is broad acceptance in the public-engagement literature that gender equity is necessary, and it is usually easy to accomplish in a randomly selected mini-public. There are claims that women in general present a different ethical perspective than men, especially one of care and welfare over rational efficiency.[18] However, the ACP did not consider proposals that were motivated by a gendered perspective. There are also claims that women tend to bring conversational styles that are more rapport building to small groups,[19] although the conversational record at the ACP revealed women to be at least as dominant and forceful as the men. Perhaps balancing gender may have acted as the most visible symbol of the inclusion that randomization promotes.

Stratifying by age is clearly crucial in deliberations about political matters. There is ample evidence that people shift in general to more conservative positions as they age, so it is vital to draft the full range of ages. At the ACP, the importance of setting public policy and especially opportunities for civic education to benefit the inheritance of youth was often repeated (see chapter 5). The tension between reinforcing traditional institutional structures and advancing democratic practice became evident because tables were populated by both young and old. The exuberance and blue-sky considerations of the younger participants were tempered by the fixed framings of those who were older. While the elder category was statistically underrepresented, their occasional confusion and disorientation demanded useful clarifications and elaborations that highlighted the perspectives and needs of older citizens.

The conversational record of the ACP shows that locality was indicated more than any other demographic dimension. In many discussions, different regional perspectives were expressed. Participants were surprised to learn about differences in government operations, regulations, and conventions between states. However, the ACP had no caucusing by region on any proposal topic, unlike the BCCAER, which included a strong "northern" voice. Participants from the large east coast cities took genuine interest in the relevant experiences of those from elsewhere in the country. Their evolving identity as an alternative national "parliament" was formed directly because they came from every corner of Australia (see chapter 18).

As in the BCCAER, ethnicity was not statistically sampled or surveyed, and there was a dearth of visible minorities in the room. James suggests that the path of the BCCAER's dialogue may have been different if the various Asian ethnicities had been represented more fairly.[20] Since participants were sourced from the electoral roll for the ACP, residents from other countries who had not gained Australian citizenship were filtered out. However, several naturalized immigrants made their mark in the ACP by telling personal stories and pointing out frequently how Australian democracy is taken for granted when not compared to situations elsewhere. Ensuring that the ACP had more than just an accidental subset of foreign-born participants would have increased its deliberative legitimacy.

A Final Note: Sampling for Political Orientation

One dimension that was not pre-canvassed was political leaning. A year following the ACP, participants were surveyed whether they subscribed to the political left or right. While there was some representation at each end, on a sliding scale most placed themselves around the middle. Survey data of participants after selection indicate that both conservative and progressive views were well represented in their choices for media consumption and the role of government. However, their political distribution against any benchmark or national average is difficult to assess, as these categories cannot be made definitive and they are moving targets through successive election cycles and opinion polls. Had they been asked in their selection questionnaire for whom they voted in the last election, trust in the ACP organizers might have been undermined and the validity of that data might have been poor.

One hazard of public deliberation that relies at least in part on self-selection is that such processes might disproportionately attract participants who enjoy political engagement and value collective benefits.[21] In contrast to the BCCAER, the survey of the ACP participants did not reveal a strong tendency to community involvement, but the willingness to participate in itself recognizes value in the public rather than just private interest. However, the prevailing expression during the ACP of personal freedom and rights as important democratic values shows that there was sufficient representation in the room of an individualist discourse in the context of democracy. More research should be done to explore how dimensions such as political leaning, ideological orientation, cultural cognition of risk, and discourse categories can be stratified effectively in random selection,[22] as these could potentially raise both the substantial and the symbolic legitimacy of public deliberation by mini-publics.

Political scientist Graham Smith summed it up well when he wrote, "The use of random selection may challenge our prejudices of what a legitimate representation entails, but it does ensure that mini-publics engage a broad cross-section of citizens with a diversity of social perspectives."[23] The main lesson out of the *near-random* recruitment procedure performed for the ACP is the need to bolster the commitment of participants from the moment of first contact right through until the deliberative process begins in earnest.[24]

NOTES

1. John S. Dryzek, *Deliberative Democracy and Beyond: Liberals, Critics, Contestations* (New York: Oxford University Press, 2000).

2. Lyn Carson and Brian Martin, *Random Selection in Politics* (Westport, Conn.: Praeger, 1999).

3. Yves Sintomer, "Random Selection, Republican Self-Government, and Deliberative Democracy," *Constellations* 17 (2010): 472–87.

4. America*Speaks*, accessed January 14, 2012, http://americaspeaks.org/.

5. On Citizens Juries, see Ned Crosby and Doug Nethercutt, "Citizens Juries: Creating a Trustworthy Voice of the People," in *The Deliberative Democracy Handbook: Strategies for Effective Civic Engagement in the Twenty-First Century*, ed. John Gastil and Peter Levine (San Francisco: Jossey-Bass, 2005), 111–19.

6. British Columbia Citizens' Assembly on Electoral Reform, *Making Every Vote Count: The Case for Electoral Reform in British Columbia: Final Report* (Vancouver: Citizens' Assembly on Electoral Reform, 2004). Its origins lie in process recommendations from Gordon Gibson, a former leader of the provincial Liberal Party, in a report he gave to the government as a consultant. Gordon Gibson, *Report on the Constitution of the Citizens' Assembly on Electoral Reform* (Vancouver: n.p., 2002), accessed January 14, 2012, http://www.citizensassembly.bc.ca/resources/gibson_report.pdf.

7. Mark E. Warren and Hilary Pearse, eds., *Designing Deliberative Democracy: The British Columbia Citizens' Assembly* (Cambridge: Cambridge University Press, 2008), 10.

8. British Columbia Citizens' Assembly on Electoral Reform, *Making Every Vote Count: The Case for Electoral Reform in British Columbia: Technical Report* (Vancouver: Citizens' Assembly on Electoral Reform, 2004).

9. Michael B. James, "Descriptive Representation in the BC Citizens' Assembly," in Warren and Pearse, *Designing Deliberative Democracy*, 111.

10. James, "Descriptive Representation," in Warren and Pearse, *Designing Deliberative Democracy*, 122.

11. Australian Citizens' Parliament website (no longer active), http://www.citizens parliament.org.au.

12. Unlike the BCCAER, the ACP had no special eligibility requirements, allowing one local government councilor to accept random nomination, unknown to the organizers.

13. Australian Bureau of Statistics, accessed January 14, 2012, http://www.abs.gov.au.

14. The complete algorithm is available, in plain English, from the first author.

15. Amy Lang, "But Is It for Real? The British Columbia Citizens' Assembly as a Model of State-Sponsored Citizen Empowerment," *Politics and Society* 35 (2007): 35–70.

16. Ibid.

17. Warren and Pearse, *Designing Deliberative Democracy*, 10.

18. Virginia Held, *The Ethics of Care: Personal, Political, and Global* (Oxford: Oxford University Press, 2006).

19. Deborah Tannen, *You Just Don't Understand: Women and Men in Conversation* (New York: Ballantine, 1990).

20. James, "Descriptive Representation," in Warren and Pearse, *Designing Deliberative Democracy*, 123.

21. For evidence that comfort with political talk, self-belief in political efficacy, and organizational membership are predictors for deliberative participation, see Lawrence R. Jacobs, Fay Lomax Cook, and Michael X. Delli Carpini, *Talking Together: Public Deliberation and Political Participation in America* (Chicago: University of Chicago Press, 2009), 43–63. The authors discuss collective benefits on p. 82.

22. John Gastil, Laura Black, and Kara Moscovitz, "Ideology, Attitude Change, and Deliberation in Small Face-to-Face Groups," *Political Communication* 25 (2008): 23–46; Dan M. Kahan, Donald Braman, John Gastil, Paul Slovic, and C. K. Mertz, "Culture and Identity-Protective Cognition: Explaining the White Male Effect in Risk Perception," *Journal of Empirical Legal Studies* 4 (2007): 465–505; John S. Dryzek and Simon Niemeyer, "Discursive Representation," *American Political Science Review* 102 (2008): 481–93.

23. Graham Smith, "Deliberative Democracy and Mini-Publics," Proceedings of the Political Studies Association Annual Conference, 2008.

24. "Near random" comes from Warren and Pearse, *Designing Deliberative Democracy*, 10.

4

GRAFTING AN ONLINE PARLIAMENT ONTO A FACE-TO-FACE PROCESS

Brian Sullivan and Janette Hartz-Karp

The Australian Citizens' Parliament (ACP) organizers faced several significant challenges. Among them were the geographic distance between participants living in a vast continent and the commitment to let the participants themselves shape the direction and design of the ACP. To address both these challenges, an Online Parliament was introduced. Whereas chapters 7 and 11 look at the deliberation that occurred online, this chapter provides the larger context for understanding the Online Parliament. Herein, we explain why online deliberation was grafted onto the ACP's face-to-face process, why the CivicEvolution platform was selected, the role it played, the participation process and rates of involvement, the challenges faced, and what would be done differently in a future initiative.

In terms of geographic distance, the ACP involved a randomly sampled person from every electorate across Australia (see chapter 3). Bringing a microcosm to a single location was expensive (airfares and accommodation) but reflected the diversity of the population. However, to tackle the challenge of *participant control of the agenda,* regional meetings were convened in many state capitals. The meetings were brief, providing sufficient opportunity to meet people and be introduced to the ACP but inadequate time to develop the agenda. The Internet offered one way to enable further deliberation, in a different way, before the Canberra event. Whereas some participants would be comfortable with large plenaries and small face-to-face deliberation groups, others would prefer the relative anonymity of being online.

Moreover, to give a clear sense of direction, it was important for each deliberative process to build on the one before it. Months of inactivity between the regional meetings and the face-to-face ACP would not be helpful. Finally, the ACP was tasked to address a very broad question—"How can Australia's political system be strengthened to serve us better?" Experts on the organizing team could have determined what they thought should be the focus, but it was deemed important that participants should do this themselves and prior to the Canberra event.

A final reason for using online deliberation was that the response rate had been far more successful than could have been predicted. Of the 8,000 randomly selected citizens who received an invitation to nominate to become a Citizen Parliamentarian, an extraordinary 2,762 registrations were received (see chapter 3). However, only 150 were needed—one randomly selected person per electorate. Rather than simply informing the remaining nominees that they had been unsuccessful, they were offered an opportunity to have a role in the overall process. They were invited to join as Online Citizen Parliamentarians (OCPs) to develop proposals that would be the initial focus of the face-to-face ACP in Canberra.

Selecting an Approach for the Online Parliament

Although there are numerous online participative tools, such as "mashups," Facebook, Twitter, wikis, private social networks like Ning, and survey tools, there are few that could be called enablers of deep or deliberative democracy. The distinctive characteristic of deliberation is that participants listen to each other's positions and, after mutual understanding and due consideration, generate group decisions based on consistency of rationales.[1] Given the difficulty of keeping participants involved for long enough to have such conversations, it is no wonder that much online participation has more to do with advocacy, dump and run, or populist voting than indepth deliberation.

We needed online-deliberation software that could deliver deep deliberation and help frame the ACP agenda. A simple aggregation of opinions would not suffice. We wanted a process to lead the participants from discussion to deliberation and hopefully find some convergence. We could not afford the cost and organization of online moderators. However, most available online tools without moderation offer unstructured dialogue and/or an aggregation of individual opinion rather than enabling deliberation. Similarly, online forums and surveys have no mechanism for understanding divergent views and developing common ground. There are some managed online solutions, such as Ascentum,[2] which use third-party mediation or facilitation to graft the process onto the tool. However, it was thought this approach could have limited the scope of issues and would incur additional cost and organization.

A further constraint was offering an asynchronous process that would allow people to participate at their own convenience. Asynchronicity offers greater possibilities for exploring the issues while simultaneously increasing the difficulty of achieving a deliberative experience. The multiple turns of dialogue, listening and responding, are much more challenging in an asynchronous environment, where each turn often necessitates a return visit in an indeterminate future. The ultimate goal of "thinking together" is complicated when people are not actually together in real time. It requires mechanisms to encourage people to return again and again. E-mail notifications, personalized calls to action, and a well-designed website can only offer a partial answer to this challenge. Generating the necessary personal motivation to return and participate is even more important than the technical elements.

Providing compelling motivation to deliberate online is not easy. Shirky evolved the concept "the promise, the bargain, and the tool" for understanding the success of websites such as Wikipedia and Flickr and the failure of countless others.[3] Good design, according to Shirky, starts with a compelling and plausible promise. Once the promise is clearly articulated, the designers and sponsors must develop a bargain that enables delivery on the promise, clearly articulating responsibilities and expectations. Only when there is a promise that motivates participation, and a bargain that encourages striving towards that promise, should the designers turn their attention to choosing a tool. We adopted Shirky's formulation, but since process is as important as a tool in online deliberation, we slightly amended it to "promise, bargain, and process."

The platform with the best fit was CivicEvolution.[4] Its tagline is "Think together to act together," and deliberation is coded into its DNA. It is designed to facilitate thinking together, not mere aggregation of private opinions. Some of the guiding principles behind the CivicEvolution platform include the requirement for participants to be self-driven and not dependent on facilitators or moderators. Participants self-manage the development of constructive output through a collaborative process. It is open to participation at any point, at any time, offering a continuum of engagement opportunities with a path toward ever-deeper involvement. These principles aligned well with the goals of the ACP. Organizers could not anticipate how far citizens could progress in a self-managed, empowered environment. Importantly, it was agreed that the functionality of the platform would be customized to the final requirements of the ACP.

The Role of Online Deliberation

Although CivicEvolution seemed to be a good fit with the ACP, it had a hesitant beginning. The first hurdle was scheduling time for the organizers to consider carefully how the online deliberation would fit into the mission of the ACP. Few of the organizers were experienced in online deliberation, and their attention focused more often on research and logistical questions. Ambivalence about the Online Parliament's place in the ACP was exacerbated by the fact that this process would not incorporate all ACPs (i.e., not all would have the capacity or the interest to work online).

Even once a small subgroup agreed to develop the Online Parliament, disagreement remained on whether its basic mission was to showcase online deliberation for government observers or, more modestly, to simply generate proposals for the ACP to consider. Although it was known that motivation to keep the OCPs involved would be pivotal to the success of the online deliberation, there was no agreed strategy to achieve this. The details of the face-to-face ACP were still being developed, and this was vital information for the creation of the online platform so that the end result would be relevant. With face-to-face deliberation, this is often done much closer to the event, so the development of the online deliberation platform had to proceed blindly in this regard. There were also innumerable practical platform challenges, such as how many participants should constitute a deliberation group, how much proposal detail would be required, and whether deliberative quality should be factored in. In sum, the CivicEvolution designer (the first author of this chapter) had to develop the Online Parliament's platform without clear organizer agreement on the purpose and direction of the online deliberation.

Online deliberation finally came to the fore of the organizing team's discussions with the decision to invite those people not randomly selected for the ACP to be Online Citizen Parliamentarians, rather than to forgo the contributions of so many willing participants. After serious debate, organizers decided that the OCPs' proposals would form the initial content agenda for the face-to-face ACP, though this decision about content agenda was strongly contested at the organizing team meetings. Alternative views were that "experts" on the organizing team should provide this input or that proposals should come through an analysis of the Q-sort methodology conducted at the regional meetings (see chapter 10).

The selection of CivicEvolution and opening the Online Parliament to all respondents resulted in two unintentional experiments. First, there were now two different groups of people engaged in a joint deliberative experience.[5] They differed in their motivation, their exposure to the ACP organizing team, the information they received, and the ways they came together. (See chapter 7 for their different perceptions as well.) Second, the topics of interest often depended on prior exposure to deliberation and information. The face-to-face ACP participants learned about deliberation and were encouraged to think systemically. The online participants were given some written guidance online, but it did not prove to be persuasive. Online participants wanted to create concrete proposals about specific government policies and services, rather than reflect on systemic concerns that addressed the topic of how to strengthen Australian democracy.

Customizing the Platform

Once the purpose of the Online Parliament was set, the focus was then on creating a process and tool to help participants shape the ACP opening agenda. The proposals developed online would serve as the opening agenda for the ACP and thereby potentially influence the final outcomes. The more tenuous promise was that the final outcomes from the ACP would be presented to the prime minister, members of Parliament, and the media, hopefully resulting in some influence on future government policy. The bargain the participants accepted was that the proposals had to meet the following criteria. They had to be developed in an open and collaborative manner with at least four other participants, and they had to fit the charge given to the ACP. Participants had to answer the questions provided as an outline for the proposal, and their proposals had to be endorsed by other online participants. The Online Parliament platform was then designed to make that happen.

The Online Process

Stage 1: Responding to the "Charge"

The Online Parliament took place over three months, from October 2008 into January 2009, several weeks prior to the face-to-face ACP in February 2009. Since the online deliberation was developing proposals that would serve as the opening agenda for the ACP, their charge was the same: "How can Australia's political system be strengthened to serve us better?" Any participant could suggest a proposal, and fifty-eight were suggested in all. Examples of their suggestions included "One man one vote," "Eliminate the preferential ballot in favor of a first past the post system," "Devise a way to hold politicians accountable for their electoral promises," and "Two Levels of Governments instead of three. Removal of State/Territory Governments." Some of the proposals were suggested and partially developed at the regional meetings, and many others were posted online.

When an idea was suggested, it was posted on the online home page along with a brief description of the problem and the proposed solution. All online participants were encouraged to browse the ideas and consider joining a team to develop the idea into a proposal. They all received periodic emails informing them about new teams and encouraging them to join a team.

Of the 58 ideas suggested, 39 attracted at least four participants, who then commenced work. Of these 39, however, 11 ultimately were classified as having too low a relevance to the ACP charge. These ideas addressed specific government policies and services rather than addressing the charge of strengthening our political system. Examples included "Make and Produce everything Locally in Australia" and "Road Laws and license age should be uniform for all states." Altogether, of the 58 ideas suggested, 31 were relevant to the ACP charge, and 27 were not. Notably, those who had attended regional meetings behaved differently online compared to those who were online-only, hereafter called OCPs.

Specifically, a sizable minority of the OCPs (41 percent) joined only low-relevance group discussions—thereby squandering their online participation in off-topic deliberation. By contrast, only 13 percent of those more fully introduced to the ACP through regional meetings made that same mistake.

An equally striking statistic concerns the depth of participation between these two groups. The OCPs outnumbered two-to-one those online participants who were part of the ACP's face-to-face process: there were 180 active OCPs, compared to just 99 who had attended regional meetings. Nonetheless, the OCPs posted just 199 comments in topic-relevant groups and 320 comments overall; by contrast, their counterparts posted a total of 1,014 comments, with 924 (91 percent) occurring in high-relevance discussions.

Clearly, there was a failure in communicating and reinforcing the parameters of the charge to the OCPs. At regional meetings, a similar tendency occurred with the ACPs' initial proposals, but there was opportunity to address it. Understandably, people chose to address issues with greater perceived immediacy and importance to them. Unfortunately, however, communicating solely online with OCPs who would also have been less invested in the process was an inadequate way to harness their effort.

Moreover, it took time to make the decision about relevance and respond. For the proponents of the unsuitable ideas, this was frustrating. There was effort made to mitigate this. Acknowledgment was given to the importance of their issue, followed by an explanation as to why that issue could not be addressed by the face-to-face ACP. Also, members of these teams were given the opportunity to continue developing their idea if they so chose. Alternatively, they were encouraged to advance another idea that still addressed their particular issue but reframed it so it focused on the charge of strengthening the political system. However, there was little take-up of either of the latter two options. Instead, these OCPs tended to drop out of the online deliberation. This highlighted the inherent tension with framing: no matter how broad, it can still be offputting, inhibiting participation, unless a clearly articulated promise (for example, some influence), makes participation worthwhile.

Stage 2: Developing the Proposals

The development of an online proposal involved following the broad outline "Define the problem you want to address," "Consider policy options," "Analyze the options," and "Make a recommendation." Participants were guided by the provision of three to five supporting questions under each of the outline headings. The expectation was that this work would be done collaboratively and deliberatively. Participants needed to discuss each question by reading and adding comments online, as well as suggesting and rating key points that would help answer the questions. There were up to eighteen questions on which participants could engage in a focused discussion. For example: "How can you explain this problem in one or two sentences?" "Who is affected by this problem? Try to consider all of the stakeholders." "Why should citizens care about this problem?" "What are other potential courses of action to deal with this problem?" and "Has anything been done or proposed to address this problem thus far?"

Rather than writing a full answer, participants were encouraged to discuss the questions and share their ideas using key points. Any participant could offer a key point, which other participants could then discuss, rate, and/or edit. Through this process of discussing, rating, and editing key points, the team developed an outline for an answer. Given past experience of online deliberation where individuals were often reluctant to write full answers or to edit others' answers, this process enabled easy collaboration. It was hoped that participants would evolve the answers over time, but this rarely happened. A set of key points would be developed by team members that captured the gist of their discussions, but there was little evidence that the teams actively edited their key points or sought convergence. The key points developed for each question were automatically compiled into a proposal. In the final phase, the team members could select which talking points would be included in the proposal and could order them to increase their coherence, discussing this online. Once the proposals were finalized, they were submitted to the team members to be endorsed. Every proposal that was endorsed by at least four team members was then posted for prioritization by all those participating in the online deliberation.

To support discussion on each question, the interface was designed to feel familiar by mimicking an e-mail application. It provided a threaded list of comments and key points for the users to browse, respond to, and rate, as shown in figure 4.1. The key points also allowed for a five-point Likert rating for agreement. The key points not only appeared in the thread of the discussion, but were extracted and displayed on the left side of the interface to act as a summary of the team discussion under each question. New content was highlighted so visitors could focus on the recent additions. New content was also reported to them via daily email reports.

From the user's home page, he or she could easily access the question workspace, and calls to action were displayed to direct the user to the most appropriate places to participate, as shown in figure 4.2. Access to the questions was organized into steps aligned with the topics "Define the problem," "Explore the options," "Analyze the options," and "Recommend a policy." Ideally, participants were expected to progress through the stages in order, starting with defining the problem. However, they often started with a solution in mind, skipping the broad exploration for the best solution. It was decided not to enforce deliberation in a predetermined sequence, but rather allow participants to proceed as they preferred, usually talking about all of the issues in the first few discussion areas. Since this was an asynchronous

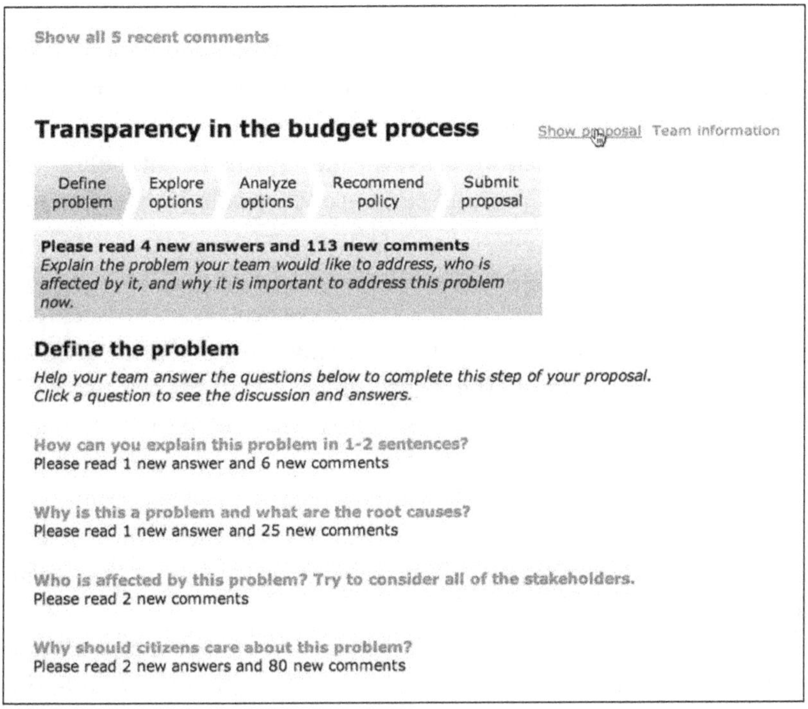

FIGURE 4.1   The interface for answering a question with discussion and key points

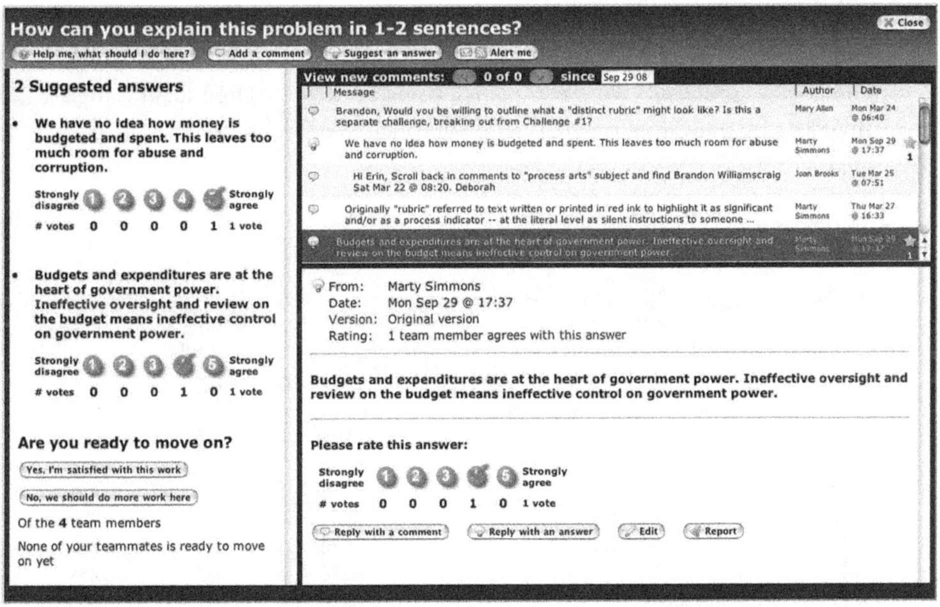

FIGURE 4.2   How the proposal appeared in the participant's home page

environment that relied on the voluntary return of every participant every time, it was unrealistic to create a fixed process with artificial constraints and expect the participants to abide by it. Instead, it was decided to maximize participation by minimizing potential impediments to engagement.

Of the eligible participants who had the means to participate online (having an e-mail address), 89 percent of those also attending face-to-face ACP events (hereafter called Citizen Parliamentarians, or CPs) signed up for at least one team, compared with 9 percent of OCPs (participating only online). Many signed up for a team but did not actually participate in the deliberation—perhaps thinking that showing support for an idea was enough. In terms of those who signed up for teams, 66 percent of CPs added at least one comment compared with 46 percent of OCPs. Similarly, more of the CPs were prolific contributors (40 percent) compared with OCPs (9 percent). The greater proportions of CPs committing time and effort to the online deliberation were understandable: the promise of influence was more motivating for the CPs than the OCPs. The CPs had a plausible narrative that justified their effort.

In terms of overall participation in online deliberation, table 4.1 shows that only 9 percent of the OCPs actually took the opportunity to do so, and fewer than 2 percent contributed three or more comments. This relatively low take-up shows the challenge of online deliberation among ordinary citizens in settings of this kind. From the 39 teams that launched their proposals, there was a total of 1,334 comments contributed by 157 participants and a total of 814 key points contributed by 101 participants. In the end, eleven proposals were completed, prioritized, submitted to, and then reviewed by the Canberra ACP and were included in the final report (see chapter 11).

Table 4.1   Online deliberation participation statistics

	ACPs		OCPs	
	Count	Pct.	Count	Pct.
Valid e-mail	123	100%	2,082	100%
Signed up for at least one team	99	80%	180	9%
Added at least one comment	72	59%	85	4%
Added 3 or more comments	57	46%	37	2%
Added 6 or more comments	44	36%	17	1%
Added a key point	52	42%	49	2%
Rated at least one answer	76	62%	91	4%

Merits and Downsides of the Online Deliberation Process

A highlight of developing the initial ACP proposals online was the powerful impact of having the top five prioritized proposals presented by their team members at the Canberra ACP opening ceremony. These online team representatives, seated at the central parliamentary table, formally presented their group's proposal to both the prime minister's representative and their fellow Citizen Parliamentarians, seated around them in the chamber, as well as to other members of Federal Parliament and invited guests, seated upstairs in the gallery. Starting the deliberations with the citizens' voices and the citizens' ideas was an ideal way to set the scene. The proposals were broad and formed a solid starting point for the face-to-face deliberations that followed. Moreover, since these proposals did create the opening agenda, there was an immediate sense that this was indeed a citizen-led parliament—the citizens had real influence over what would be discussed. A number of ACPs said how important this was in terms of being a clear disjuncture from the usual government top-down directed engagement. Additionally, ACPs gained confidence that their everyday wisdom was sufficient to understand and deliberate complex governance issues.

On the downside, some members of the organizing team thought the online proposals were not sufficiently visionary or innovative. Moreover, only around half of the Canberra ACP participants had submitted ideas to the online proposals, and therefore not everyone had participated in the agenda setting. For these reasons, much of the first day of the Canberra ACP was dedicated to all participants working in small groups to develop new proposals. An additional downside was the unintended consequence of some online deliberators feeling considerable "ownership" of their proposals and loyalty to their fellow team members who were not attending the Canberra event. Some of these participants noted that insufficient weight was being given to the fact that their teams had invested considerably more time and thought into developing their proposals than the short proposal-development sessions at the Canberra event. As a consequence, rather than being willing to put self-interest to one side to listen to others and stay open to others' rationales and viewpoints, a few were committed to defending and strongly advocating their proposals to others. Even towards the end of the deliberations, some still felt the same, expressing their disappointment or frustration with the ACP when their proposals were not prioritized.

Much was learned about desirable surface-level design. The format for the proposals was too long and complex. Participants were asked to discuss and answer thirteen questions. Each of them was valid and important, but as a whole, thirteen was too many. One colleague on the organizing team remarked, "I wouldn't ask my graduate students to complete such an onerous task." A direct result of the myriad questions was that the conversation became too scattered. Participants avoided this by expanding the conversation in the first few questions to cover all issues, as they saw fit. Only near the end, when they were pressed by time to complete their proposals, did they actually visit the other questions and input their key points. The most recent applications of CivicEvolution have reduced this to four basic questions: "What do you want to change?," "Why is it important to our community?," "How can the change be made?," and "Where do we start?" Additional cues are provided to encourage participants to consider different perspectives, but the focus remains on presenting a concise format that is not overwhelming.

We now recognize that the user interface was also too complex and not sufficiently user-friendly. The CivicEvolution platform has been in constant evolution toward simplicity and a more intuitive, deliberative, and collaborative process. However, it is the challenge of eliciting deeper and repetitive online engagement that remains the greatest obstacle to deliberation. Most people are content with superficial engagement. For example, clicking a "Like" button is seen to be a legitimate form of participation. This was evidenced by the numbers of people who clicked to join a team but never went further. For others, leaving an opinion and comment constitutes engagement. Neither of these constitutes deliberation. Notably, Facebook is now promoting what it calls "frictionless sharing"—sharing that occurs automatically when something else is done, like selecting a song from a playlist or "liking" a cause. However, when there is no intention behind the act, it makes sharing meaningless. Deliberation cannot occur without intention.

The goal of voluntary, self-directed deliberation requires even greater depths of engagement. The participants must be challenged and motivated, but not overwhelmed. This is often referred to as being in a state of flow.[6] It is the condition of finding a task sufficiently challenging and interesting to be absorbing, so individuals feel intrinsic motivation. This requires a delicate, adaptive process of incrementally increasing the challenge in response to the participant's skill and success. However, enabling participants to reach the stage of real immersion in online deliberation is anything but easy. Participation is purely voluntary, and the motivation has to be justified at every decision point and often reestablished. Each return by a participant is the result of a decision to engage.

This is closely aligned with the three principles behind good games: autonomy, mastery, and purpose.[7] Autonomy means you participate at your own pace and time. Mastery means you are improving your skills and learning. Purpose implies you find meaning and value in the task. All three are essential to ensuring a high level of ongoing engagement, a definite prerequisite to constructive collaborative deliberation. Another prerequisite is the existence of a continuum of possibilities for engagement, including simple rating by clicking, through to sharing opinions, refining key points, and deliberating over differences.

Conclusion

There are few examples in the literature where online deliberation has been integrated with face-to-face processes in ways that are innovative and add value without adding significant cost. The Australian Citizens' Parliament demonstrated one example of how this could be done. There were many lessons learned as a result. While most who participated in the online deliberation found it to be worthwhile, and many said they enjoyed the experience and learned a lot as a result, the key learning for the organizers was that truly deliberating online, without the support of synchronicity and a moderator, is a very difficult task.

Online deliberation is not a common experience, and attempts to introduce it are competing with a long history of much more shallow and often more entertaining online activities. Every asset that can be mustered, including game-design principles and flow, needs to be utilized in order to engineer a compelling user experience. This is much easier to achieve in a face-to-face engagement, where an effective facilitator is far more entertaining and warm than the best software interface. Even easier for face-to-face deliberation is the fact that participants usually need to be attracted to the deliberation space just once. However, this is also the weakness of face-to-face deliberation—its limited reach and greater demand for resources and the typical lack of comprehensive follow-up and continuity of effort.

The Online Parliament was important to the ACP not only because of the competent proposals it developed—almost all of which were integral to the ACP's final recommendations—but also because it demonstrated how geographic distance and insufficient time and money can be overcome to achieve a modicum of deliberation. Achieving deeper deliberation online without the support of moderation will be an iterative process, each iteration learning from and improving upon the last. The online deliberation at the ACP was an important step in this process.

NOTES

1. John S. Dryzek, *Discursive Democracy: Politics, Policy, and Political Science* (Cambridge: Cambridge University Press, 1990); and John S. Dryzek, *Deliberative Democracy and Beyond: Liberals, Critics, Contestations* (New York: Oxford University Press, 2000).

2. See http://www.ascentum.ca.

3. Clay Shirky, *Here Comes Everybody: The Power of Organizing Without Organizations* (New York: Penguin Press, 2008).

4. One of the authors of this chapter, Brian Sullivan, is the founder of Practical Evolution, LLC, and the designer and director of the CivicEvolution platform.

5. It should be noted that there is some overlap between these two groups. Some OCPs were later selected as replacements for those randomly selected ACPs who had dropped out of the process prior to the Canberra event for health or other reasons. There was also some, but less movement in the other direction. A few ACPs who could no longer attend the Canberra event persisted as OCPs. The statistics noted here relate to their final status as OCPs or ACPs rather than their initial status.

6. Mihaly Csikszentmihalyi, *Flow: The Psychology of Optimal Experience* (New York: Harper and Row, 1990).

7. Daniel H. Pink, *Drive: The Surprising Truth About What Motivates Us* (New York: Riverhead Books, 2009).

PART II

EXPLORING DELIBERATION

The central purpose of the ACP was to harness the power of democratic deliberation, and the chapters in part II provide a portrait of that deliberation. Most of the chapters in this part are based on the transcripts produced from the recorded table conversations at the ACP. The chapters demonstrate a range of useful approaches to studying the deliberation itself.

Chapters 5 and 6 showcase the interpretive approach. Ron Lubensky presents a story arc in the ACP in "Listening Carefully to the Citizens' Parliament: A Narrative Account," and suggests critically that a storied perspective of deliberative activity may enhance public acceptance of it. Then Laura W. Black and Lubensky show how the CPs themselves effectively used stories during their Canberra assembly in "Deliberative Design and Storytelling in the Australian Citizens' Parliament." In chapter 7, John Gastil applies social-scientific approaches to assessing deliberation in both the Online Parliament and the ACP in "What Counts as Deliberation? Comparing Participant and Observer Ratings."

Through an interpretive study reported in chapter 8, "Hearing All Sides? Soliciting and Managing Different Viewpoints in Deliberation," Anna Wiederhold and Gastil look at how the ACP welcomed, discouraged, and generally handled attitudinal diversity through different forms of discussion and dialogue. Chapter 9 returns to the social-scientific mode, with Joseph Bonito, Renee Meyers, Jennifer Ervin, and Gastil aggregating the transcript data to look at speaking-turn inequality during the various ACP discussions in "Sit Down and Speak Up: Stability and Change in Group Participation."

5

LISTENING CAREFULLY TO THE CITIZENS' PARLIAMENT: A NARRATIVE ACCOUNT

Ron Lubensky

Deliberative public engagement is not yet a topic that is well-known outside its academic and practice communities.[1] Invariably I have to explain what it is before talking more about it. Sometimes I try to describe the Australian Citizens' Parliament (ACP) project, which I helped organize and study. It is rarely an easy task.

My explanations about the ACP often degenerate into defenses of public engagement as a whole. I face oft-told stories about the democratic deficit and voter ignorance, although not always using those terms.[2] In response (and sometimes preemptively), I have paraphrased the survey comments of participants after the ACP was complete. Most, who had never done anything like this before, wrote generously about the process and their experience of it. For instance, one Citizen Parliamentarian (CP) said that the ACP gave "an appreciation of my role in the governance of country. I now feel that I have enough knowledge to participate in a constructive way." Another used that same word—"appreciation"—when reflecting on the ACP: "It has given me a greater appreciation for the difficulties of governing in Australia" and "restored some faith in our politicians and opened my mind to the other view."

In my experience of deliberative processes, such appreciation is common. CPs commented more on the effect of the process than on its various outcomes. The activity of public engagement left a lasting mark on them, and to get us past the abstractions of deliberative political theory, we should share their stories.

Thus, my task in this chapter is to open a window to the story of the ACP's participants, from their own perspectives. I take a social-constructionist stance in the research into and rendering of this story. This means that I am not authoritatively claiming a master story from which all interpretation of the ACP should follow, nor am I claiming that the story line presented here is the only one. Instead, I am demonstrating that a reflexive, storied approach to analyzing the events, based on narrative methods of discourse analysis, provides useful insight into the process and the capacities of participants.

The Plot

The organizers created a comprehensive agenda that included preparatory activities leading to a face-to-face assembly for four days in Canberra. The participants worked through a series of steps to arrive at an outcome that had a predetermined format: a list of proposals for national democratic improvement. This agenda effectively frames the story.

In narrating their story, I have reduced that agenda to five overlapping activities that follow an alphabetical dramatic arc of rising intensity leading to resolution: *Gather, Hope, Inquire, Judge,* and *taKe* (see table 5.1).[3] These activities can be mapped to most deliberative processes, although the emphasis and boundaries may vary.

For the purpose of briefly demonstrating the constructionist method and its usefulness in this chapter, I have prepared a "mini-story" of the

Table 5.1   Narrative arc of deliberative process

Gather:	Receive an invitation, make contact, enter a hospitable space, meet and begin to know one another. Be welcomed. Set the norms of civil behavior. Feel safe.
Hope:	Establish why we have been gathered. Express our individual and mutual goals and aspirations. Appreciate what there is. Articulate the problems that we want to solve. Imagine a future. Believe we can reach a conclusion.
Inquire:	Explore the facts, concepts, each other, ourselves. Share. Tell stories. Find surprises. Make empathetic, appreciative, inclusive, open, sincere, civil, cooperative gestures. Expand, diverge, envision, emerge.
Judge:	Harvest, theme, make choices, prioritize, categorize, synthesize, negotiate, seek consensus, collaborate, converge.
taKe:	Take up and take on. Consent to judgments, prepare outcomes, commit to action, next steps, archive documents, reflect on process, disseminate agreements, celebrate.

experiences of the younger participants and the shepherding of proposals about youth engagement and education. I invite you to read my commentary critically. It is intentionally written in the present tense to bring you into the scene.

Gather

Invitations

The story of every participant who attended the ACP begins with the happy surprise of receiving a compelling and attractive invitation in July 2008. From the strong response, one applicant from each of the 150 federal lower-house electorates is randomly selected to participate in the ACP (see chapter 3). Eighteen participants are aged from eighteen to twenty-four years of age. Unlike many of the older married participants who accepted the invitation in spite of their partners' cynicism, all of the young CPs tell me that they had been encouraged by their parents and friends when I ask them why they accepted the invitation. As one says, "I wanted to learn something new. I am twenty years old and I don't really know much about politics and what goes on around Australia. Plus I wanted the experience. I thought it would be fun."

For many older participants and a few of the younger ones, the ACP provides an opportunity to identify with—and be recognized for—participating in an initiative of national significance. Consider the reasons given by CP Dan, from whom we will hear again later. He says that he wants "to gain more experience and understanding of politics. Being part of the younger generation, I believe that some of my thoughts and ideas can be put forward and better the Australian political system."

Many older participants speak of feeling "privileged," "honored," and "important" about their inclusion. But younger participants generally express their sense of good fortune at having "an opportunity to contribute as a young person" and to "have a say." They are "ready for adventure."

Regional Meetings and the Online Parliament

Their first contact with organizers occurs at one of fifteen regional meetings aimed to introduce them to the project, to practice the deliberative method of small-group interaction, and to start them thinking together about how to strengthen Australia's democratic system. The CPs show a range of engagement styles in these early gatherings.

The Adelaide regional meeting, for example, is attended by Skye, who at eighteen years of age is the youngest CP and would become something of a celebrity in Canberra. During this initial orientation meeting, however, she is wide-eyed and shaking. She speaks timidly but takes everything in eagerly. At a Melbourne meeting, twenty-one-year-old medical student Robert, who had been up all night working as a hospital intern, remains determined to pay attention and contribute. At a meeting in Sydney, nineteen-year-old Nick pays attention but hangs back.

At a different meeting in Melbourne, seven CPs gather for the first time, including young Sharlene and Debbie. After their introduction and some brainstorming about Australian democracy, they take up the idea of a national curriculum for learning civics in schools. In the absence of table facilitation at the regional meeting, tension rises as an older woman, Ellen, presses her case strongly without acknowledging the perspectives of the others:

ELLEN: They just need to get back to teaching basic history, and within that, the history of our democracy, our democratic system.
SHARLENE: Well, Australian history should be first, I think, in my o[——] . . .
ELLEN: Of course! Well, it should be . . . not . . . not only . . .
DEBBIE: Not in grade 5, but later on maybe in high school . . .
SHARLENE: No. . . . When we're doing, when we're back doing, what was it, "SOSE," when that was actually like social, the Study of Society and Environment . . .
ELLEN: Well I think the reason . . .
SHARLENE: . . . that's something that is relevant to our own country.
ELLEN: The reason *my* generation is fairly well informed on politics is because we were taught . . . history . . . and politics . . . in school.
SHARLENE: Yeah, well, I think it needs to be done.

In addition to the regional meetings, CPs also have the opportunity to take part in the Online Parliament to generate an initial slate of proposals (see chapter 4). Only half of the youngest cohort sign in, and only two make multiple and substantial contributions. The proposal about a civics-education curriculum is copied online, but it does not gain sufficient participant support to advance.

Meeting in Canberra

On February 3, 2009, the 150 selected participants gather in Canberra. Many traveled from far across the country. The opening session is held in the grand House of Representatives chamber of Old Parliament House.[4] CPs occupy the seats where previous generations of members of Parliament had sat, and some tremble with excitement and pride. They are welcomed into their new roles by speeches from the event's distinguished co-chairs, a government minister, and the ACP organizers.

To begin proceedings, five proposals are introduced by the participants who had helped develop them during the Online Parliament. Kenneth, one of the older CPs, introduces the proposal he helped create about public engagement through education. He receives warm applause after he speaks:[5]

> Our group's proposal is to empower the citizens of Australia politically, and empowerment needs several things. It means that we need to have political ideas and attitudes. We need to have capabilities that we can use in the political arena. We need to have the techniques and skills to use those capabilities. We need to have opportunities to use our political capabilities and of course, we need to have awareness of where those opportunities lie. . . . [We] believe that through this experience of being involved in politics at the educational level, these students will then, as they progress through their lives, feel more empowered to engage in politics in the wider sense.

At the start of each day in the Members' Dining Room, CPs are randomly seated at twenty-three tables and reintroduce themselves to their tablemates. The youngest CPs rarely identify themselves by electorate, although it is on their name tags. But by the third day even the older CPs introduce themselves instead by their general home locality:

DAN: Hi, I'm Dan from Sydney. I'm having a reasonable time, it's interesting hearing people list out their ideas, so, yeah, it's been enlightening for me in lots of ways.
ALISON: Alison from Melbourne. This is amazing, it's mind blowing and wonderful to hear so many perspectives on things that I've . . .
FACILITATOR: Where in Melbourne, sorry, just that I've got on my mind those Victorian fires.

ALISON: I'm from metropolitan Southeast.

FACILITATOR: Right.

ALISON: So the areas they're talking about, I know people in them.

On this occasion the room had just heard a morning report that bushfires were raging across northeast Victoria, with devastating loss of life and property. The participants and facilitators are isolated from the rest of the world, including their families. Gathered, they share their worry.

Hope

In their first small-group exercise on Day 1 in Canberra, CPs cast their vision forward three days to imagine what a successful ACP would look like. Many of the older participants focus on the outputs in hope that the ACP would have substantial influence on government. Several participants also hope to demonstrate the value of the engagement process:

IAN: It's a really important initiative, and you never know it could be the start of something very interesting in Australia in terms of, you know, the way the government, the way our democracy works. So it's good to be a part of it.

FACILITATOR: Yep, okay.

SHARLENE: My ideal weekend . . . I think everyone will . . . gain more knowledge and understanding of the political system . . . for a common view perhaps or discuss why they've come to that decision to that view. So just to really get a vast knowledge of what everyone else is thinking and why.

FACILITATOR: Excellent.

SHAUN: I think the involvement in the process creates success in itself and finding out about other people too. I would hope that at the end of this that there would be at least two proposals that would go forward that was backed by solid arguments and were compelling proposals that government would actually seriously address.

At his table, CP Doug is optimistic but restrained in his expectations. To these CPs, the question about the ACP's "success" is ambiguous. Did the organizers mean success for the process as a whole, or personally for the individual participants? Doug works from the latter interpretation. Notice how the CPs are already seeking mutual agreement:

DOUG: I think tangible results are going to be hard to see because it's going to take time. I was very excited to be part of this purely for, [CP] Katrina said it, to learn a bit more about politics in this country, I don't know a lot, I don't know much at all but I'm willing to learn. I'd like to see that there's other people out there in the same boat that I'm in. . . .

FACILITATOR: Is there somebody else who would like to say what success would mean to them?

AMY: I agree with everything Doug just said, well everything, and at the end I would like to say that we hope we can contribute something of value to make this a precedent for the following years to come if possible.

Some of the older participants speak sarcastically, revealing their attitude of cynicism. When the facilitator asks, "What do we want to achieve here?" the outspoken CP Ed says, "Maybe dot points. That's going to help us drive this country into the future."

The first exercise relating to content occurs in the multiround style of a World Café (WC).[6] Between rounds the participants disperse to sit at new tables of their choice. In the first round, they address the question of what they "appreciate in a democratic system that works well." Young Robert makes an early contribution at his table: "Being secure in the knowledge that the government is acting in our best interests." A lively discussion then teases out some nuances about the safety and security afforded by good government, but neither this CP nor another young CP, Lory, participates further, even with prompting by the facilitator.

Responses at other tables mention hopes about the Constitution, social and political inclusion, voting, access to politicians, accountability, openness, and vigilant media. At one table, the young participants identify signs of a healthy democracy, but they struggle to link them to particular structural features:

FACILITATOR: So when do we know it's at its best?

ANAND: When people don't complain. [laughter]

ED: Well I think when we've got fair and equal representation in the decision-making process. [pause]

ADAM: I don't know about when it's working, but there is some evidence that Australia is a great country to live in, so something's got to be right.

FACILITATOR: How do we know when it's right?

ED: We live in harmony and peace with each other, I suppose.

ADAM: That's it.

FAY: I suppose when everyone's happy, something's working.

Inquire

The next day, the participants move past abstractions such as these and thrash through concrete proposals for reforming Australian politics and government. They modify, combine, and add to the list of proposals from the Online Parliament to generate a list of fifty-two ideas. As the participants work through various agenda exercises, these proposals are recorded and synthesized in real time behind the scenes by the academic "Theme Team," who receive suggestions and comments via notebook computers at each of the discussion tables.

The following conversation occurs during an Open Space session at a table that attracts participants interested in the proposal "Empowering citizens to participate in politics through education":[7]

WAYNE: I think that the major problem is that most, well not most but a lot of people vote on what their grandfather, their father and their mother all say. . . . You know, you just vote because your Dad voted Labor and I vote Labor, or Liberal or National or Greens or whatever.[8]

FACILITATOR: So do you think that's a good family tradition?

WAYNE: No. It's stupid. They should be taught more at school to get involved in politics and understand where each party is coming from, what their pros and cons are, rather than just go along with whatever a person who is older than them has told them that that's the way it is.

JANE: Yeah, and that's where I think the education of the youth needs to come in. There's no education in schools on how our politics works. . . .

FACILITATOR: (turning to Lars) What do you think is a factor in Denmark, that has not compulsory [voting] but [still] a high level of participation?

LARS: Well, I think it is because, one, it's a small country. You possibly therefore, we feel closer engagement with our politicians. I'd like to say too that I think we should give citizens the right to not participate, if they so choose. . . .

VIV: But something has to be put in its, you can't just take the enforced, the compulsory vote away, without putting in an education system or something like that.

LARS: Oh, exactly, exactly.

This all-in conversation shows participants collaborating to build knowledge and making sense of the question about whether education is a more democratic alternative to Australia's compulsory voting law. While the topic is ostensibly about all citizens, they frame education as a matter just for youth. Active facilitation provides probing questions that open opportunities for all participants to bring in new ideas and reflections. Wayne brings a storied perspective about why leaving voting to family units may be insufficient, Lars relates the situation in his native Denmark, and Viv offers a summarizing coda.[9] They work their way down to the implied question about how education can inspire youth towards independent political judgment:

JANE: It's only as people seem to get older that they take more interest in politics.
LARS: Once you get a mortgage!
JANE: That's what I've found, like when I was young I didn't care, and my friends didn't care. And it's as I've gotten older and as friends around us have gotten older that there seems to be more developing and interest in what the government is doing and who's who and you know.

Viv and Moira articulate an answer and their summary is entered into the table notebook computer for transmission to the Theme Team:

VIV: Yeah, harness that passion and idealism and if, you know, and marry it up with education.
MOIRA: Say, education of the young, make them aware, enthusiastic, and passionate about issues.
VIV: And maybe if it's not compulsory to vote, they'll feel it's a privilege and they'll leap on it, in an ideal world [laughs].

From the start, young CP Skye hardly says a word. But during the Open Space session, she chooses to join a table talking about a proposal to "Ensure the Expertise of Ministers."[10] Skye asks question after question about how a ministerial office works, such as "Could the minister, once selected for that particular portfolio, then address his own staff by advertising for a person in that field, like the CEO of a hospital or, to be his second person?" Later she asks, "Don't they kind of get an advisor? They're an advisor to him through research?" And again, "So would there the secretary and all those ministries and all that, would they be experts in that field?"

At another table, there is prejudice against the capacity of teachers to present politics in an objective manner. The participants miss CP Donna's point that people can learn from each other rather just than relying on the authority of teachers:

DONNA: Well this [the ACP] is a prime example of how to educate the others. To me this is . . .
ROSS: You've got to get, with the schooling you've got to get unbiased views of educating people because there's a lot of teachers that are say unionist teachers and they lean . . .
ALISTAIR: One way or the other.
ROSS: . . . so there's no sway.
ASAD: They're never on the fence, they're always totally extreme left or totally extreme right.

These conversations about political education are usually about electoral voting decisions rather than the operation of government or the potential of practicing democracy in school:

ZOE: Do you think it would be helpful if teenagers were given the option to vote?
SHARLENE: Yes, I do.
IAN: What do you call teenagers? Do you mean under eighteen?
FRANK: Fourteen to eighteen.
ZOE: To get people involved at a young age while they're learning about it.

That idea is sent through by table notebook computer to the Theme Team.
At another table, Kenneth is having trouble getting others to see his perspective of politics relating generally to institutional decision-making activities rather than just to the structure of government and voting, even though he had introduced it during the opening plenary session:

MAXINE: What would you feel as a teacher? You said you're a teacher?
MURNI: . . . It's quite dry and unless they see that relevance and the connectedness . . . , writing to members of Parliament and all that, it's not going to mean much. . . .
KENNETH: I would like to see it based on real issues in the schools, for example if the school was coming up with an issue like "let's change the

starting hour," instead of that just being decreed, that the students should be invited to create a political process to do that. . . .

MAXINE: They do that somewhat when they elect their sports captains.

On Day 3, a table of three young participants and older CP Ellen realize the problem that different Australian states follow different school curricula:

ANDY: I would have to definitely agree that it is very important to have [history] in the education system. I'm sort of confused how people missed it because I had excursions in Year 6 down to Canberra where we did political stuff and . . .

ADAM: Are you in New South Wales?

ANDY: Yeah.

ADAM: That's New South Wales's curriculum and the other states don't have it.

ANDY: In Year 7 I had Australian history and we did federation and all stuff about conscription and World War I; we did all the referendums going through the 1940s through to 1960s.

ELLEN: Sorry, was that in your history?

ANDY: Yeah, that was compulsory into Year 10, and that was in the school certificate so everyone in the state had to do that. . . .

SKYE: In South Australia there's nothing. There's absolutely nothing.

ANDY: They should all have the same.

Thus, this conversation ties their desire for education about politics in school to the proposal about "harmonization of state laws."

Judge

On Day 3, with a weighted ranking procedure operated through the tables' notebook computers, the CPs identify and prioritize democratic values and then, with those in mind, rate the various proposals. There is little time to talk through their comparisons, but Dan makes a case for encouraging the political engagement of youth:

DAN: It may not be anything to do with you but I know I seem to come back to "youth engagement in politics" because in twenty years' time down the track, when all these things come up, I'm going to be your age. I'm going to be like all the guys up the back there [the expert panel]. We're going to be forties, fifties, or whatever. . . . you've got to still look at what I'm going to be turning into.

KATHY: Is that so bad?

DAN: . . . I reckon you ask any general kid off the street [like me], . . . and ask them about politics, they're going to have no clue what you're even on about. They probably won't know who Liberal and Labor are.

At many tables, participants suggest that two proposals—empowering citizens through education (labeled "Proposal D") and youth engagement in politics ("Proposal K")—should be amalgamated or grouped together. One table divides into discussion pairs to decide and then report back before making their ratings:

ASAD: What is the most important for you in the long term?

HILTON: "Youth engagements in politics," in the long-term strategy I think [Proposal] K.

MARTIN: . . . Getting the youth involved is one thing, but shouldn't we get everyone involved? Because we've got a long time before we have to worry about the youth actually taking over and taking charge. Shouldn't everyone be engaged in education about our politics?

ASAD: I agree, you've got, every three or four years you get a new government and the youth from the age of say six or seven have got five or six terms before they get into government, anyway. . . .

GAY: [Proposal] D is number one.

PENG: Yeah, I agree with that.

MARTIN: We had [Proposal] M, which was "Empowering citizens to participate in politics through community engagement." See, I'd love that one to be in community engagement/education.

SHERYL: You've got D, K, and M?

HILTON: Yep, D, K, and M.

In a fishbowl exercise on Day 3 before prioritizing the proposals,[11] nominated participants relate proposals to the democratic value identified earlier as "freedom":

SHARLENE: The biggest one for me and my fellow peers, I think, will be youth politics . . . through the education system. A point that was raised yesterday that I think was fantastic that if you don't like something you can do something about it. . . . If you don't like how the politicians are running the county or what they're doing, you can become a politician. I think that's such a magnificent freedom. . . .

BRUCE: . . . I certainly agree with the young lady from Victoria, get youth engaged in politics. The youth are the future in this country and if we want to maintain our freedom we've got to make sure the next people coming along have the same feelings that we have and get them to do the dirty work over the next thirty years!

taKe

On the final day, the top proposals are summarized in speeches delivered to a government representative. Here are parts of what CP Sharlene says in support of the "youth engagement in politics through education" proposal:

> Good morning, everyone, my name is Sharlene and I'm going to be talking about youth engagement in politics. . . . I think we need to start from a lot further down in primary school when we're sponges and ready to learn. I think also a lot of us are forgetting that voting is compulsory. . . . So many of our youth are walking into voting booths with absolutely no idea as to who to vote for and why, that's something that needs to be addressed. . . . A lot of you seem to think . . . that we don't want to learn, this is untrue. If we are given the tools in the right way we will explore them, we will learn and we will help to shape your nation. I promise you, give us the chance and we will.

Near the end, Skye is interviewed on stage, by virtue of being the youngest participant in the ACP. "This has been a pretty big learning experience for me," she says, "because I didn't know a thing about politics when I came here. And I just feel like I know a lot now, and I feel like I can go home and read the paper and just turn straight to politics and understand it." Warm laughter and applause follows. One of the lead facilitators interjects, "That's all right. Here's a question. What, apart from turning to the politics section in the paper, do you have any sort of wild ideas about what you might want to do with your life or anything?" Skye earns encouraging laughter and applause when she replies, "I'm going to work for the first woman prime minister!"

The lead facilitator then invites the oldest participant, the ninety-year-old Elizabeth, to the stage. He asks, "What advice have you got . . . for Skye as our youngest Citizen Parliamentarian here?" Elizabeth says, "Oh, learn all you can, join in all you can, participate in all you can, and give all you've got." To this, the assembled CPs give a standing ovation. Outside, a special photograph is taken of all the young participants. Two weeks later, Skye gains employment in the office of her elected state Member of Parliament.

Conclusion

It is no coincidence that the mini-story I have just rendered reads like a documentary screenplay or radio broadcast. Contemporary documentary-making practice reveals a story mainly through the actions and words of its subjects, ideally with limited or no narration at all.[12] Invariably, such documentaries demand an empathetic regard that challenges surface judgment; however, a constructionist storytelling demands more transparency.

There is a recognizable hint of the story genre of youth maturation and acceptance by an adult world.[13] Rendering a story that aligns with a meta-narrative helps readers make sense of what occurred and provides associative meaning that makes it memorable. Perhaps if the broadcast media sought and recognized some entertaining story genres evolving in deliberative activity, we would see more compelling mainstream coverage.

At the ACP, there were incidents of adultist positioning ("*my* generation is fairly well informed") that deflated young people and inhibited their participation.[14] In a deliberative process, the perspectives of youth are recognized and the dominating habits of adulthood are tempered, but not without substantial intervention by facilitators. The conversations show how different people view learning and education. Recent school graduates are comfortable with the modern pedagogic practice of learning collaboratively and constructively through the group performance of problem-based learning and role-play.[15] This is in contrast to many older participants, who believe that education is for children and learning should primarily still be a didactic process of fact dissemination by a teacher-authority. There is also the tendency of conservative citizens to view democracy (and education) as a set of institutions with historical legitimacy rather than as a set of evolving everyday practices, which demands different pedagogic treatment. Still, many did realize the collaborative adult-learning potential of deliberation.

The mini-story illustrates how participants become aware of the complexity of their task. In this case, they began with distinct proposals to consider, but then realized through their discussions how there were substantial and often unpredicted overlaps between them.

My depiction reveals the need for improvements in process design and facilitation to help participants understand each other better and recognize more clearly the implications and values embedded in different perspectives. More reframing guidance by facilitators would be useful. In a nutshell, participants need more time and assistance to unpack and reflect on what they say to each other.

By only choosing to follow the themes of youth and education in this rendering, I necessarily shifted attention away from other narrative perspectives of the ACP. It is important that I reiterate that this is just one story from the conversational landscape of the ACP. I could present others, such as the evolution of certain proposals as participants became more informed, or the adaptation of the online-proposal stakeholders during face-to-face deliberation. The more stories one reads, the more nuanced one's understanding of deliberation becomes. By vicariously witnessing the immediate proceedings rather than just judging its outcomes, one can construct a more compelling picture of what makes deliberation worthwhile, in spite of its occasional shortcomings.

NOTES

This chapter is a revised extract from a more complete PhD dissertation.

1. Scholars and practitioners use several overlapping combined terms: *deliberative processes, civic engagement, public deliberation, facilitated public participation*. They are all a mouthful. Perhaps we need a new ironic term along the lines of a "murder of crows."

2. The democratic deficit describes the perceived failure of politicians and public servants in a democracy to satisfy the ideal expectations of the public.

3. We are used to literary, theatrical, and cinematic drama typically following the three-act script of *setup, complication* (usually referred to as *confrontation*), and *resolution*.

4. This now houses the Museum of Australian Democracy: http://moadoph.gov.au/ (accessed January 17, 2012).

5. This is only an extract of the monologue. Omitted text is replaced with ellipses. The reduction here and in other quotes in this chapter is due to space constraints.

6. For details about the World Café process, see The World Café, accessed January 17, 2012, http://www.theworldcafe.org/.

7. For details about Open Space format, follow the links from Open Space World, accessed January 17, 2012, http://www.openspaceworld.org/.

8. In Australia, the Liberal and National parties represent the conservative side of politics.

9. In narrative analysis, text is divided into conversational episodes that display strong cohesion, with a concluding statement ("coda") that performs a recognizable communicative action, like summarizing.

10. In the Australian system of government, the executive comprises elected members of Parliament of the governing political party, who lead one or more (a "portfolio" of) governmental departments as "ministers."

11. Nominated participants have a conversation on the stage, while the rest of the assembly witness and reflect on what is said.

12. Australian readers would be familiar with the *Australian Story* format presented on ABC Television (http://www.abc.net.au/austory/, accessed January 17, 2012). Over radio and the Web, BBC, Radio Netherlands, and National Public Radio (U.S.), among others, present similar self-told documentaries.

13. Akin to the classic German *Bildungsroman*.

14. *Adultism* describes the disrespect that adults may exhibit to deny youth of developmental opportunity and voice. See John Bell, "Understanding Adultism: A Key to Developing Positive Youth-Adult Relationships," 1995, FreeChild Project, accessed January 17, 2012, http://www.freechild.org/bell.htm.

15. Problem-based learning (PBL) is a learning theory that promotes learning in challenging simulated situations. Participants must collaborate to plan actions and design appropriate solutions as if they were really "on the job." Instructors conduct themselves as mentors rather than authorities. For example, see Cindy E. Hmelo-Silver, "Problem-Based Learning: What and How Do Students Learn?" *Educational Psychology Review* 16 (2004): 235–66.

6

DELIBERATIVE DESIGN AND STORYTELLING IN THE AUSTRALIAN CITIZENS' PARLIAMENT

Laura W. Black and Ron Lubensky

Over the past decade, several deliberation scholars and practitioners have discovered the importance of personal stories in public deliberation.[1] Stories describe experiences that relate to some kind of problem. They are told through the eyes of a character, who typically is both the protagonist and the storyteller. When people tell complete stories, their tale has a clear beginning and end, plus something in the middle, like a surprising turn of events, that makes it seem worthwhile to the listeners, who derive meaning from its telling.

The Australian Citizens' Parliament (ACP) provides a special opportunity to examine the role of storytelling in deliberative events because it provides a complete transcript of the small-group discussions that constituted the heart of its process. Though the organizers provided the Citizen Parliamentarians (CPs) with complex analytic tasks each day, the CPs sat in small groups of just six or seven persons each and found the time to tell stories.

It is our contention that one cannot understand what transpired at the ACP until one takes stock of those stories, and that is the purpose of this chapter. We investigate the stories citizens told about their own — and other people's — experiences, as well as how the other CPs responded to these stories. In addition, the variety of discussion methods at the ACP lets us consider how those influenced the telling of stories over the course of the four-day event.

What Stories Accomplish

Storytelling is an innate part of human life, a fundamental way that we make sense of our social world.[2] From infancy on, we listen to and learn from stories, and stories are pervasive through many aspects of our adult lives. Stories reproduce cultural values, and many of our fundamental understandings of morality come to us in narrative form.[3] We use stories to describe events in our lives, give meaning to these events, and even make sense of who we are.[4] Thus, it should not be surprising to find that people in deliberative forums exchange personal stories.

Deliberation involves both analytic and social purposes (see chapter 7), and storytelling has implications for how participants accomplish these tasks. Even humble "introduction" stories can help deliberators accomplish social tasks by building relationships, displaying values, and establishing a shared understanding of their goals and priorities.[5] Stories also bring deeply held values and beliefs into the conversation and can thereby invite perspective taking and dialogue in the group.[6]

Stories can accomplish analytic tasks by helping group members build arguments and think through the implications of different policy choices.[7] Stories provide examples of people's experiences related to the issue at hand and can influence the group's decision making by pointing out positive or negative aspects of a proposal or by critiquing expert sources.[8] These "argument stories" can be adversarial, in that they highlight divisions among deliberators to sharpen disagreements within the group, or they can be consensus-building stories, which are told in a way that demonstrates connections between different people's experiences and promotes a collaborative approach to problem solving. Finally, some stories told during deliberation can be used to help frame a vision for the future, which can enable people to imagine how policies might influence their communities in the long term.[9]

Research Questions and Method

The ACP may have elicited a rich variety of stories by using a varied set of deliberative methods.[10] The primary format was similar to a 21st Century Town Meeting, but the organizers added many other processes.[11] On Day 2, participants engaged in a World Café discussion that involved switching tables every fifteen minutes.[12] Day 3 featured a "fishbowl" session, in which nominated participants talked with each other on stage about an issue while everyone else listened. The third day also involved complex, inter-linked prioritization exercises to finalize a set of proposals for presentation to public officials on Day 4. Given that storytelling is always influenced by its context, we expected these different deliberative methods to shape how stories were told and responded to by others.

To examine the link between discussion format and storytelling, the first author of this chapter examined a manageably sized random sample of twenty-four group tables, including six from each day (approximately one-quarter of all discussions). Within each table discussion, the basic unit of analysis is the "storytelling event," which involves both stories and the responses they elicit.[13] Responses often occur immediately after the story was told, but they can also appear much later, so long as they directly refer to the events of the story.

The first analytic step involved the first author reading through the selected transcripts and identifying story-telling events within each small-group task session demarcated by the organizers. Next, the analysis looked across the different groups to discern any larger patterns in story content and function. Finally, storytelling patterns across the ACP's different days and discussion formats were compared to test the expectation that delibera-tive design influenced storytelling.[14]

Day 1: Aspirations and Analysis

Our analysis begins with Day 1 of the ACP. After an extended formal wel-come, only half an afternoon remained. The time for discussion at each table was divided into four segments: introductions, aspirations for the ACP, analysis of some of the proposals, and reflections about the discussion.

Introductions

As an icebreaker exercise, facilitators asked CPs to provide their name and an object that held special meaning for them. Two tables had explicit story-telling events in the introduction. At Table 2, many CPs chose objects that centered on their family. Several of these involved brief stories, such as one from a CP who introduced himself by sharing how his eyeglasses showed a connection to his father. Other CPs responded to his story and some made comments about their own fathers. At Table 23, the facilitator engaged in a great deal of casual conversation before the official introductions. He asked several questions about CPs' specific experiences, such as "Did you do any of the Online [Parliament] work?" He also talked about his own personal experiences over the past few days, which sparked several CPs to share stories about traveling to the ACP, dealing with the heat, seeing the sights, and so on. Subsequently, several CPs introduced themselves via stories and commented about each other's experiences. For example, one CP chose the object of his wedding ring, which he was not wearing: "Hello, everyone, my name's Antony. My thing is my wedding ring. I don't wear it though, because I'm an electrician, and it's very dangerous to wear rings. . . . Hence, I forgot it. I remembered on the flight, and I thought, oh well, so that's a little something." "Fantastic," the facilitator replied. "That is fantastic, thank you very much." Two speakers later, another CP commented, "I never wear my wedding ring. I always forget it." During the introductions, several other CPs told stories about specific experiences in their lives. At the end of the introductions, the facilitator talked more about wedding rings and told a story of how he had caught his ring on things when he was falling. After his story, several CPs joked about the "dangers of marriage." The content provided in these stories is fairly trivial and is not directly related to the policy proposals that CPs were about to deliberate about. Yet it may have been helpful in the more socio-relational aspects of the group's dynamics.

Aspirations for the ACP

The next task faced by groups that day was to discuss their aspirations for the ACP. In the six tables analyzed for this project, *only* Table 23 engaged in any substantial storytelling during this task. All other groups were involved in making lists of very general statements about what they hoped the ACP would accomplish. Speaking turns were very brief, and statements were at a very abstract or general level.

When the group at Table 23 took on this task, their conversation involved lengthy stories from multiple group members and over several speaking turns. Most of these stories were about how CPs had contacted either politicians or media outlets in their area prior to coming to the ACP. In this group, group members directly solicited stories by asking questions such as "Anybody been contacted by their local Members about the weekend?" In response to this question, one CP said,

I was waiting for Cathy King,[15] who I dearly respect, to ring me because I know they had a press release about this, and I thought it is her place to ring me. I am not ringing her, and I'm not usually backward in coming forward. . . . It was an exercise, an interesting exercise for me, and so the fact that she didn't contact me—and I know her and I support her in government, it says everything to me that most of the MPs probably think this is an absolutely absurd thing.

This example, which offers a story of personal experience with a clear evaluative statement at the end, was one of many stories offered in this group. During this conversation, the facilitator acted as the scribe, encouraged the group to "keep going—it's good to listen to," and told them he tried to "get the side comments" on each story. In this way the facilitator actively encouraged storytelling.

General, Hypothetical Examples

The third task of this day was analysis of two different policy proposals. Again, for most groups the conversations around this task involved very little storytelling. Several CPs provided general examples that followed a narrative form, but were not actual stories of personal experience. These examples followed a general story structure by having characters experience a series of events, yet they were hypothetical and vague. These examples are not really stories, but are worth noting because they were pervasive across all days of the ACP.

Argument Stories

In some cases these more general examples were responded to with personal stories. For example, in response to a hypothetical example about education, one CP replied, "It's like that with teacher registration, and states do deals sometimes and other don't." A third CP stated, "I taught in Queensland, and now I teach in South Australia. And they've got to deal with my registration. I was afraid that I had to find somewhere else at that time and have to start again. I don't know if they've changed that." This personal story supported the group's argumentative position about the proposed policy. It was one of the few personal stories told in this particular group on this day, and it seems to have been inspired by the more generalized storied example.

Other groups offered argumentative stories after being asked for personal examples by the facilitator.

Day 2: World Café

During the second day of the ACP, participants engaged in a modified World Café, with table discussions divided into fifteen-minute rounds. CPs sat at their original tables for the first round, then, after an audible gong, they dispersed to tables of their choosing for each successive round. This allowed participants to speak to a wider range of people and, potentially, to develop ideas by building on suggestions at different tables.

During these conversations the table facilitators served as the recorders, and CPs were told that the goal was "exploring the question, getting every-body's contribution, and to try and connect diverse perspectives."[16] The three rounds focused on a succession of three questions: "What are the things we like best about our democracy? How can our democracy be more like this more often? What can be learned from this?" After the World Café rounds of dialogue, the CPs had a chance to respond to presentations by expert panelists, and the day finished with an Open Space period to discuss particular proposals.

Overall, the table discussions on Day 2 involved far more storytelling events than any other day. Every table discussion in this study had at least a few storytelling events, and several segments of the day featured conversa-tions centered on personal stories. Along with hypothetical examples and argument stories, like those on Day 1, CPs offered interesting variations, and we highlight the most illustrative stories from this day.

Stories That Demonstrate Democratic Values

The conversations began with a call to discuss things that the CPs liked best about Australia's democracy. These discussions quickly focused on democratic values and abstract concepts, such as one's basic "rights." CPs often explained their stated values by offering stories that showed how the value looked in practice or why they believed it was important.

One interesting example comes from Kel, a CP at Table 3, who had men-tioned the value of freedom. Early in the conversation, a CP named Ken-neth stated, "I just wanted to ask for clarification from Kel that it's actually freedom, if you could be a bit more specific." This request prompted the following storytelling event:

KEL: Okay, my background, my parents are Estonian, from Estonia, if you know where that is?

DONNA: Yes.

KEL: Baltic State, okay next to Russia . . . Lithuania, Latvia. My mum and dad immigrated here at the end of the Second World War, okay, on a visa, which means that they'd been sponsored to get here.

KENNETH: My father, too.

KEL: Yes, and to see the visa's impression and the stories from my parents of what they had to put up with between the Russians and the Germans and the atrocities which the Russians did to my parents' country was never printed or documented because they were the Allied Force. So the Germans got everything documented and printed to show how they were the Russians, 500 percent worse. And of course all of my family, that's all my relatives, okay, were all shot. All because my mum's got royal blood and the Russians shot anyone with royal, like if you had royal blood or you were a schoolteacher or you were a lawyer, a solicitor, a town mayor, anyone with any notoriety that could create an uproar was just shot. Anyway, my mum got out, the only way she got out of . . . Estonia was that the service dressed her up as a servant's girl.

DONNA: Which got her through?

KENNETH: You're talking about very fundamental freedoms to . . .

KEL: So the freedom we have in this country is that we do not have that oppression.

Soon after Kel finished his story, another CP commented, "Really we don't appreciate [our freedom] because we don't have sufficient of your background to know what it is. We don't appreciate what we've got." Other CPs agreed. The facilitator, who had been quiet during the storytelling event, thanked Kel for "putting it in context." Notably, the facilitator did not redirect the group to move on to another topic or prompt them to write "freedom" on a list. Instead she said, "We have freedom, yes. And just doing this and really talk[ing] about it is an amazing experience for some."

The group continued to talk about Kel's situation of growing up without an extended family, and a few other group members told similar stories about coming from or visiting other countries that had considerably less freedom than Australia. Other CPs offered alternative stories to show how freedoms were eroding, and they expressed concern that their valuable freedom could be diminished. This conversation about freedom took most of the time allotted to this discussion segment and was filled with stories. The discussions at other tables during this time also included a lot of stories.

Kel's story demonstrates how groups can use stories to bring rich detail to their conversations, encourage perspective taking, and help groups consider a range of alternative views. Yet what really makes Kel's story interesting is what happened next.

After the discussion about values, Kel and a fellow groupmate, Ida, ended up at another table together when the gong sounded and the groups all reconstituted. Early in the discussion, a CP told a story of how she came from a country where she had been discriminated against. Later, Ida brought up Kel's story and prompted him to tell it again to this new group of people. Kel recounted a slightly shorter version of his story to again support ideas about not taking freedom for granted. The group members agreed with Kel's sentiment, and the conversation continued on this topic for some time.

Soon, though, Kel used his same story to make a more controversial point that immigrants to Australia should be required to learn the English language. This sparked a disagreement among group members and a conversation about the political ramifications of mandating language use. One CP told a hypothetical story that supported Kel's argument, and Kel later gave further details about his personal experience in support of his claim. Overall the discussion of this issue was respectful and reasoned, and stories were used to support arguments. One of the interesting things here is the way that a story that was used in one context as support for a democratic value is moved into a new context and used to make specific policy arguments. This points to the versatility of stories in deliberation, and also can help alert facilitators to pay attention to the ways in which stories are told and responded to in the group. The World Café model lends itself to stories being transported from one group to another, but the way the story is taken up and used can vary depending on the group members, the task at hand, and the topic of discussion.

Secondhand Stories About Indigenous Issues

The other distinct storytelling pattern in the third day occurred when groups were prompted to consider how Indigenous Australians were included or excluded from Australian society. The initial prompt came from the plenary session, in which the speaker offered a brief story—a hypothetical narrative in which Australia was colonized by Brazil and CPs had to change their customs to accommodate Brazilian cultural norms. The speaker called on the CPs to discuss issues of identity and action and ended with a hypothetical future narrative in which racial equality had been achieved.

Some groups did not answer this plea to consider the challenges facing Indigenous Australians, but it was taken up by all six of the groups we examined in this study. Several of these groups told stories, all of which were secondhand tales of other people's experiences. For example, one group had a lengthy discussion that centered on the challenges Indigenous Australians face in the education system. Their exchange, bookended by stories from one CP, portrayed Indigenous Australians as very "different" and unable to learn "in the way that we teach them." The stories were told in a way that was sympathetic to Indigenous Australians' struggles. Yet they portrayed this group as people who are different and unable to be fully included in the taken-for-granted educational system. Even when pushed by the facilitator to avoid stereotyping and be more specific about the people they are describing, CPs told stories that strongly construed Indigenous Australians as an abstract and anonymous other. This trend was especially notable in light of the presence in the room of Lowitja O'Donoghue, an Indigenous Australian who was a distinguished co-chair of the ACP.

In a society where direct contact with Aboriginal culture is rare, secondhand stories are understandable. They can be valuable by bringing minority issues into the forum. But the narrative constructions evident in these secondhand stories could come from often-retold stories that attenuate prejudicial views. In this discussion, the stories were not used to make arguments about particular policies or actions. Instead, they illustrated the complexity of a problem and expressed a discouraged sympathy. It seems CPs recognized barriers to mutual understanding and inclusion, but were unsure how to address them.

Days 3–4: Listing and Ranking

During the last two days of the ACP, the table discussions focused on analyzing and refining policy proposals, ranking proposals, then preparing to present the top proposals to public officials. These discussions involved very little storytelling. Most centered on making lists, summarizing, editing, voting, and offering brief statements of support or contention. A great deal of the conversation focused on the issue of time: CPs and facilitators talked about how much time was left for the task, when the gong would sound, how long the day would be, and so on. Although concern about time was common throughout all four days, it was pervasive across all six tables during these last two days.

Swapping Stories During Breaks

In contrast, there was a great deal of storytelling that happened during the breaks—when the groups moved away from the agenda-set tasks and into more personal discussion. A few of the transcripts for Days 3 and 4 included records of conversation that occurred during these breaks, though most of these informal exchanges were inaudible. CPs talked about where they went the previous night, what happened during dinner, how they were coping with the extreme heat, whom they talked to during breaks, and what they were learning through the ACP. Some CPs talked explicitly about how they were changing their perspectives through participating in the ACP and what they planned to do when they returned home. They also shared stories about events happening in Australia at the time, like the bushfires in the state of Victoria (see chapter 5).

Given the paucity of stories during the actual deliberative tasks on these days, it was interesting to see so many stories during the breaks. This is likely one of the advantages of a lengthy, residential deliberative event. It seemed that the storytelling events happening during these down times were animated, interactive, and lengthy. We might presume that CPs had plenty of time for storytelling in the evenings and other informal times that were not audio recorded as data for research. We suspect that these off-the-record stories helped CPs bond with each other, make sense of their experiences at ACP, and think together about what they might do when they returned home.

Future Stories

The final kind of story that was evident in these discussions, especially on Day 4, was what we call "future stories." These were hypothetical narratives told by CPs about what they planned to do when they left Canberra and went back to their home communities. Some of these visionings occurred organically, whereas others were prompted through the agenda. Most involved imagined interactions with the press or public officials, and some began by referring back to real experiences CPs had had prior to arriving in Canberra.

One particularly lengthy, collaboratively told future story occurred at Table 3. This storytelling event involved three different CPs, and it spanned twenty-four speaking turns. Jeremy began the exchange with this statement:

> I'm going to go off on a tangent here, if I may or do you want to keep on that theme? I, my take on it is [that] if we all went back and approached our local member—either online or phone or both to see what their take was on the issues raised by Citizens' Parliament and get their feedback—they will go, "Well, I don't know anything about it." "Well, go and see [Prime Minister] Kev. He'll give you the hard copy." You know what I mean? To keep it alive in the political arena. But they start getting e-mails from us or letters or phone calls. That's going to motivate them, I think, to take an interest, so it doesn't just stay in Canberra. You know what I mean?

Several other CPs joined in with comments like "your local rep might not even know," "you'll say to the secretary who you are," and "just say 'could he please get in contact with me?'" The group proceeded to construct a lengthy narrative that spelled out the steps they could take to contact the representative, get his or her attention, and ask for feedback on the proposal. The storytelling event ended when Jeremy, the primary storyteller in this case, said, "You've got to say 'within a week' or something. . . . [H]ave a look and give them a timeline. Otherwise you, otherwise it will all be forgotten, you know."

At the end of this storytelling event, which was limited by time, the facilitator redirected the conversation by summarizing a key message from the story and adding it to the list of ideas they were compiling. At that point the group moved away from storytelling and back to list making. The story, which was even labeled as a "tangent" by Jeremy, was treated simply as a list item—that CPs could contact their local public officials.

Conclusion

Generalizing across the entirety of the ACP, we observed surprisingly few well-developed stories, with many being brief, hypothetical, or very general.

By contrast, past research has found a great deal of storytelling in online dialogues and more exploratory, slow-paced face-to-face issue forums.[17] We attribute this difference, in part, to the CPs' constant sense of urgency: much of their discussion focused on making lists, offering brief statements, ranking, voting, and summarizing themselves—none of which lent itself to storytelling.

That said, when stories emerged at the ACP, the tellers often used them to support their arguments or add information to a group's analysis. CPs' stories also served a relational function by helping group members get to know each other.[18] Some groups shared personal stories during the early introduction period, and many of the breaks between official deliberative tasks featured relational bonding storytelling about CPs' experiences at the ACP itself.

In addition, some important stories told during the ACP raised questions about power and inclusion.[19] Sometimes CPs' stories about their own experiences, such as Kel's story about his family, offered new perspectives and helped CPs think critically about an idea.[20] In the ACP, however, secondhand stories about Indigenous Australians could negatively stereotype a group of historically underrepresented and marginalized people. These stories raised questions about race, power, inclusion, and oppression, but the broad and busy agenda did not permit groups to adequately address such concerns.

Moving to our principal research focus, we did find that the different discussion formats at the ACP influenced the character of storytelling. In particular, the World Café on Day 2 featured far more storytelling than any other session, in part due to the values-based questions they posed.[21] More discussion of personal experiences with public problems could help CPs develop a vocabulary for values, beliefs, and ethics. Moreover, the World Café method itself allows people to share their stories and experiences across tables, which can enrich conversations throughout the forum.

Beyond discussion format, we also discovered that most of the stories found in this analysis occurred in a group where the facilitator either asked explicitly for personal stories or at least modeled and encouraged storytelling as a group norm. The story-generating facilitators often encouraged the groups to provide detailed examples about their ideas, whereas their counterparts focused more on time constraints. The practical point here would not be to make the facilitator the lead storyteller and center of the conversation. Quite the opposite: providing more opportunities for storytelling could ultimately limit the facilitator's influence and help participants develop a richer understanding of their common values and experiences.

Finally, we found that the most interesting of the numerous hypothetical stories were future-oriented ones that focused on actions CPs could take when they returned to their home communities. These stories seemed to help CPs articulate a shared vision for themselves as representatives and actors in the public sphere. These stories emerged principally toward the end of the ACP. We suspect that the ACP experience itself helped participants envision themselves as public agents—the protagonists of future stories about civic life. It could well be that telling and hearing these kinds of stories, particularly as a collaborative small group, can help produce the shifts in political efficacy, identity, and agency that chapter 17 shows participants felt even a full year after the ACP had ended.

NOTES

1. See, e.g., Laura W. Black, "Deliberation, Storytelling, and Dialogic Moments," *Communication Theory* 18 (2008): 93–116; Laura W. Black, "Listening to the City: Difference, Identity, and Storytelling in Online Deliberative Groups," *Journal of Public Deliberation* 5, no. 1 (2009): art. 4, accessed January 8, 2012, http://services.bepress.com/jpd/vol5/iss1/art4; Francesca Polletta and John Lee, "Is Storytelling Good for Democracy? Rhetoric in Public Deliberation After 9/11," *American Sociological Review* 71 (2006): 699–723; David M. Ryfe, "Narrative and Deliberation in Small Group Forums," *Journal of Applied Communication Research* 34 (2006): 72–93; Iris Marion Young, "Communication and the Other: Beyond Deliberative Democracy," in *Democracy and Difference: Contesting the Boundaries of the Political,* ed. Seyla Benhabib (Princeton: Princeton University Press, 1996), 120–35.

2. Jerome Bruner, *Acts of Meaning* (Cambridge, Mass.: Harvard University Press, 1990); Walter R. Fisher, "Narration as Human Communication Paradigm: The Case of Public Moral Argument," *Communication Monographs* 51 (1984): 1–22; W. Barnett Pearce, *Making Social Worlds: A Communication Perspective* (Malden, Mass.: Blackwell, 2007).

3. Richard Bauman, *Story, Performance and Event: Contextual Studies of Oral Narrative* (Cambridge: Cambridge University Press, 1996); Charles Briggs, *Disorderly Discourse: Narrative, Conflict, and Inequality* (New York: Oxford University Press, 1996).

4. There is a vast literature on the connection of storytelling and identity. For reviews, see Kristin M. Langillier, "Personal Narratives: Perspectives on Theory and Research," *Text and Performance Quarterly* 9 (1989): 243–76; Charlotte Linde, *Life Stories: The Creation of Coherence* (New York: Oxford University Press, 1993); Elinor Ochs and Lisa Capps, "Narrating the Self," *Annual Review of Anthropology* 25 (1996): 19–43.

5. Black, "Listening to the City"; Pearce, *Making Social Worlds*; Katherine Cramer Walsh, *Talking About Race: Community Dialogues and the Politics of Disagreement* (Chicago: University of Chicago Press, 2007); Young, "Communication and the Other."

6. Black, "Deliberation, Storytelling, and Dialogic Moments."

7. Francesca Polletta, "Just Talk: Public Deliberation After 9/11," *Journal of Public Deliberation* 4, no. 1 (2008): art. 2, accessed January 8, 2012, http://services.bepress.com/jpd/vol4/iss1/art2; Black, "Listening to the City"; Polletta and Lee, "Is Storytelling Good for Democracy?"; Ryfe, "Narrative and Deliberation in Small Group Forums."

8. Heather L. Walmsley, "Mad Scientists Bend the Frame of Biobank Governance in British Columbia," *Journal of Public Deliberation* 5, no. 1 (2009): art. 6, accessed January 8, 2012, http://services.bepress.com/jpd/vol5/iss1/art6/.

9. Black, "Listening to the City."

10. Janette Hartz-Karp and Lyn Carson, "Putting the People into Politics: The Australian Citizens' Parliament," *International Journal of Public Participation* 3, no. 1 (2009): 9–31, accessed January 8, 2012, http://www.iap2.org/displaycommon.cfm?an=1&subarticlenbr=375.

11. On 21st Century Town Meetings, see America*Speaks*, accessed January 8, 2012, http://www.americaspeaks.org.

12. On the World Café model, see The World Café, accessed January 8, 2012, http://www.theworldcafe.com.

13. Elaine Hsieh, "Stories in Action and the Dialogic Management of Identities: Storytelling in Transplant Support Group Meetings," *Research on Language and Social Interaction* 37 (2004): 39–70.

14. On this analytic method, see Thomas R. Lindlof and Bryan C. Taylor, *Qualitative Communication Research Methods,* 2nd ed. (Thousand Oaks, Calif.: Sage, 2002); Anselm Strauss and Juliet Corbin, *Basics of Qualitative Research: Grounded Theory Procedures and Techniques* (Newbury Park, Calif.: Sage, 1990).

15. The participant's Member of Parliament.

16. Instructions offered to all the CPs by lead facilitator, Max Hardy, in the introduction of the day.

17. For comparison, see Black, "Deliberation, Storytelling, and Dialogic Moments"; Black, "Listening to the City"; Polletta, "Just Talk"; Polletta and Lee, "Is Storytelling Good for Democracy?"; Ryfe, "Narrative and Deliberation in Small Group Forums."

18. See Black, "Listening to the City" on "introduction stories," and Young, "Communication and the Other," on greeting and storytelling.

19. See also Wamsley, "Mad Scientists Bend the Frame of Biobank Governance in British Columbia"; Walsh, *Talking About Race.*

20. Black, "Deliberation, Storytelling, and Dialogic Moments."

21. Poletta, "Just Talk."

7

WHAT COUNTS AS DELIBERATION? COMPARING PARTICIPANT
AND OBSERVER RATINGS

John Gastil

As a matter of convenience, commentators often refer to events like the Australian Citizens' Parliament (ACP) as exercises in "democratic deliberation." This parallels the casual way we use the word when we say a jury has left the courtroom to "go deliberate." A more careful use of terms, however, leads us to ask whether, in fact, the jury will deliberate, or just reach a verdict hastily, without discussion or reflection. Likewise, one can ask whether the ACP—and the Online Parliament (OP) that preceded it—produced a fully deliberative process, let alone a democratic one.

To answer those questions, I provide in this chapter a particular conception of democratic deliberation and a pair of analytic approaches. I begin by distinguishing rigorous deliberation from democratic social relationships so that one can assess the two elements independently. I then look at each from two perspectives—that of trained outside observers and then that of the participants themselves. As students in my undergraduate course on public deliberation, the observers in question studied the same definition presented herein. Though they undoubtedly applied that definition with uneven precision, I believe they did so conscientiously, and at the very least, their perspective—thousands of miles removed from the ACP itself—provides a useful counterpoint to the subjective experience of the Citizen Parliamentarians (CP) themselves.

A Conception of Democratic Deliberation

In *Political Communication and Deliberation,* I refined a definition that I had developed earlier in collaboration with two graduate students.[1] That conception of public deliberation distinguishes the analytic and social aspects of such a process. To say that one has conducted a rigorous analysis, the following criteria must be met:

- Create a solid information base
- Prioritize the key values at stake
- Identify a broad range of solutions
- Weigh the pros, cons, and tradeoffs among solutions
- Make the best decision possible

But events like the ACP that strive to yield public deliberation want not only rigor but also democratic social relationships among the participants. This requires doing the following:

- Adequately distribute speaking opportunities
- Ensure mutual comprehension
- Consider other ideas and experiences
- Respect other participants

There exists no single method for assessing such criteria.[2] Chapters 5 and 6 use a qualitative approach to assess aspects of deliberation, and chapter 14 uses the same criteria presented above to look at facilitation at the ACP. Another alternative is the systematic content coding demonstrated in chapter 9, but this chapter relies instead on the perceptions of participants and outside observers, using survey items derived from the analytic and social dimensions described herein. By using those data, I hope to show the degree to which the OP and ACP met a common set of criteria for democratic deliberation.

Assessing Deliberation in the Online Parliament

Though this chapter does not examine discussion transcripts in detail, it is still helpful to get a feel for what deliberation looked like when it occurred in an OP session. The discussions themselves, after all, are what the participants reflected on while filling out their surveys, and they are what student observers considered when making their ratings. With that in mind, consider the case of the online group that developed a proposal for a Bill of Rights. Below is a condensed excerpt from December 30, 2008:

BRAD: Many people feel that by not having a Bill of Rights Australians are at risk of human rights violations. The feeling is that basic freedoms and rights are better protected in countries that do have such a document.

RITA: Hi, Brad, I think this is a great description and here is some comments that I found useful too. [She provides links to commentaries and articles online.] In many countries with a written constitution, constitutional development in the second half of the twentieth century was dominated by concepts of human rights. For example, Canada and South Africa gained Bills of Rights while the United States saw an existing Bill of Rights expanded through judicial interpretation. . . . Australia stands apart from these developments. As a result, according to Spigelman CJ of the Supreme Court of New South Wales, within a decade, British and Canadian court decisions in many areas of the law may become "incomprehensible to Australian lawyers." . . .

BRAD: Hi, Team. Have a look at this. [He cites a newspaper article.] Let's see if we can come up with something better and quicker than our pollies [politicians].

DON: I just wonder (and some commentators have also) how much in touch the average politician is with their constituents on this and many other issues. Or is it a case of resisting what they see as the possibility of interference in their political agendas from the judiciary?

BRAD: Hi, Team. After reading a few recent pieces I am starting to doubt the track we are on. [He cites three articles and opinion pieces.] I don't like the idea of giving more power to judges and politicians to meddle in our lives. We should be able to live in a decent, civilized society with basic protections that come from laws that give genuine protection to us.

Online exchanges like this show give-and-take, meaningful response to previous comments, disagreement, and other hallmarks of an engaged discussion. Many of the postings in the OP, however, were closer to monologues, dealt with confusions about procedure, or consisted of other exchanges not so clearly indicative of deliberation. Thus, I turn now to the views of observers and participants to get a better sense of the overall quality of the OP's discussions.

Observer Ratings of the OP

To get an independent assessment of the OP, I assigned students in my winter 2009 undergraduate political deliberation course the task of studying the transcripts for the fifteen OP discussions that had sufficient discussion to merit evaluation. With a total of 57 valid assessments completed, this meant that there was sufficient overlap to calculate interrater reliability among the student assessments (i.e., roughly four students independently assessed each transcript), and the result was a decent reliability score.[3]

For the sake of simplicity, I summarize here just the overall ratings given to the fifteen transcripts the students analyzed. When they were asked to combine their micro-evaluations into a summary assessment of the degree to which the discussion met the criteria for deliberation, the average score on a scale from 1 (strongly disagree) to 5 (strongly agree) was 3.6. Around that mean, OP transcript ratings distributed rather evenly, from a low of 2.7 to a high of 4.3.

In sum, the student observers agreed that those transcripts they studied showed signs of deliberation—but did not meet a very high standard. In only three cases did they lean toward saying the groups failed to deliberate (giving a score below 3), but in only two cases did they give a strongly favorable rating (a score above 4). Moreover, recall that these assessments came from only the fifteen most loquacious online groups. Ratings for the others would have likely fallen even lower.

OP Self-Assessments

Did participants in the OP view their experience the same way? To find out, I examined two separate surveys. First, I surveyed those OP participants who showed up in Canberra for the ACP, and that yielded ninety-one responses. Second, a year after the ACP, while conducting follow-up surveys with the ACP participants (chapter 17), I also surveyed those who had only taken part in the OP ($N = 41$). By looking at these two surveys, I could compare the fresh perspectives of those who had just taken part in the OP before arriving in Canberra against the recollections of OP-only participants who had no further direct investment in the ACP, plus the luxury of distant hindsight. Though this confounds two factors (involvement and proximity), it certainly provides distinct OP samples; any similarities they share suggest a consistency of OP experience.

Table 7.1 Ratings of deliberative quality given by respondents to surveys of participants in both online and face-to-face deliberation (OP + ACP), as well as those who only participated online (OP Only)

	Analytic process ("rigorous")		Social process ("respectful/fair")	
Rating	OP + ACP	OP Only	OP + ACP	OP Only
Very low	2%	0%	0%	0%
Low	4%	12%	2%	10%
Moderate	44%	51%	19%	46%
High	40%	32%	51%	39%
Very high	10%	5%	29%	5%
Total	100%	100%	100%	100%
N	93	41	91	41

Table 7.1 shows responses to two survey items assessing the analytic and social aspects of deliberation. The first question asked, "In your own opinion, how rigorous, thoughtful, or careful were the Online Parliament discussions?" On a five-point scale from 1 ("very low") to 5 ("very high"), 50 percent of those who later attended the ACP gave a score above the midpoint, whereas only 37 percent of those who only took part in the OP gave similar ratings. In both cases, the modal response was simply to give the midpoint rating—essentially rating the OP as "moderately" deliberative.

To self-assess the social process, respondents answered this question: "In your own opinion, how respectful and fair were the Online Parliament discussions?" Even more of those who took part in the OP and ACP together gave a rating above the midpoint (80 percent), but almost half as many OP-only respondents (44 percent) gave a similar response. As with the analytic process, the OP-only respondents' modal rating was the scale midpoint ("moderate").

Summary

Overall, it is fair to say that those who participated in the OP and ACP together were more effusive about the OP's deliberative quality than both those who observed it from a distance and those who participated only in the OP. Those who brought their OP experience to the ACP raved about the OP's democratic social process and gave qualified praise to the rigor of its analysis of Australian politics. Others likewise gave higher ratings to the social process than the analytic but were, on balance, more skeptical that its deliberative analysis met a high standard.

Assessing Face-to-Face Deliberation in Canberra

For two reasons, one could expect that the ACP would earn higher ratings on deliberative criteria than did the OP. First, the OP had been designed relatively late and with a degree of haste, as it was a response to an unanticipated level of interest in the ACP itself (see chapter 3). By contrast, the ACP was designed over a period of many months and reflected the organizers' years of experience arranging similar—and successful—processes. Second, the OP was a preliminary affair, rather than a main event, and its participants may have sensed that difference. Chatting asynchronously online with strangers to develop policy proposals is one thing, but meeting with fellow citizens face-to-face in the Old Parliament House building in the nation's capital is something else. That difference in magnitude, coupled with the more careful design, likely yielded a higher-quality deliberative process.

One of the challenges in studying deliberation in the Canberra sessions of the ACP is the sheer volume of textual data produced by four days of transcripts, with two dozen separate table discussions and various plenary sessions each day. Before turning to survey and observational data, therefore, it is worthwhile to take a glimpse again at what the transcripts show. In particular, they illustrate that CPs were willing to question one another in a respectful manner. Consider this example, in which one CP stresses the importance of the aforementioned Bill of Rights, while another CP challenges that assertion without seizing control of the floor:

KEL: I'd like to, you know what's wrong with the way we're going without a Bill of Rights or why is there a need, why is it a major discussion topic?
DONNA: Because as the world's changing there is going to be a need for a lot of protection.
KEL: Well, what is it?
DONNA: Well, it's happening now, if you have a look at one case; that doctor that was arrested. No charge, no evidence, no charges, no nothing, he had no rights.
KEL: Yeah, but that's been sorted out now, hasn't it?
DONNA: Yeah, but how would you like it if your son was carted away for so long, kicked out of the country?
KEL: Yeah, but this is where you learn from that process. Because that has happened and now it's been sorted out it would be very unlikely if it happened, it wouldn't happen again.
DONNA: It's going to happen more and more, let me assure you.[4]

As with the OP excerpt, this represents a relatively deliberative moment, but it is just that—one moment in a stream of interaction that ranged from polite chitchat to acerbic argument. The question at hand is, what did observers and participants see in the totality of the ACP's discussions?

Observer Ratings

When the students in my winter 2010 public deliberation course read these same transcripts, they also saw considerable evidence of deliberation. I assigned each student one or two table days each from Days 2 and 3 of the ACP because those two days covered the heart of the deliberation that occurred at the event. Thus, one student examined the transcript for Table 1 on Day 2, whereas another focused on Table 1 from Day 3—a completely different group of people, owing to the random reassignment to tables each day at the ACP.

Two main results came out of these observational ratings. On balance, students rated the ACP's social process more favorably than its analytic process, and they gave higher ratings to Day 2 table discussions than to those occurring on Day 3. As for the details, in every case the students used a rating scale from 1 (very low) to 9 (very high). When asked to give summary ratings, 70 percent of the 51 student raters said that the ACP's deliberation on Day 2/3 was no higher than a 6 on the nine-point scale. By contrast, 63 percent rated the social process as a 7 or higher.

Table 7.2 averages ratings across the two days to compare which aspects of the deliberative process received the highest and lowest scores. The one item that most contributed to the low/moderate analytic scores was this one: "Recognizing the limitations of one's own preferred solution and the advantages of others." Student raters gave an average score of 4.3, well below the scale midpoint. With a standard deviation of 1.9, this meant most ACP table discussions ranged from roughly 2–6 on the nine-point scale. As for the generally positive social ratings, the highest scores (mean = 7.2, SD = 1.5) went to this item: "Speaking plainly to each other, asking for clarification when confused, and generally understanding the content of the discussion."

When students were asked to judge the two ACP days separately, figure 7.1 shows that their analytic ratings were higher for Day 2 than for Day 3 (5.5 vs. 5.0), as were the social process ratings (7.0 vs. 6.1). Given the small number of ratings, there were few more detailed statistically significant differences, but these two did stand out: Day 2 rated much

Table 7.2   Average observer ratings of the ACP on Days 2–3

Rating item	Mean (1–9 scale)	Standard deviation
Discuss personal and emotional experiences, as well as known facts	5.8	2.0
Reflection on values	5.5	1.8
Brainstorming/developing a range of different solutions	5.6	2.2
Recognizing the limitations of one's own preferred solution and the advantages of others	4.3	1.9
Developing refined opinions/judgments in light of what I have learned	4.9	2.2
Taking turns in conversation to ensure a balanced discussion in which nobody is denied the chance to speak	6.2	1.9
Speaking plainly to each other, asking for clarification when confused, and generally understanding the content of the discussion	7.2	1.5
Listening carefully to one another and considering what is said, especially when there is disagreement	6.2	1.8
Showing respect to one another	6.8	2.1

Minimum $N = 48$ ratings.

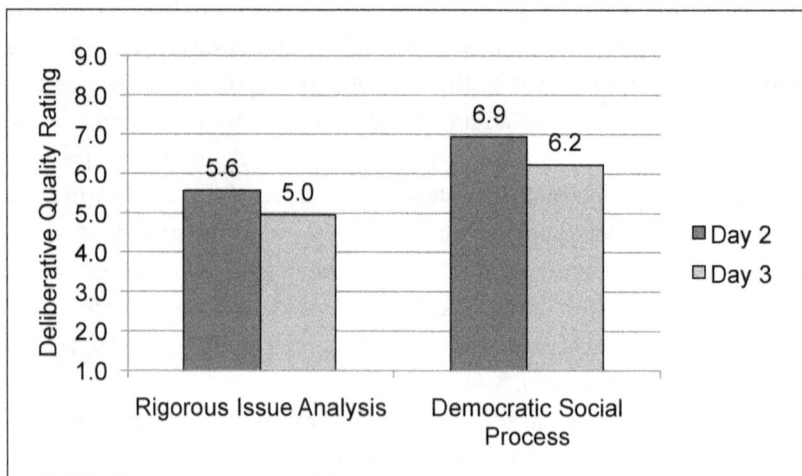

FIGURE 7.1   Average observer ratings of the ACP, broken down by day

Table 7.3 Citizen Parliamentarians' self-assessments of democratic deliberation at the ACP

	Analytic process			Social process		
Frequency	How often do you believe participants just stated positions without justifying them?	How often do you believe participants truly expressed what was on their mind?	When weighing the different choices for strengthening our political system, how regularly did participants consider the downsides of the choices?	How often do you feel that other participants treated you with respect?	When participants expressed views that were different from your own, how often did you consider what they had to say?	During the discussions, to what extent did you try to bridge conflicting views held by different Australians?
Never	14%	1%	2%	0%	0%	11%
Occasionally	62%	6%	31%	1%	3%	28%
Often	14%	11%	40%	5%	8%	26%
Very often	8%	43%	19%	9%	32%	21%
Almost always	2%	39%	8%	85%	56%	14%
Total	100%	100%	100%	100%	100%	100%

Minimum $N = 140$ survey responses.

higher in terms of ACP participants' providing personal information (6.2 on Day 2 vs. 5.0 on Day 3) and reflecting on their values (5.8 vs. 4.7).[5] Considering the activities on those days at the ACP, it makes sense that the exploratory nature of Day 2 would get better ratings on these items than would Day 3.

ACP Participant Ratings

Did the CPs see it the same way? Toward the end of the final day of the ACP, participants rated their experience using survey items similar to those used by the observers. In this case, however, the participants reflected on the totality of their experience, rather than one or two table days' worth of discussion. Before we look at their particular responses, evidence of the CPs' commitment to the ACP—and the research accompanying it—came in the 95 percent survey response rate for this survey: 143 of the 150 participants completed the brief post-deliberation survey.

Regarding the analytic aspect of their task, the CPs saw strengths and weaknesses. Eighty-two percent said that CPs "truly expressed what was on their mind" at least "very often," and 76 percent reported that fellow CPs only "occasionally or never" just expressed "positions without justifying them." Though participants reported a good degree of honesty and justification for their positions, less often did they consider the cons as much as the pros of the various proposals advanced for reforming Australian politics. Though 40 percent believed that CPs "often" considered the "downsides" of the various choices, only 27 percent said this happened "very often" or "almost always."

By contrast, the CPs' ratings of the social aspect of deliberation appear more enthusiastic. Eighty-five percent said they "almost always" felt that the other CPs treated them "with respect." In turn, 88 percent reported that they considered "what others had to say" when others expressed views different from one's own. More mixed results came from the third item, which was slightly oblique to the core definition of deliberation. When asked the extent to which one tried "to bridge conflicting views held by different Australians," 39 percent said they did so only "occasionally" or "never." Only 35 percent reported doing so "very often" or "almost always." In other words, the CPs felt they received and gave respect, but only a minority tried to use that goodwill to build consensus across the apparent lines of difference at the ACP.

Summary and Comparison

Both outside observers and the participants themselves agreed on this much: the ACP met a high standard for a democratic social process among the participants by maintaining a spirit of equality, mutual respect, and consideration of diverse views. The participants themselves, on balance, saw the ACP as a rigorous analytic process, with some qualifications, whereas the observers had a less sanguine assessment.

Comparing the ratings of the OP and ACP, it is fair to conclude that the ACP met a higher standard for both the analytic and social aspects of its process. As stated at the outset of this section, that likely reflects the greater investment on the part of both ACP process designers and the participants themselves, relative to their OP counterparts.

There exists no bright line between deliberative and non-deliberative, but one could summarize these data in two ways. Though observers and participants generally agreed that the OP and ACP had deliberative qualities, when it came to assessing the analytic aspect of the process, the observers saw "adequate" OP deliberation and a "good" ACP process. By contrast, the OP participants themselves (especially if taking part in the later ACP) saw their online discussions as "good," and the ACP's participants saw their process as "great."

Conclusion

In the long run, analyses such as these will only have considerable payoff when compared across a wider range of deliberative processes. The particular conception of deliberation used herein has not yet been applied widely across different political issues and contexts, but, with some trepidation, I would venture to make the following comparative notes based on my own observations of similar events. Following the style of my uncle, Raymond Gastil, who edited the annual volume *Freedom in the World,* I would offer these comparison cases to get a sense of what processes are "more" or "less" deliberative than the OP and ACP.[6]

At the bottom of that spectrum, I would argue that the typical online political discussion, such as those that e-thePeople facilitated, is less deliberative than was the OP.[7] The former tends to give way to invective and unfocused argument, whereas the OP maintained a focus and purpose in its sustained discussions to a sufficient degree that it proved useful as a prelude to the ACP (see chapter 11).

Between the OP and the ACP lie a number of processes, such as the typical Deliberative Poll or a National Issues Forum. These comparison processes engage one or more issues for a period of hours or days, respectively, and the net result is a group of participants who better understand the issues, have new factual information to consider, and come away with modest—or occasionally striking—changes in their attitudes. In essence, such processes model a robust civic education, whereas the ACP pushed participants farther in their issue analysis and raised higher the level of mutual regard and consideration.

Above the ACP, I would place intensive small-group processes like the Citizens' Jury, the Oregon Citizens' Initiative Review (modeled on the Citizens' Jury), and the British Columbia Citizens' Assembly. These have the benefit of a smaller body of citizens, which permits the group to move farther faster, and they often have a more precise question to address, such as what law to propose or whether to support a specific policy.

Returning to the assumption that animated this chapter, it is never enough to assert that one or another event was deliberative by virtue of its very design. In this spirit, such comparisons would benefit from more systematic measures and observational procedures, which may come in time. It is the aspiration of this chapter—and, more generally, this entire volume—to make strides toward such comparative tools.

NOTES

1. John Gastil, *Political Communication and Deliberation* (Thousand Oaks, Calif.: Sage, 2008), drew on the earlier essay, Stephanie Burkhalter, John Gastil, and Todd Kelshaw, "A Conceptual Definition and Theoretical Model of Public Deliberation in Small Face-to-Face Groups," *Communication Theory* 12 (2002): 398–422.

2. See John Gastil, Katie Knobloch, and Meghan B. Kelly, "Evaluating Deliberative Public Events and Projects," in *Democracy in Motion: Evaluating the Practice and Impact of Deliberative Civic Engagement*, ed. Tina Nabatchi, John Gastil, Matt Leighninger, and G. Michael Weiksner (Oxford: Oxford University Press, 2012); Laura W. Black, Stephanie Burkhalter, John Gastil, and Jennifer Stromer-Galley, "Methods for Analyzing and Measuring Group Deliberation," in *Sourcebook of Political Communication: Methods, Measures, and Analytic Techniques*, ed. Eric C. Bucy and R. Lance Holbert (New York: Routledge, 2010), 323–45.

3. Coefficient alpha for multiple raters was 0.71. To get a sense for the level of intersubjective agreement, consider that on a five-point scale, the most discrepant ratings of overall deliberative quality were scores of 2, 3.5, 4, and 4.

4. This excerpt was identified by research assistant Phuong Phillips.

5. Both results are significant on independent sample t-tests at $p < 0.10$.

6. The best first reference on that series is Raymond D. Gastil, "The Comparative Survey of Freedom: Experiences and Suggestions," *Studies in Comparative International Development* 25 (1990): 25–50.

7. This and the cases that follow are described in John Gastil and Peter Levine, eds., *The Deliberative Democracy Handbook: Strategies for Effective Civic Engagement in the 21st Century* (San Francisco: Jossey-Bass, 2005), as well as Gastil, *Political Communication and Deliberation*.

8

HEARING ALL SIDES? SOLICITING AND MANAGING
DIFFERENT VIEWPOINTS IN DELIBERATION

Anna Wiederhold and John Gastil

In any complex deliberative process, a tension exists between welcoming new and different ideas and maintaining a clear focus on the problem at hand. When faced with this dilemma, organizers of the Australian Citizens' Parliament (ACP) hoped to err "on the side of breadth" by privileging varied perspectives, divergence, and innovation over consensus. They hoped to reach a certain level of convergence by its end, but only if that agreement reflected a "collective intelligence" emerging out of rich discussions.[1]

Deliberative scholars and activists contend that public discussions between diverse publics can lead individuals to develop greater empathy with one another and a better understanding of their own positions.[2] Though universal in their embrace of "diverse perspectives," it remains unclear how, exactly, the organizers of deliberative events manage the aforementioned tension between openness and focus—between ongoing divergence and degrees of convergence.

To address that issue, we scrutinize the transcripts from both the plenary sessions and small-table discussions at the ACP. We focus on how event organizers, facilitators, and participants solicited and managed different perspectives and opinions during the ACP. In the end, we will argue that one can distinguish deliberative and dialogic diversity, both of which help to serve three functions—brainstorming, blending, and building.

Concepts and Method

We begin by making a simple distinction between deliberation and dialogue. Public deliberation—the clear focus of this volume—entails the rigorous and respectful examination of a problem to reach a shared judgment or decision. Public dialogue, by contrast, involves the open-ended exploration of different perspectives and experiences to reach mutual understanding—though not necessarily a decision.[3] By these definitions, the ACP was principally a deliberative event, though it contained dialogic features. Herein, we explore both aspects of the event.

To develop a more refined model of the interplay of deliberation and dialogue, we systematically analyzed transcripts of both plenary and table discussion sessions at the ACP. The first author used a method called action-implicative discourse analysis to compare the deliberative practices of the Citizen Parliamentarians (CPs) to the normative ideals of deliberative democracy as expressed in plenary sessions. This method derives from "grounded practical theory," an epistemology that seeks to reconstruct communicative practices by analyzing contradictions, discursive strategies, and situated ideals.[4] The first step involved analyzing argument strategies and discursive moves across the long stretches of discourse at the ACP. Next, repeated inductive analyses of the transcripts (and supplementary documents) revealed those discursive practices that might extend or challenge existing theory.

More specifically, our analysis investigated three phenomena: how structural features of the ACP affected the management of diverse perspectives, what expectations were expressed to the CPs during the plenary sessions, and how CPs and organizers dealt with different viewpoints in actual practice.

ACP Structural Design for Dialogue and Deliberation

We begin by considering how structural features of the ACP constrained or enabled the expression of diverse perspectives.[5] Of the influential structural factors, the most prominent were deliberative format and strategic process design. Previous research has found that the exploratory phases of a public event tend to draw out divergent thinking, whereas consensus seeking tends to be encouraged more during decision-making phases.[6]

Each day of face-to-face deliberation was highly structured, with the primary format incorporating elements adapted from the 21st Century Town Meeting.[7] These repeated the following sequence: facilitating deliberation at small tables, recording ideas via networked computers, identifying themes in the streams of network data, then getting CPs' reactions to those themes by asking them to weight their priorities.[8] On Day 2, the ACP also utilized World Café and Open Space deliberative formats to encourage exploration.[9] Since we were interested in exploring the role of diverse perspectives in public deliberation, analysis of the table discussions focused primarily on Day 2 because the World Café and Open Space formats utilized on that day claim to allow the most space for opinion divergence.

Beyond the issue of specific discussion formats, the ACP's design also reflected deeper strategic decisions about where to locate the event in the life history of a public issue. Communication scholar Shawn Spano provides a useful framework for thinking about these choices by identifying six typical stages for public engagement: (1) identifying the issue, (2) eliciting different views, (3) framing the issue, (4) generating options for action, (5) deliberating and deciding, and (6) implementing public agreements.[10]

These stages oscillate between openness and divergence and convergence and closure. By the time CPs arrived in Canberra, they were already at Stage 4 (generating options for action). After all, the ACP process began long before the four-day meeting. Prior to the main event in February, discussions at regional meetings and in online forums created space for the elicitation of different views. These processes better articulated the ACP's focus on political reform, and the Online Parliament identified eleven specific proposals, which helped set the agenda for the face-to-face deliberations in Canberra (see chapters 4 and 11).

As the following section shows, the ACP's organizers were cognizant of these design considerations, and they tried to keep participants' expectations in line with the opportunities and limitations they had built for the CPs. The main point here is simply to better recognize that the ACP, like all deliberative events, was the product of format design choices that enabled a particular kind of dialogue—and a particular sort of deliberation. By drawing on different discussion practices across the four days of Canberra meetings—and by prefacing the main event with additional processes—the ACP was at least able to reap the benefit of multiple designs.[11]

Setting Expectations for the ACP

On arriving in Canberra, the CPs could not have had a clear sense of what would unfold in the next four days. A deliberative event like the ACP takes people outside of normal public life and places them in, if not an "ideal speech situation,"[12] then at least an exceptionally structured one, as described above.

To help the CPs form reasonable expectations for the event, organizers and the ACP co-chairs frequently addressed the entire ACP in plenary sessions over the four days of deliberation. On Day 1 of the ACP, event organizer Lyn Carson addressed the participants in a plenary session, outlining the four-day meeting as follows:

> Day 1, that's today, is a chance to understand and decide what you want to achieve in this place, and the facilitators will lead you through that. On Day 2, you'll have a chance to broaden your perspectives and hear from other people, the guests that Fred mentioned and your fellow participants. Important to always bear in mind those guidelines that Lowitja was kind enough to reinforce. By Day 3 you're going to have to determine what's important to you and on the final day, that's devoted to consolidating and delivering those agreed recommendations and we want those to be tight and coherent.

In the plenary explanation of events, Day 2 is the only day about which the organizer offers more than a procedural description. Interestingly enough, in describing Day 2, the day which structurally allows for the highest level of divergence, she also issues a cautionary reminder regarding the rules of engagement. The event organizer's emphasis on Day 2 indicates both the importance of this divergence to the deliberative process, but also the concern and discomfort that often accompanies the relinquishing of organizational control necessary to provide space for this sort of open discussion.

During these plenary sessions, speakers predominantly used three distinct rhetorical strategies to set expectations regarding the role of divergence in the small table discussions: they offered examples of desirable divergence in their procedural explanations, they directly modeled ideal behavior personally, and they celebrated those panelists and participants who engaged in productive divergence by holding them up as exemplary.[13]

Process Explanations

Every new session began with an explanation of the particular deliberative format being employed, as well as a reminder of procedural expectations. On Day 1, this was especially prevalent, as event organizers sought to clarify what they meant when they asked people to deliberate. For example, ACP co-chair Lowitja O'Donoghue began the first day by reminding participants of the goals of the forum: "To provide the space and the opportunity for dialogue and deliberation on how Australia's political system can be strengthened to serve us better. To enable participants to explore different ways to achieve this through deliberative processes that facilitate participant understanding of different views. Learning new ideas, testing assumptions, identifying values, and weighing options and developing priorities."

By setting exploration, understanding, and assumption-testing as goals, O'Donoghue's description of the forum suggested that participants would be delving deeply into one another's ideas. ACP co-chair Fred Chaney reiterated this expectation when he explained that most conversations would be facilitated in small group settings "so that you can actually genuinely exchange views and ultimately every view, every person here will get a chance to prioritize and to engage in ways that means that no one will be silenced by the noisier people."

In addition to emphasizing the exchange of diverse perspectives, on multiple occasions plenary speakers stressed the importance of listening. As co-chair Chaney said on Day 1, "It's not going to be a great noisy debate, it's going to be a case of using your voice, your ears, and your minds to encompass what other people are saying and to assess what you think and what you're saying, in the light of that."

Another common theme was the need to hear from a large number of people. As ACP co–lead facilitator Max Hardy said on Day 2, "You're not in here to argue for what you think should happen but you're here to create a space for lots of different ideas to emerge." On multiple occasions speakers reminded participants that they did not need to reach consensus. Rather, scribes were directed to record the majority view and any strongly held minority opinions. Then, once a multitude of different options had been proposed, participants were asked to consolidate ideas. Plenary speakers often spoke of the group's "combined influence" and how the value of this event emerged through the development of "collective wisdom."

Modeling Deliberation

Additionally, plenary speakers expressed their expectations for how they hoped citizens would share their diverse perspectives by modeling ideal behavior and celebrating exemplary participants. Model speakers and parliamentarians were spotlighted for their performance, applauded as sorts of deliberative "heroes."[14] These participants embodied the beliefs and values associated with deliberative success. Heroes became symbolic representations of how the process should work. For example, on Day 2, co-chair O'Donoghue drew attention to an expert panelist to heroize him—making an example out of his contributions to the deliberative process: "I'd like to make a special mention at this point of how proud I was of Mark Yettica-Paulson today. [*Applause*] A young Aboriginal brother who actually introduced a new perspective today to the issues that we've been dealing with which will be ongoing now from now on I think in terms of your discussion. So I was proud of him." Not only did Lowitja celebrate the fact that Mark Yettica-Paulson introduced a previously unheard perspective, but she also encouraged other Parliamentarians to incorporate his contribution into their ongoing discussions.

Brainstorming and Blending for Deliberative Diversity

In reviewing the plenary speakers' expressed expectations, the first author of this essay identified *brainstorming* and *blending* as two primary functions diverse perspectives can serve in deliberative practice. We count these both as means of establishing an event's deliberative diversity, namely, a macrolevel variety of opinion and ideas.[15]

Brainstorming Ideas

In brainstorming, organizers emphasize the accumulation of a large quantity of possibilities. Similar to aggregative models of democracy, everyone has an opportunity to share opinions in a comparable manner to a poll or verbal vote. In contrast, *blending* encourages interaction between opinions through the cross-pollination or amalgamation of ideas. As participants hear a variety of perspectives, they are encouraged to integrate others' viewpoints into their own, transforming oppositional views into new proposals situated on common ground. In the ACP, the CPs' interactions with one another largely reflected plenary speakers' expressed expectations. In the table discussions, substantial discursive evidence suggests the actual practice of both brainstorming and blending functions in the Citizens' Parliament.

During a Day 2 plenary session, organizer Lyn Carson stated, "We're really keen to capture as many ideas as we can." Her statement perfectly sums up this first type of divergence, *brainstorming*, as it functioned in the ACP. The idea here is to throw out as many ideas as possible, accumulating a large pool which can be refined at a later time. The 21st Century Town Meeting is especially conducive to the brainstorming function because that deliberative format is specifically designed to take a large quantity of information and distill it down to key points.

That said, the sessions characterized by brainstorming had a frantic quality, as participants struggled to get all of their ideas recorded in limited spurts of time. From the very opening of sessions on Day 1, organizers and the two co-chairs incessantly referred to time limitations, reminding participants that "we have an incredibly tight schedule" and "we have a lot of ground to cover." The tension between wanting to address a large number of issues and needing to do so within a finite amount of time contributed to the development of a contradictory and often frustrating situation (see chapter 6). As one participant, Brent, remarked on Day 3, "It's like, 'Fix the world in a sentence.'" "Diversity of perspectives" in the ACP primarily manifested itself in this report-like aggregation of statements, without time for engagement. Each individual's contribution could be happening in isolation from one another. An unidentified female commented at the end of Day 2 (the day structured to allow the greatest amount of divergence), "It appears just as an observer and with a couple of conversations that I've had with other people that the process is about gathering as much data as the researchers can possibly get out of us and not a lot of, I guess, engaging or facilitating but more just quick just let's get information, let's sort of really approach this as a research project. And I appreciate that it is. But it's just an observation as a participant that I and fellow other people have had."

Plenary speakers responded to this comment contemplatively, stating that public deliberation "is designed in a way to give people space to think and information you need to think well together." In practice, however, deliberations like the ACP can end up functioning as less of an in-depth discussion and more like a polling system that crafts its survey questions by eavesdropping on the themes it hears in small-group conversations among strangers that would normally never occur or happen only in private spaces, like workplaces and living rooms.

Blending Voices

In contrast to brainstorming, *blending* is characterized by the cross-pollination—rather than simple accumulation—of ideas. Event organizers sought this function of diverse perspectives in designing the World Café. Co–lead facilitator Max Hardy explained this process on Day 2: "Getting everybody's contribution and to try and connect diverse perspectives, that is, over a period of time in the World Café you'll be picking up things from other people, you'll be getting ideas and merging them, looking for insights and just sharing some collective discoveries. That's the idea of the World Café. In other words, you just have a good chat, you learn stuff from each other, and you try and make sense of all the things that you've heard throughout the process."

During the Café, CPs talked for fifteen minutes about an issue at one table, then a gong would sound and CPs would scatter to new tables to discuss the issue for another fifteen minutes with a new group of people. After several rounds of this, each table's scribe (an ACP volunteer) submitted key ideas to the theme team. As participants maneuvered quickly through these fast-paced conversations, ownership of ideas was easily lost amid all the movement. Facilitators asked participants to share good ideas that they had heard in previous rounds, and the result was similar to a brainstorming session during which every response is recorded, no matter how banal or outlandish.

One conflict arose from the blending of ideas when a panelist on Day 2 spoke about two similar, yet meaningfully different, proposals as if they were one. The CP who authored one of the proposals was outraged that his idea had been misrepresented. As this example illustrates, one risk of blending is that, when people *do* take ownership of their ideas, changing even minute details might be interpreted as a perversion of the original concept rather than an improvement.

The Building Function of Dialogic Diversity

In response to the limitations of brainstorming and blending, we would like to suggest that a third type of diversity can emerge in public forums.

Brainstorming and blending have been categorized above as two types of *deliberative* diversity because exploration of diverse viewpoints happens at the macro-level when notes are compiled from disparate table conversations. In contrast to deliberative diversity, *dialogic* diversity consists of engagement with difference at an interpersonal level.

In this section, we will elaborate on one particular manifestation of dialogic diversity—the *building* function. This idea is informed by the writings of French political theorist Chantal Mouffe, who has explicated a democratic model she calls "agonistic pluralism."[16] Agonism occurs when citizens seek to transform conflict in such a way that oppositional perspectives are no longer perceived as a pathology or enemy to be destroyed but as an adversary (i.e., someone whose ideas we combat but whose right to defend those ideas we respect).

As defined herein, "building" is the product of an agonistic interaction between participants' ideas. An agonistic interaction is a type of productive conflict, in which the goal is to engage in difference, challenging and problematizing one another's views so that everyone thinks more deeply about issues, aware of a greater level of complexity. Differences in opinion become the invaluable material needed to construct, or build, new proposals and ideas.

Given the structural constraints of the ACP, opportunities for this function of diversity were severely limited. During the Open Space session on Day 2, however, citizens finally had a chance to talk at length with one another about their ideas. Participants signed up to explore the issues of greatest interest to them. Facilitators were told that "whoever comes is the right people," "whatever happens is the only thing that could have," and "whenever it starts is the right time." This session provided the most space for creativity, innovation, and engagement with one another's ideas because time was less of a constraining factor. Participants had forty-five minutes of unstructured time to talk about one issue of interest.

During this time, citizens often challenged one another through the posing of questions. Questions and responses often led to deeper explanation and refinement of thought through rearticulation. Take, for example, this dialogue between participants Gillian, Janet, and Terry. The group is discussing ways to empower citizens through community, and the majority viewpoint expressed to this point has lamented the heavy hand of lobbyists in government affairs and limited opportunities for citizen involvement. General agreement among group members has led to several bridging comments in which each speaking participant echoed the sentiments of the previous speaker. Gillian breaks this trend toward consensus, initially framing her critique of the majority argument by posing a question:

GILLIAN: But how can you correct this, I mean you've got to correct it but are you going to put any ways accessing ways of how you . . . correct it.

JANET: It's not about correcting it, it's about balancing it.

GILLIAN: We're not even balancing, I don't . . . ?

JANET: But I do think that's something that could take time, many years.

GILLIAN: Mitigated, if that's the right word. Take the power out of it.

TERRY: We'll never be spending as much money getting those points of view of business and professionals getting their point of view across, but I do think that governments—parliamentarians—do a bit of a balancing act themselves. They know—they do know the coal industry has a particular point of view, and it's going to argue its point of view, not necessarily the public interest. And they do . . . a bit of balancing, but nevertheless, in these processes, you do actually have to have the voices there. If they only hear from the coal industry and they don't hear from consumer groups or environment groups or whatever, then it's very hard for them to say we disagree with the coal industry. If they can point to voices from those other ordinary citizens' interests, then it does make it easier.

Through a series of questions, Gillian pushes Terry to elaborate on his initial polemics on the current system. Rather that talking in the generalities that characterized early moments in this conversation, Terry delves into a more detailed explanation of his perspective when pushed to do so by Gillian's questions.

In an analysis of a different set of public discussions, communication scholars Jay Leighter and Laura W. Black argue that "raising the question" sometimes functions as a way of drawing attention to issues that have been overlooked or obscured in group discussion.[17] Furthermore, framing arguments as questions softens the challenge to fit a more collaborative setting by creating space for counterarguments in the form of clarification.

The building process requires substantially more time and space than the deliberative diversity processes we discussed earlier. One reason for this may be that politeness norms often moderate the direct assertion of counterarguments, so dialogic diversity manifests itself most commonly as series of questions. Creating the space for challenges, emotions, and difference in deliberation is vital for the development of more richly complex democratic interactions.

Conclusion

When it comes to managing a diversity of perspectives, we have shown that this can be thought of as either deliberative (i.e., engagement occurring at the macro-level of the larger event) or dialogic (i.e., engagement occurring at the micro-level of personal interaction). Furthermore, we have outlined three functions of diversity that fall within these larger categories: *brainstorming* encourages the collection of multiple perspectives by inventorying ideas together, *blending* integrates perspectives to develop different ideas through a process of bricolage, and dialogic *building* occurs when discussants encounter differences that challenge them to think more deeply about their own perspectives and, at the very least, elaborate their own ideas in more complex detail.

In practice, this building function may be underutilized in deliberative practice, but it holds much potential for transforming the ways people engage with views and experiences that deviate from their familiar lifeworld or cultural orientation. The ACP shows how the structure of a deliberative format can inhibit the building function; however, the ACP also offers hope that this form of engagement remains attainable in large deliberative settings. Appropriately enough, it is our wish that both scholars and practitioners engage in their own building dialogue on how best to create space for dialogic exchange within more formal deliberative structures.

NOTES

1. Janette Hartz-Karp and Lyn Carson, "Putting the People into Politics: The Australian Citizens' Parliament," *International Journal of Public Participation* 3, no. 1 (2009): 15, 24.

2. See Michael X. Delli Carpini, Fay Lomax Cook, and Lawrence R. Jacobs, "Public Deliberation, Discursive Participation, and Citizen Engagement: A Review of the Empirical Literature," *Annual Review of Political Science* 7 (2004): 315–44.

3. John Gastil, *Political Communication and Deliberation* (Los Angeles: Sage, 2008), 33–37.

4. Robert T. Craig and Karen Tracy, "Grounded Practical Theory: The Case of Intellectual Discussion," *Communication Theory* 5 (1995): 248–72; Karen Tracy, *Challenges of Ordinary Democracy: A Case Study in Deliberation and Dissent* (University Park: Pennsylvania State University Press, 2010).

5. Anthony Giddens, *The Constitution of Society* (Berkeley: University of California Press, 1994).

6. Shawn Spano, "Theory and Practice in Public Dialogue: A Case Study in Facilitating Community Transformation," in *Facilitating Group Communication in Context: Innovations and Applications with Natural Groups*, ed. Lawrence Frey (Cresskill, N.J.: Hampton Press, 2006), 271–98.

7. See America*Speaks*, accessed January 12, 2012, http://americaspeaks.org.

8. Carolyn J. Lukensmeyer, Joe Goldman, and Steven Brigham, "A Town Meeting for the Twenty-First Century," in *The Deliberative Democracy Handbook: Strategies for Effective Civic Engagement in the Twenty-First Century,* ed. John Gastil and Peter Levine (San Francisco: Jossey-Bass, 2005), 154–63. For more detail on the Australian variant, see "21st Century Dialogue," accessed January 12, 2012, http://www.21stcenturydialogue.com.

9. Sandy Heierbacher, "NCDD's Engagement Streams Framework," January 1, 2009, National Coalition for Dialogue and Deliberation, accessed January 12, 2012, http://ncdd.org/rc/item/2142.

10. Spano, "Theory and Practice in Public Dialogue."

11. This reflects the organizers' commitment to using diverse methods. See Lyn Carson and Janette Hartz-Karp, "Adapting and Combining Deliberative Designs: Juries, Polls, and Forums," in Gastil and Levine, *The Deliberative Democracy Handbook,* 120–38.

12. The term comes from work by Jürgen Habermas. For an ambitious attempt to articulate that ideal in practice, see Ortwin Renn, Thomas Webler, and Peter Wiedemann, eds., *Fairness and Competence in Citizen Participation: Evaluating Models for Environmental Discourse* (Dordrecht: Kluwer Academic, 1995).

13. Past research has shown how each of these teaching strategies can yield better outcomes during and after forums. John Gastil, "Adult Civic Education Through the National Issues Forums: Developing Democratic Habits and Dispositions Through Public Deliberation," *Adult Education Quarterly* 54 (2004): 308–28.

14. The word "hero" here is borrowed from organizational communication literature. For a detailed discussion of organization heroes, see Terrence E. Deal and Allan A. Kennedy, *Corporate Cultures: The Rites and Rituals of Corporate Life* (Reading, Mass.: Addison-Wesley, 1982).

15. In definitional terms, this amounts to a variety of solutions to a problem, or different perspectives on the nature of the problem itself (Gastil, *Political Communication and Deliberation,* 18–21).

16. For a detailed discussion of this theory, see Chantal Mouffe, *The Democratic Paradox* (London: Verso, 2005).

17. James L. Leighter and Laura Black, "'I'm Just Raising the Question': Terms for Talk and Practical Metadiscursive Argument in Public Meetings," *Western Journal of Communication* 74 (2010): 547–69.

9

SIT DOWN AND SPEAK UP: STABILITY AND CHANGE IN GROUP PARTICIPATION

Joseph A. Bonito, Renee A. Meyers, John Gastil, and Jennifer Ervin

Public forums such as the Australia Citizens' Parliament (ACP) have the potential to engender personal transformation, group learning, and social and political change, but that potential is realized only if participants actually deliberate. More precisely, deliberation does not work (and, in fact, is not really *group* deliberation) if only one or a few participants monopolize a discussion.[1]

Like most large-scale deliberative events, the ACP used a mix of plenary sessions and small-group discussions. In the plenaries, all participants gathered together in the Members' Dining Room to hear a small number of individuals—such as policy experts, public officials, or selected ACP members—speak and answer questions. However, to counterbalance the relative passivity of those sessions, the bulk of the ACP consisted of group discussions convened at twenty-three small tables in the Old Parliament House dining room. A typical discussion table consisted of seven Citizen Parliamentarians (CPs) and a facilitator.

The issue addressed in this chapter is whether the ACP succeeded in its efforts to create truly deliberative discussions at these tables, at least in terms of relatively equal participation. Such equality cannot be taken for granted, as past research shows even carefully crafted deliberative events, such as the 1996 USA Deliberative Poll, become monopolized by just a few members, with others remaining silent.[2] And although equality of participation does not equate with the more fundamental question of equal speaking *opportunity*,[3] it is necessary to begin setting a baseline for what kinds of talk distributions one can hope to achieve in a highly structured deliberative process.

Theorizing Participation in Small Groups

Research on small-group communication shows that discussion participation is anything but equal.[4] When defined as taking a turn to speak during a discussion (i.e., a "speaking turn"), participation rates vary considerably among the members of a typical small group. In some cases, a few participants dominate from the beginning, and that dominance persists throughout a group's discussion. In other cases, dominance develops gradually, becoming clearer by a discussion's end.[5] What's more, there is evidence that pairs of participants hold the floor for the majority of discussion, in effect "locking out" those who might otherwise wish to contribute.[6] In effect, the longer one waits to participate between speaking turns, the less likely one will continue contributing to a discussion.

What group characteristics are responsible for, or at least correlate with, variance in participation? Groups, such as those at the twenty-three tables at the ACP, often vary on many dimensions, but some of those differences are more dynamic than others. For example, group size is a fairly static characteristic, though it can change. In fact, it did change for some ACP groups, with individual members leaving during discussion—sometimes through the remainder of an entire session. The process of a group discussion also has dynamic qualities. An ACP discussion group's excitement about the topic of Australian politics, for instance, waxes and wanes when it develops a novel civic-reform idea only to discover later that it won't work.

Before searching for causal explanations of differences in participation equality, it is important to start with a richer description of the extent of those differences within and between the small groups at the ACP. In doing so, we hope to establish something of a baseline for looking at equality of speaking turns in deliberative events. With the level of concern that went into organizing the ACP, establishing discussion norms, and bringing in professional facilitators, the ACP provides a good starting point for seeing what level of equality is feasible in a public deliberation, at least in terms of the crude measure of speaking turns per person. (For more detail on these features of the ACP, see chapters 13 and 14.)

Analyzing Deliberation at the Group Level

We approach the problem of participation in the ACP at the group level of analysis because we believe there is much to learn by evaluating group dynamics. The ACP provides a unique opportunity to examine how the dynamics of group participation change over time. During the course of the ACP, participants moved from group to group such that no two groups across the four days contained exactly the same members. More specifically, the ACP used a version of a 21st Century Town Meeting model for its small group discussions on Days 1, 3, and 4, so we focus on those days of the ACP.[7]

Although group membership and tasks/topics/issues varied across the days, the organizers imposed a relatively stable structure on the discussions. Each group had a facilitator, whose primary mission was to support the deliberative component of the interactions by asking questions, playing devil's advocate, and keeping the discussions on track, though the participants were not obligated to follow the facilitator's guidance.[8] In addition, group discussions were occasionally augmented by the presence of "experts" on some issues, who responded to questions. The experts did not usually stay with a table for the duration of that session (nor were their speaking turns counted in the analyses presented herein). The purpose of imposing such structure on all the discussions was to improve the quality of the process and outcomes, although previous research has shown that these types of well-intentioned interventions can yield mixed results.[9]

Group-level analyses, gathered from individuals within groups (as is the case here), provide the opportunity to evaluate homogeneity and heterogeneity of participation rates in these ACP table discussions. Participation in a given group is considered homogeneous when there is little variation in the amount of contributions provided by members, and participation is heterogeneous if substantial variation exists.[10] This approach allows us to compare groups within each of the discussion days based on homogeneity and heterogeneity of individual participation rates within each group.

An Overview of Speaking-Turn Distribution at the ACP

We begin our analysis by examining the frequency statistics for speaking turns at the group level. The frequency of turns for groups on Day 1 ranged from an average high of 120 speaking turns to an average low of 54 turns. The intensive table work on Day 3, which required specifying evaluative

Table 9.1 Distribution of the Index of Speaking Inequality (ISI) for an array of small discussion groups

Description	# of groups	Group size	Lowest ISI	Highest ISI	Avg. ISI	SD
2001 CR	42	3	6	90	37	22
2007 JPSP	33	5	15	101	39	19
2007 NCA	15	6	29	85	40	14
Bonito CM	30	4	11	88	48	21
1998 CM	45	5	13	39	52	19
1999 CM	73	4	17	95	56	19
Unpublished	57	6	11	114	57	20
1988 Soc	29	6	29	105	68	18
1996 NIC	4	19–20	67	86	76	10

NOTE: Full citations for these data sources are provided in the chapter endnotes.

criteria and then applying those to dozens of different policy proposals, yielded a tremendous increase in participation across most of the groups, with an average high of 357 turns, though the average low was only 69 turns. Finally, the briefer discussions on Day 4 returned to averages similar to Day 1, with an average high of 119 participation turns and an even lower average low of just 30 speaking turns.

These findings suggest, generally, that groups varied tremendously in their overall number of speaking turns on any given day. Although the number of Citizen Parliamentarians (CPs) in these groups was relatively stable (roughly seven CPs per group), some groups obviously talked more than others and likely spoke in shorter bursts—with more interjections and exchanges of turns per minute.

The minimum and maximum statistics also show that in some groups there were members who did not participate at all. Four groups on Day 1 had at least one silent member, as did five groups on Day 3 and four groups on Day 4. At the other end of the spectrum, there were members who participated extremely frequently in some groups, with several groups having a member who took several hundred speaking turns on Day 4.

Measuring the (In)Equality of Speaking Turns

These overall statistics do not tell us anything about the distribution of these speaking-turn totals. Were these reflective of widespread participation by a majority of group members, or were they due to vocal domination by just a few members? To assess the degree of distribution of speaking turns across the members of each ACP table discussion group, we created an Index of Speaking Inequality (ISI). The ISI is simply a group's coefficient of variation (i.e., standard deviation divided by the mean) multiplied by 100.[11] ISI measures the extent of speaking-turn inequality in a group, taking into account how much total talk occurred in that group. More equal sharing of turns and more turns overall lowers the CV, not unlike the Gini coefficient, commonly used to index income inequality. Importantly, the ISI considers equality independent of any given group's mean; thus, groups will have comparable ISI values assuming a constant relationship between their means and standard deviations (e.g., if Group A's mean and standard deviation are exactly twice those of Group B).

From the standpoint of a deliberative-democratic theorist or practitioner, the aim would be to have a low ISI score in all groups, or at the very least, no groups with high ISIs. The distribution of speaking turns does not precisely represent the more fundamental idea of equality of speaking *opportunities,* but when dispersion scores become high, it indicates the foreclosure of at least some group members' chances to get their views into a discussion and/or the most quiet members' reticence or unwillingness to speak.[12]

Before applying the ISI to the Australian case, we begin by setting baseline expectations using previously collected data. To facilitate comparisons among groups in plain words, we set cutoffs at 50, 75, and 100. A score below 50 indicates *high equality,* whereas a score from 50 to 74 indicates *moderate equality.* A score from 75 to 99 shows a *low equality* distribution, and we label a score of 100 or more as *high inequality.*

Table 9.1 shows how ISI scores varied in numerous small discussion groups for which turn-taking data were readily available. This set consists principally of eight laboratory groups, but it also includes four groups from the 1996 National Issues Convention (NIC). Table 9.1 shows that in most of these studies, one or more groups achieved a score of high equality (i.e., ISI < 50), with the exception of the 1996 NIC, which had relatively large groups of nineteen or twenty persons each. Only one study had every group meet the high-equality standard, with three studies including one or more groups that score as highly unequal. The average ISI score was in the high-equality range for four studies (from 37 to 48), with the four having averages showing moderate equality (from 52 to 68), and one (the NIC study) at the low end of the low-equality range, with an average of 76.

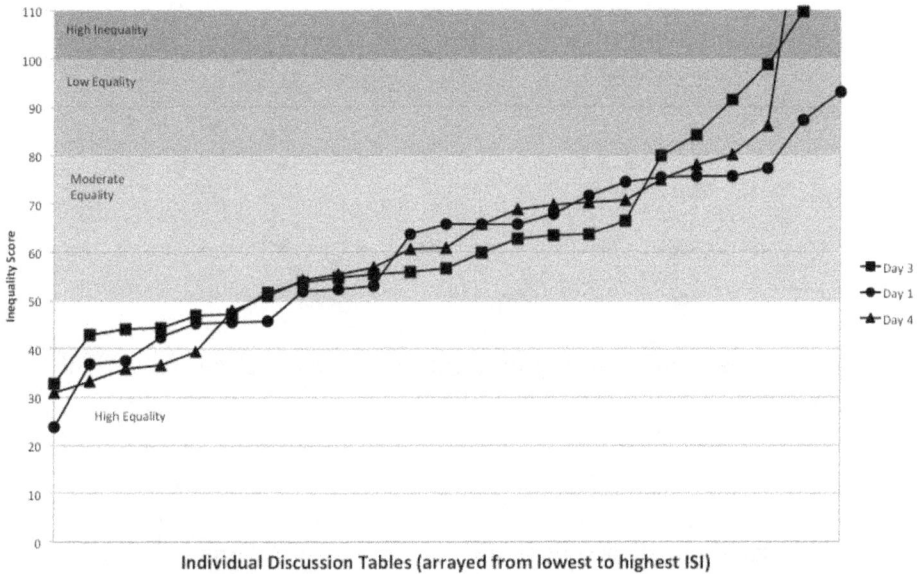

FIGURE 9.1   Speaking turn dispersion for ACP discussion tables on Days 1, 3, and 4, excluding facilitators

Looking at figure 9.1, we can see that the frequency of speaking turns on Day 1 is quite unevenly dispersed in the groups, as measured by the ISI. It merits mention that this figure—the central descriptive result of this chapter—excludes the facilitator from the analysis. If the facilitator is included as a group member, the median ISI increases by roughly five points. As some illustrations below will show, this generally reflected the high frequency of speaking turns taken by the facilitators themselves.

The average ISI score for Day 1 was 67.9 (SD = 16.0), indicating moderate equality across the twenty-three groups. The figure shows that most of the groups on this day achieved a moderate level of speaking-turn equality, whereas seven achieved high equality (i.e., an ISI below 50).

A look at the actual frequencies of speaking turns in one of the most unequal groups shows that, indeed, there are clear differences in the frequency of speaking turns across the team members. Table 9.2 shows that in this group, three members take very few speaking turns, four members speak fairly regularly, and the last two members speak most often. Chiara

Table 9.2   The frequency of speaking turns in a
low-equality group on Day 1 of the ACP

Participant	Speaking turns
Ferdinand	124
Hilton	139
Janet	194
Nick	43
Ray	20
Kathy	145
Olga	31
Chiara (facilitator)	253

especially seems to be a very prominent speaker in this group, though she
is the facilitator and her loquacity might be expected. But Janet, Kathy, Hilton, and Ferdinand are also far more frequent contributors than are Nick,
Ray, and Olga. In this group, then, it appears that most of the participation
was produced by half of its members.

The Day 3 data show very different participation patterns. On this day,
more groups show lowered dispersion indexes, as indicated by the average
ISI of 63.9 (SD = 16.1), suggesting greater equality in speaking turns. Figure 9.1 indicates that several groups on Day 3 demonstrated fairly evenly
dispersed member speaking turns. By our metric, we count six groups as
having high equality, eleven achieving moderate equality, and five having
low equality.

Table 9.3 shows the actual frequency of speaking turns for the most equal
group, whose members shared speaking turns fairly equally. Five of the
members produced fewer turns than the other three, but generally, the speaking-turn distribution was fairly homogeneous across members. If we exclude
Stuart (the facilitator), we can see that only two of the seven members in this

Table 9.3   The frequency of speaking turns in the
most equal group on Day 3 of the ACP

Participants	Speaking turns
Albert	15
Darleen	22
Jillian	42
Mary	46
Tim	56
Jeremy	102
Stan	113
Stuart (facilitator)	158

group were dominant, compared to four members of the low-equality Day 1 group (shown in table 9.2). Additionally, the frequency of participation in this discussion between the most dominant members (Stan and Jeremy) and the rest of the group was at an average ratio of 3:1 turns. This compares to a difference of 5:1 turns on average between the more dominant members and the rest of the table members in the Day 1 example.[13]

On the fourth and final day of the ACP, the results looked very similar to the previous days, an average ISI of 71.1 (SD = 19.5). Figure 9.1 shows that in six groups, speaking turns achieved high equality, but most stayed in the 50–75 ISI range of moderate equality.[14]

Conclusion

Equality of opportunity to speak stands out as one of the most important indicators of democratic deliberation. It parallels the basic democratic principle that each member of an association has an equal vote in the end. That said, fully equal participation in groups is not always expected or desirable. Researchers have found that in participatory decision making—the practice of encouraging and weighing input from different stakeholders—equal participation does not always improve the quality of a group's performance.[15] In some cases, productivity increases when high-status group members (e.g., elders, leaders, or official supervisors) provide clear expectations and goals for the group's more novice members. Even when equal participation is encouraged and valued in small democratic groups, such as cooperatives, some degree of inequality in participation persists.[16]

Nonetheless, the purpose of deliberation in general, and of the ACP specifically, is to create a context in which participants feel comfortable and even compelled to participate to some degree, and that should result in a modest level of speaking-turn equality. Our data show that the ACP, with its emphasis on structure within and across groups, accomplished this objective to a good extent, though many of the groups seated at tables in the Old Parliament dining room displayed a level of inequality in participation rates that clearly privileged the contributions of some of their members over those of others.

Using our shorthand measure of equality, the Index of Speaking Inequality, we conclude that the greatest balance of speaking turns occurred on what might have been the most important juncture of the ACP—the third day, during which groups discussed and rated the top policy recommendations for reforming Australian politics. Before and after that day, fewer groups achieved high levels of equality. On the last day, as the ACP's work wound to a close, the equality achieved the day before disappeared in many of the groups. Perhaps both facilitators and group members recognized that the principal task of the ACP had been largely accomplished, freeing them to revert to more conventional patterns of unequal speaking turns. That said, the more striking finding across the three days is the relatively similar distribution of ISI scores across the discussion tables.

What is needed in future research—and what these data can eventually provide—is information regarding whether members tend to participate similarly across discussions. Should participation for a given member vary (i.e., she participates frequently during one discussion but infrequently during another), then that is evidence that something about the group influenced the individual's participation. If, however, a member tends to participate infrequently across all discussions, then something about that member, independent of the group and its interaction patterns, is responsible for decisions to participate. Future research on this question will help us distinguish individual- and group-level influences.

We conclude this chapter on a practical note. Over five decades ago, researchers identified group members' structuring communication as integral to group processes, and more recently, investigators of self-managing teams have found in-group structuring behaviors to be essential for team success.[17] Because poorly managed group interaction can lead to ineffective communication processes, practices, and products,[18] structuring procedures (e.g., round-robin discussion formats) that organize the flow of members' comments often prove helpful in ameliorating these problems. This task can be effectively undertaken by the group itself if sufficient training and practice is provided.[19] Some deliberative events have devoted an entire day or more to such training.[20] Though costly in terms of time, such procedures might help groups facilitate themselves with an eye toward equality of speaking opportunity.

NOTES

1. Stephanie Burkhalter, John Gastil, and Todd Kelshaw, "A Conceptual Definition and Theoretical Model of Public Deliberation in Small Face-to-Face Groups," *Communication Theory* 12 (2002): 398–422.

2. Tom A. Smith, "The Delegates' Experience," in *The Poll with a Human Face: The National Issues Convention Experiment in Political Communication*, ed. Maxwell McCombs and Amy Reynolds (Mahwah, N.J.: Lawrence Erlbaum, 1999), 39–58.

3. Measuring opportunity provides even greater measurement challenges and likely requires a mix of subjective perceptions and direct observations of nonverbals, since those moments in which an individual remains silenced may have no clear verbal markers. John Gastil, *Political Communication and Deliberation* (Thousand Oaks, Calif.: Sage, 2008).

4. Joseph A. Bonito and Andrea B. Hollingshead, "Participation in Small Groups," *Communication Yearbook* 20 (1997): 227–61.

5. M. Hamit Fisek and Richard Ofshe, "The Process of Status Evolution," *Sociometry* 33 (1970): 327–35; Robert K. Shelly and Lisa Troyer, "Speech Duration and Dependencies in Initially Structured and Unstructured Task Groups," *Sociological Perspectives* 44 (2001): 419–44; Robert K. Shelly and Lisa Troyer, "Emergence and Completion of Structure in Initially Undefined and Partially Defined Groups," *Social Psychology Quarterly* 64 (2001): 318–32.

6. Kevin C. Parker, "Speaking Turns in Small Group Interaction: A Context-Sensitive Event Sequence Model," *Journal of Personality and Social Psychology* 54 (1988): 965–71; Garold Stasser and Laurie A. Taylor, "Speaking Turns in Face-to-Face Discussion," *Journal of Personality and Social Psychology* 60 (1991): 675–84.

7. Carolyn J. Lukensmeyer, Joe Goldman, and Steven Brigham, "A Town Meeting for the Twenty-First Century," in *The Deliberative Democracy Handbook: Strategies for Effective Civic Engagement in the 21st Century*, ed. John Gastil and Peter Levine (San Francisco: Jossey-Bass, 2005), 154–63. Day 2 used a World Café format—akin to "buzz groups"—that discussed a topic or problem for some minutes before rotating to another table with another set of participants working on a different problem. Because the discussion format for Day 2 differed fairly drastically from those used on the other days, we decided to exclude it from our analysis. For more on the World Café approach to discussion, see "The World Café Community," accessed January 30, 2012, http://www.theworldcafecommunity.org.

8. Janette Hartz-Karp and Lyn Carson, "Putting the People into Politics: The Australian Citizens' Parliament," *International Journal of Public Participation* 3, no. 1 (2009): 9–31.

9. Beatrice G. Schultz, "Improving Group Communication Performance: An Overview of Diagnosis and Intervention," in *The Handbook of Group Communication Theory and Research*, ed. Lawrence R. Frey, Dennis S. Gouran, and Marshall Scott Poole (Newbury Park, Calif.: Sage, 1999), 371–94.

10. Our approach is similar to a study that used within-group variation to assess climate strength in organizations. See Jeremy F. Dawson et al., "Organizational Climate and Climate Strength in UK Hospitals," *European Journal of Work and Organizational Psychology* 17 (2008): 89–111.

11. Arthur G. Bedeian and Kevin W. Mossholder, "On the Use of the Coefficient of Variation as a Measure of Diversity," *Organizational Research Methods* 3 (2000): 285–97.

12. John Gastil, *Democracy in Small Groups* (Philadelphia: New Society, 1993); Gastil, *Political Communication and Deliberation*.

13. The dominant members being Tracy, Catherine, David H., and Luke, with the facilitator excluded.

14. Note that a recording error meant that one of the twenty-three tables was not recorded that day.

15. Philip Yetton and Mike Crawford, "Reassessment of Participative Decision-Making: A Case of Too Much Participation," in *Decision-Making and Leadership*, ed. Frank Heller (Cambridge: Cambridge University Press, 1992), 90–111.

16. Gastil, *Democracy in Small Groups*.

17. Norman R. F. Maier and Richard A. Maier, "An Experimental Test of the Effects of 'Developmental' vs. 'Free' Discussions on the Quality of Group Decisions," *Journal of Applied Psychology* 41 (1957): 320–23. See Charles C. Manz and Henry P. Sims Jr., "Leading Workers to Lead Themselves: The External Leadership of Self-Managing Work Teams," *Administrative Science Quarterly* 32 (1987): 106–29; J. Richard Hackman, "The Psychology of Self-Management in Organizations," in *Psychology and Work: Productivity, Change, and Employment*, ed. Michael S. Pallak and Robert O. Perloff (Washington, D.C.: American Psychological Association, 1986),

85–136; J. Richard Hackman, "The Design of Work Teams," in *Handbook of Organizational Behavior,* ed. Jay W. Lorsch (Englewood Cliffs, N.J.: Prentice Hall, 1987).

    18. SunWolf and David R. Seibold, "The Impact of Formal Procedures on Group Processes, Members, and Task Outcomes," in Frey, Gouran, and Poole, *Handbook of Group Communication Theory and Research,* 395–431; SunWolf and Lawrence R. Frey, "Facilitating Group Communication," in *The Handbook of Group Research and Practice,* ed. Susan A. Wheelan (Thousand Oaks, Calif.: Sage, 2005), 485–510.

    19. Joseph C. Chilberg, "A Review of Group Process Designs for Facilitating Communication in Problem-Solving Groups," *Management Communication Quarterly* 3 (1989): 51–70; W. Mayon-White, "Problem Solving in Small Groups: Team Members as Agents of Change," in *Tackling Strategic Problems: The Role of Group Decision Support,* ed. Colin Eden and Jim Radford (London: Sage, 1990), 78–90; Frances Westley and James A. Waters, "Group Facilitation Skills for Managers," *Management Education and Development* 19 (1988): 134–43.

    20. The Oregon Citizens' Initiative Review, for instance, did this in 2010—devoting the first of its five-day deliberations to training in deliberation and argument analysis. For more information, visit "Citizens' Initiative Review," accessed January 30, 2012, http://healthy democracyoregon.org/citizens-initiative-review.

PART III

THE FLOW OF BELIEFS AND IDEAS

Whereas part II explored the nature of deliberative activity, the chapters in part III focus on the evolving content of deliberation. The ACP aimed to prioritize a set of proposals for improving the Australian political system, and these chapters assess the degree to which the CPs got that job done. In chapter 10, "Changing Orientations Toward Australian Democracy," Simon Niemeyer, Luisa Batalha, and John Dryzek present the detailed results of a hybrid approach called Q methodology that indicates how attitudinal patterns shifted over the course of the ACP about government and politics. In chapter 11, "Staying Focused: Tracing the Flow of Ideas from the Online Parliament to Canberra," John Gastil and John Wilkerson use computer-aided content analysis to measure the surface features of talk during the Online Parliament and ACP to see when different proposals rose to the top of the CPs' agenda. Finally, in chapter 12, "Evidence of Peer Influence in the Citizens' Parliament," Luc Tucker and Gastil show that interpersonal influences played an important role at the Canberra meetings; the authors use complex network analysis to show that CPs' priorities at the ACP came to reflect those whom organizers randomly seated them beside.

IO

CHANGING ORIENTATIONS TOWARD AUSTRALIAN DEMOCRACY

Simon Niemeyer, Luisa Batalha, and John S. Dryzek

The Australian Citizens' Parliament (ACP) addressed a single broad issue—the nation's political system. How did participation in this unique event influence participants' orientations toward that system?

We begin by describing our approach to measuring attitude change—involving an extended version of Q methodology. We then identify the basic orientations that Australians have toward politics and examine how those changed over the course of the ACP. We find that participants' orientations changed significantly, most notably through increased contentment with Australia's liberal democracy. This finding is perhaps a bit surprising in the context of a process that subjected aspects of Australia's political system to critical scrutiny. We consider the factors that might have accounted for this shift, as well as their implications.

Q Methodology

We measure and describe participants' orientations to Australia's political system using one of the most well-developed systematic approaches to the study of human subjectivity, Q methodology. This method is appropriate because it enables fine-grained measurement of participants' subjective beliefs.[1]

Q methodology begins by drawing a sample of statements relevant to the issue or phenomenon under study to implement as a "Q sort." A Q sort represents an individual's reaction to a set of statements about a particular domain—in this case, Australian democracy; it is therefore a model of the *entirety* of an individual's orientation to that domain. We gathered statements from actual dialogue using a wide range of sources—including old and new media, World Cafés conducted by the newDemocracy Foundation in the lead up to the Citizens' Parliament, and a report from the 2020 Summit (a gathering run by the Australian government in 2008; see chapter 2).

We drew a sample of forty-eight statements from this larger pool to comprise a manageable number for use in the Q sort at the ACP.[2] These items were selected to encompass the broadest possible range of potential orientations toward Australian politics. The set included statements originally used in a prior study of Australian discourses of democracy.[3]

Participants completed the Q sort at four stages during the ACP process. At each stage each participant was asked to order the statements into a set of eleven categories along a scale from "most disagree" to "most agree." In doing so, participants assigned a score to each statement from −5 to +5, with the requirement that their ratings approximate a normal distribution (i.e., fewer statements can be placed in the extreme categories).

The first Q sort was done as soon as participants consented to be selected; the second (stage 2) at the regional meetings that were conducted around Australia in the lead up to the main event. The third and fourth Q sorts (stages 3 and 4) were obtained, respectively, immediately before and immediately after the main meeting of the ACP.[4] The number of Q sorts at each stage varies considerably.[5] Forty-eight individuals provided usable Q sorts at all four stages of the research, and it is these individuals whom we examine in this chapter.

Four Orientations Toward Politics

Using inverted-factor analysis combining the Q sorts of the forty-eight who completed all four stages, we sought to identify patterns across the individual ACP participants.[6] Each factor represents an ideal type position, how a hypothetical individual whose beliefs perfectly matched the factor in question would sort the forty-eight statements.[7]

Figure 10.1 represents schematically the main characteristics of each of the four factors, which appear as partially overlapping rectangles. Each rectangle contains the main elements of its corresponding factor as represented by selected Q-sort statements. Statements that fall within two or more factors appear in the areas of overlap.

A: Liberal Democratic Contentment **B: Moralistic Leadership**

Aust' society evolutionary, not revolutionary (5)

Aust' is a great democracy (6)

Respect for difference is important (15)

Slightly pessimistic about capacity of voters to grasp issues (37)

Democracy IS a meaningful term (1)

Democracy id about individuals rights (16)

Aust' is NOT particularly democratic (39)

The Aust' political system is not particularly remote from voters (35)

The two-party system is not a problem (36)

Australia needs leaders of high principles (23)

Governments can/do share power with voters (20)

There IS a difference between Aust' political parties (33)

Know enough about democracy, do NOT feel ridiculous voting. (13)

Not voting is NOT an effective form of political expression (48)

Voters need to understand issues before voting (2)

Money is too influential in politics (3)

Democracy should make you feel like you are important (24)

Australia DOES NOT need leaders of high principles (23)

We do not get the gov'ts that we deserve (32)

Racism is not acceptable in politics (31)

Voting does not ensure equality (27)

Not always cynical about government (19)

Disagreement is OK (43)

Republicanism is OK (17)

We are equal at the ballot box, at least (27)

Against minority domination (12, 14)

Female representation is not an important issue (25,30)

Voters are easily brainwashed (28)

Self interest can be detrimental to politics (21)

Existing consultation is not effective (45)

Free markets do not always work (29)

Too much vested interest influence in politics (34)

Slightly optimistic about capacity of voters to grasp issues (37)...but

Political System is NOT capable of change (7)

The wealthy dominate politics (9)

Voters do not have enough input into politics (11)

Politicians are response to parties, not voters (41)

Voters should be able to vote on specific issues (38)

Aust' is fairly democratic (39)

Voters are NOT responsible for failures by gov' (47)

Difficult to influence politics beyond voting (10)

Two party system is corrupt and politicians remote (40, 35)

Deliberation followed by voting favourable (46)

C: Anxious Majoritarianism **D: Discontented Participationism**

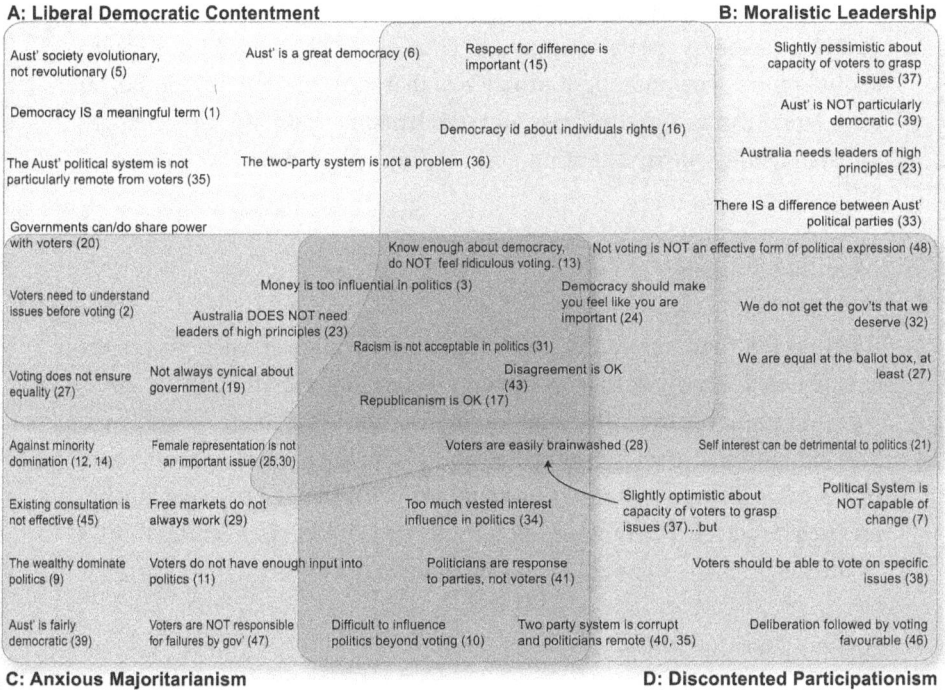

FIGURE 10.1 Schematic representation of factors

For many statements, figure 10.1 shows that there is actually a good deal of agreement across the four factors. Overall, there is considerable agreement that money is too influential in politics (statement 3); that individuals do not feel ridiculous voting, being confident in their abilities (13); that republicanism is acceptable (17); that people should be able to influence politics (24); that races and cultures are equal (31); that disagreement is fine (43); and that not voting is not acceptable (48).

Aside from that common ground, the Q sort revealed interesting differences across the four factors. These make it possible to understand how the factors diverge from one another. Below, we construct a distinctive narrative from the set of statements associated with each particular factor, and this makes clearer what each orientation represents.

Liberal Democratic Contentment

This orientation holds that Australian democracy, although imperfect, is meaningful and works well, as governments do share power with citizens.

We have a well-functioning party system that nurtures the disagreement that is a necessary part of democracy. Thus, there is no need to be cynical about politics. The only slight problem is that money is too influential, but our system can adapt to address any problems that do arise. Citizens have a responsibility to pay attention and vote, and should be able to exercise influence.

Moralistic Leadership

Whereas this view agrees that Australia's system of government works reasonably well, it argues that we deserve better. We are all equal when we vote, but money is too influential in politics. The key to better government is leadership that puts into practice moral principles, such as those found in the Bible. A robust democracy would feature decency, active citizenship, and debate across different views, all motivated by what individuals think is in the public interest, not their private interests.

Anxious Majoritarianism

The third orientation will grant that we live in a democracy but believes the system is distorted by the influence of the rich, corporations, vested interests, and the power of various minorities who have too big a say. Likewise, there is no reason for the interests of minorities and women to be promoted. Informed voting has particular importance: this is where the majority can express itself, and there is no need for citizens to be active in politics beyond voting.

Discontented Participationism

The final perspective holds that the Australian political system is remote, closed, and inflexible. We are not well served by a conflict-based party system that serves itself rather than the voters, where corporate lobbyists and vested interests have too much say. Politicians don't listen at all between elections. We deserve much better government than what we have. It would be great if we could vote on specific issues, not just on party platforms. Politics should involve much more in the way of citizen participation that discusses legitimate disagreements and influences public policy.

What Changed During Deliberation?

These four narratives represent the main orientations among participants during the ACP. Individuals' locations in relation to the factors, however, were not necessarily constant over the course of the process, and these changes can be investigated in a number of different ways.[8] Most straightforwardly, we can extend the standard approach in Q methodology and examine how factor loadings change. A factor loading is a measure of agreement between an individual (or, more specifically, his or her Q sort) and a factor, where "+1" represents complete agreement and "−1" complete disagreement.

The first approach to observing changes during the ACP process simply involves using the average factor loadings (that is, the average across all the citizens) for each of the factors at each measurement stage. Figure 10.2 shows the results of this analysis. It reveals that, for the most part, there were relatively small changes in average agreement with any given factor at each Q sort stage. The exception concerns a large increase in the average level of agreement with Liberal Democratic Contentment following participation in the main ACP meeting. More modestly and gradually, agreement with Factor B also increased over the course of the ACP. Anxious Majoritarianism increased slightly during the early phases of the research, but then returned to its original strength following the deliberative event. Discontented Participationism decreased gradually from beginning to end. But the real story was the increasing contentment with Australian democracy, associated with Factor A, and this is what we seek to investigate and explain.

The use of average factor loadings is useful for providing a sense of the overall changes that occurred during the ACP. However, if one looks only at averages, one can overlook other important changes. For example, the variation in commitments can increase while the average stays the same. Or, when the average does increase, one needs additional information to know which participants contributed to the change. The result could simply reflect a strengthening of the factor from within, where individuals already sympathetic to it fortify their position. Alternatively, it could be the result of supporters of another factor "migrating" toward it to cause its increased average.

One way in which the nature of the changes that have occurred can be explored involves plotting the position of each individual on the "factor map" provided in figure 10.1 at different stages of the research. This has

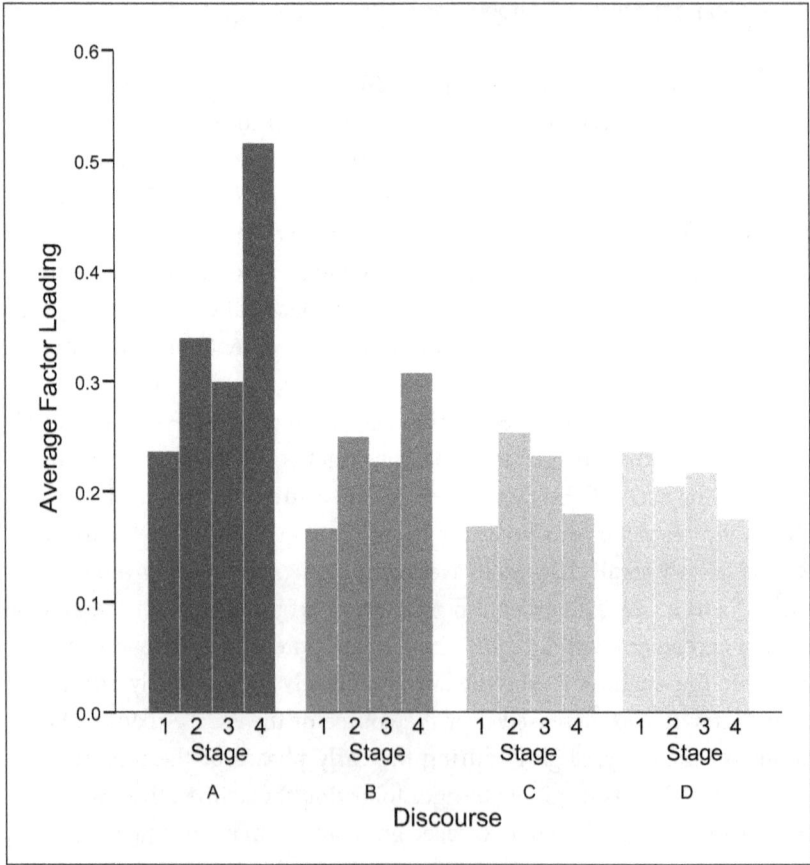

FIGURE 10.2   Average factor loadings for the four factors

been done in figure 10.3, which shows the migrations between stage 1 (recruitment) and stage 4 (post-deliberation). Each of the arrows in the figure represents the "migratory path" of a single individual from stage 1 to stage 4.

The actual location of the arrows is schematic; it is not possible to represent the positions precisely in two dimensions. In general, the further toward the edge of a factor, the higher the agreement with that factor (i.e., higher factor loading). Where an individual has a significantly strong loading on more than one factor, the position is shown in the overlap between the factors, with the exact position determined by the relative strength of the competing factor loadings. There are also some individuals who do not have a significant association with any of the factors at stage 1. In these cases, the arrows begin just outside the factor on the map closest to the

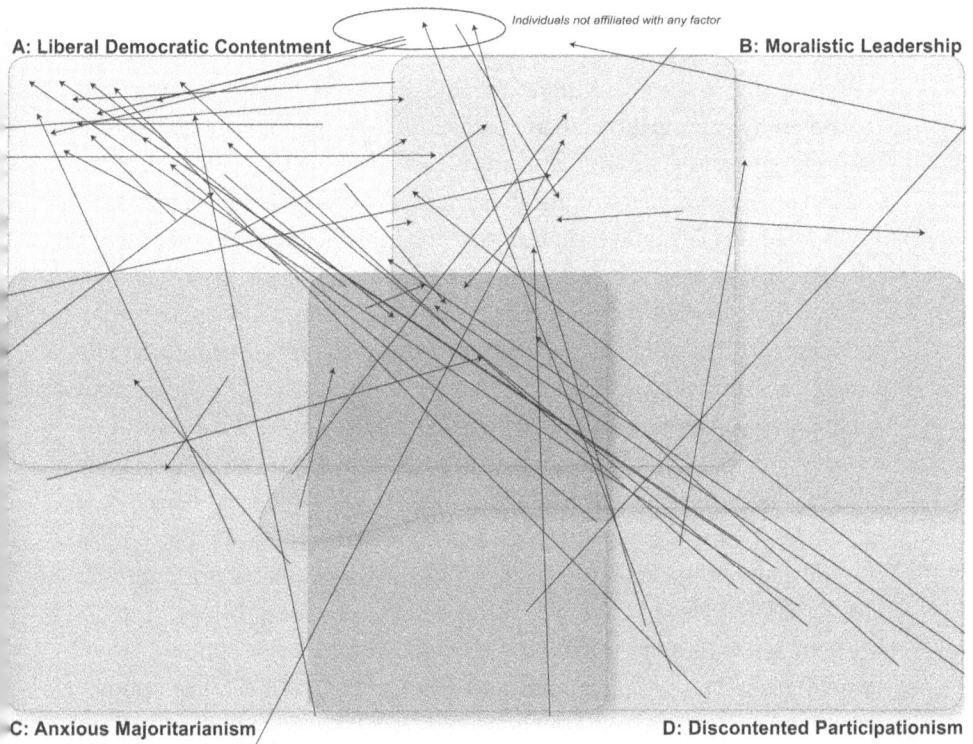

FIGURE 10.3   Factor migrations between stage 1 and stage 4

factor/s with which they are most strongly associated. Finally, an even smaller number of individuals are not inclined toward any factor (i.e., their loadings are near zero for all factors); they have been gathered into an oval at the top of the map.

Figure 10.3 shows a strong movement toward Liberal Democratic Contentment during participation in the ACP from a number of directions. Most striking is the migration of individuals from the bottom right to the top left of the figure. In other words, those individuals who began the deliberative process as Discontented Participationists tended to transform into Contented Liberal Democrats. In addition, those individuals who began with some association with Liberal Democratic Contentment strengthened their affiliation by the end of the process.

Most of the rest of the movements are either toward Factor A exclusively or toward the overlap between Liberal Democratic Contentment and Moralistic Leadership. There is a tendency for those individuals who were almost, but not quite, significantly associated with Liberal Democratic Contentment at the outset of the study to increase their loadings on both it and Moralistic Leadership over time.

By the end of the ACP's main meeting, Anxious Majoritarianism and Discontented Participationism are both close to being nonviable. That is to say, by stage 4 there are very few individuals attaching themselves to these factors, and where they are, they also have a significant association with another factor. (The lone exception was one individual uniquely loaded on Discontented Participationism in the final research stage.)

Overall, it appears the main effect of the ACP was to increase participants' satisfaction with Australia's existing system of parliamentary democracy. This conclusion is also borne out by the results from an additional survey, in which participants were asked to rate five options on a scale of −5 ("strongly dislike") to +5 ("strongly like"). Of the five options—*maintaining the status quo, developing a more inclusive form of government, developing a minimalist form of government, increasing moral leadership,* and *improvements in equal treatment of citizens*—it is the *status quo* option that gains more support than any other options (the average score increasing from 0.6 to 1.6 between research stages 1 and 4), although the *inclusive* option is most favored at the end of deliberation (2.4, up from 1.7). Of the five options, responses to these two were the only ones that changed significantly from stages 1 to 4.

Why Did People Change?

Why did these changes occur? In particular, what accounts for the sizable increase in support for Liberal Democratic Contentment? We divide the impacts of the ACP into two categories: the cognitive impact that changed the way that participants perceived Australian democracy and their place in it, and the affective impact on people's feelings toward politics and government. Liberal Democratic Contentment could have strengthened as a result of working through ideas about Australian democracy, weighing up the alternatives, and finding them lacking (cognitive). Alternatively, this increased satisfaction with existing Australian politics could have emerged via processes that made people "feel" better about their system of government (affective). The distinction between these two effects is somewhat artificial as cognitive reasoning and affective dimensions interplay strongly,[9] but it is possible to sort out their relative roles.

Cognitive Impacts

Despite the scale of the task presented to participants, there was at least some opportunity for cognitive deliberation about Australian governance, which resulted in the final recommendations made by the ACP. The recommendations themselves do appear to have resulted from deliberation, although many of them may well have been extant among the participants prior to the event. Deliberation also resulted in withdrawal of a proposal that had been developed by a group online to implement a system of "first-past-the-post" voting and replace it by optional preferential voting. Here we see a cognitive process that ended up favoring something closer to the status quo—that is, compulsory preferential voting, at least at the national level. (On the character of ACP deliberation, see part II of this volume.)

However, the availability of such an example does not demonstrate that participants were able more generally to work through the many features of Australian governance to arrive at well-developed positions that reflect the sort of process ascribed to idealized forms of deliberation.[10] Australia's political system is complex, with an equally complex history. Developing a working knowledge of it is asking a lot, even within the relatively generous time constraints of the ACP.

Affective Impacts

One possible way to understand the effect of the ACP process, particularly in respect to the move toward Liberal Democratic Contentment, is in terms of a shift from a situation where citizens do not identify with their system of government, to one in which they do. The social-identity perspective within social psychology, concerned with the factors that determine whether people behave according to their personal identity ("I") or a social identity ("us"/"we") can account for this shift.[11] For example, one ACP participant said, "I heard about a 'we' and an 'us' . . . . [I]f I'm sitting here, which I am, then I think I'm becoming part of the 'us.'" (On the emergence of shared identity in the ACP, see chapter 18.)

The question here is the degree to which the observed changes can be explained by identity dynamics: a shift from an "I" to an "us" in which there is not only an identification with the larger deliberative group, but also with the political system that is supposed to meet their collective needs.

The features of the ACP together with social-identity processes offer a plausible explanation for why people moved toward a position we describe as (liberal democratic) contentment. The ACP generated a very positive feeling among its participants. Self-esteem effects resulting from identification with a pre-existing group often operate through positive distinction favoring the in-group in relation to out-groups.[12] However, these effects can also work in a bottom-up fashion, within intragroup relations, rather than through intergroup processes, where no comparison out-group is readily available.[13] In this case, the simple observation of other in-group members' behavior may lead people to assimilate general characteristics of the in-group, resulting in shared identity.

This dynamic is also more likely to apply in situations in which group members share observations or experiences with each other. Intragroup communication helps to shape similarities between group members. From these underlying similarities, norms and values are created that help to define an emergent social identity.[14]

The ACP process contained all the necessary elements to create a shared social identity. Such a deliberative process privileges dialogue over formal debate, as participants work together to identify common interests and the best means by which they can be met. An ideal deliberative design should "create respectful, educational, purposeful, egalitarian spaces."[15] And it is just such a space in which a collective identity can flourish.

In addition to the group identity, participants in the ACP became familiar with "the" political system as well as effectively becoming part of a type of political system (however temporarily). In other words, they became members of an in-group with some perceived political power. From a social-psychology perspective we know that shifts in identity are followed by shifts in self-perception and consequently in social perception.[16] We suggest that as a social identity of Citizen Parliamentarian was being crafted, in-group stereotypes that define the participants as insightful in politics, a group with a say, and a group with (relative) power, also emerged. This comes very close to the archetype of the politically competent figure. The movement toward Liberal Democratic Contentment may therefore be an indication of participants' emerging identification with the political establishment and, consequently, approval of that establishment.

Summary

There may well be other factors influencing increased satisfaction with the existing political system. There is a possible framing effect where at least one distinguished speaker framed the process as one of improving an already good system. And this positive framing was also reflected in the way in which group discussions were organized.[17] There was a dramatic (and traumatic) bushfire in nearby Victoria over the weekend of the main event, possibly leading to a display of national solidarity. And the simple fact that the process took place in the dignified surroundings of Old Parliament House may have led participants to identify with the system in which that building played such a significant part. Finally, in working through proposals, participants did indeed learn a great deal about the political system as it stood, much of which may have translated into a newfound appreciation—a good example of how cognitive deliberation can have affective consequences.

These effects add to, rather than contradict, our overall contention that the ACP process served to form not only a shared identity with the deliberating group, but also with the very system that they were charged with improving—a system that had heretofore been distant from their everyday experience (see chapter 18).

Conclusion

Analysis of the changes in positions of Citizen Parliamentarians reveals a shift toward greater appreciation of the current political system. We interpret this change as at least partially resulting from the emerging group identity as Citizen Parliamentarians as well as identification with the political system at large. That a major effect of the ACP was to improve identification with the existing parliamentary system might seem to detract from more cognitive accounts of deliberation, which treat outputs as well-reasoned recommendations. However, to point to the importance of affective processes is not to diminish that of cognitive ones, and, as we have argued in the case of the ACP, there is a feedback loop between these effects.

This interplay of cognitive and affective processes could account for an apparent contradiction where the greatest subjective change was in favor of the status quo, but in terms of stated preference there was a strong move toward more inclusive forms of governance. The two findings are not entirely incompatible, but might point to an unfinished deliberative process, which was strong on appreciative developments, but did not (and perhaps could not, given serious time constraints for such a lofty issue) permit contestation of the finer points of parliamentary reform.[18]

Regardless of the strength and completeness of the cognitive impacts, the affective impacts that took place are significant and, arguably, beneficial.

Trust in existing political institutions grew, and, our explanation of how this happened notwithstanding, we recognize the irony that a process designed to subject the status quo of Australian parliamentary democracy to critical scrutiny ended up increasing its approval of that very system. Given the general framework of the ACP, both in terms of design and the physical setting, such an outcome was perhaps inevitable. Whether or not the outcome can be called "deliberative"—and we think it can, with some qualification— the ACP example is exemplary of the need for sensitivity to both the affective and cognitive impacts of deliberative designs, both of which need to be accounted for in deliberative democratic theory.

NOTES

1. For introductory treatments of Q methodology, see Steven R. Brown, *Political Subjectivity: Applications of Q Methodology in Political Science* (New Haven: Yale University Press, 1980); Fiona Dziopa and Kathy Ahern, "A Systematic Literature Review of the Application of Q-Technique and Its Methodology," *Methodology: European Journal of Research Methods for the Behavioral and Social Sciences* 7, no. 2 (2011): 39–55.

2. This is in the middle of the range common in Q studies.

3. See John S. Dryzek, "Australian Discourses of Democracy," *Australian Journal of Political Science* 29 (1994): 221–39. An analysis comparing the results from the ACP with Dryzek's original study using a benchmarking method can be found in Simon J. Niemeyer, "The Q-Block Method and an Alternative: Benchmarking the Australian Discourse of Democracy," *Operant Subjectivity* 34, no. 1 (2010): 59–84.

4. The shape of the grid approximates a normal distribution such that there is a smaller number of statements that could be allocated in the "most agree" and "most disagree" columns and a greater number of statements in the middle columns. The quotas for the respective columns (−5 to +5) were 2, 3, 4, 6, 6, 6, 6, 4, 3, and 2 statements, respectively.

5. Of the 3,000 individuals who agreed that they would participate in the ACP if selected, at stage 1, 220 provided usable Q sorts, most of which were performed online, the remainder by post. There were 144 viable Q sorts provided at the regional meetings (stage 2), 119 before the ACP (stage 3) and 134 afterward (stage 4).

6. Unlike common "R"-factor analysis, which seeks patterns across variables.

7. Technically, we used principal-components factor analysis followed by Varimax rotation.

8. For a more complete list of methods that can be used, see Simon J. Niemeyer, "The Emancipatory Effect of Deliberation: Empirical Lessons from Mini-publics," *Politics and Society* 39 (2011): 103–40. See also Kersty P. Hobson and Simon J. Niemeyer, "Public Responses to Climate Change: The Role of Deliberation in Building Capacity for Adaptive Action," *Global Environmental Change* 21 (2011): 957–71.

9. Justin Storbeck and Gerard L. Clore, "On the Interdependence of Cognition and Emotion," *Cognition and Emotion* 21 (2007): 1212–37.

10. Simon J. Niemeyer and John S. Dryzek, "The Ends of Deliberation: Meta-consensus and Inter-subjective Rationality as Ideal Outcomes," *Swiss Political Science Review* 13 (2007): 497–526.

11. Michael A. Hogg, "Uncertainty, Social Identity, and Ideology," *Advances in Group Processes* 22 (2005): 203–29.

12. Henri Tajfel, "The Achievement of Group Differentiation," in *Differentiation Between Groups: Studies in the Social Psychology of Intergroup Relations,* ed. Henri Tajfel (London: Academic Press, 1978), 77–100.

13. Tom Postmes, S. Alexander Haslam, and Roderick I. Swaab, "Social Influence in Small Groups: An Interactive Model of Social Identity Formation," *European Review of Social Psychology* 16 (2005): 1–42.

14. Postmes, Haslam, and Swaab, "Social Influence in Small Groups."

15. Lyn Carson, "Creating Democratic Surplus Through Citizens' Assemblies," *Journal of Public Deliberation* 4 (2008): 3.

16. See, e.g., Rina Onorato and John C. Turner, "Fluidity in the Self-Concept: The Shift from Personal to Social Identity," *European Journal of Social Psychology* 34 (2004): 257–78; Ana-Maria Bliuc, Craig McGarty, Katherine Reynolds, and Daniela Muntele, "Opinion-Based Group Membership as a Predictor of Commitment to Political Action," *British Journal of Social Psychology* 37 (2006): 19–32.

17. See Nicole Curato and Simon Niemeyer, "Appreciative and Contestatory Inquiry in Deliberative Forums: Can Group Hugs Be Dangerous?," paper delivered at Deliberative Democracy in Action conference, June 6–7, University of Åbo.

18. Although Curato and Niemeyer, ibid., do offer some caution that more contestatory modes of deliberation involving the challenging of ideas may have been underemphasized.

II

STAYING FOCUSED: TRACING THE FLOW OF IDEAS FROM
THE ONLINE PARLIAMENT TO CANBERRA

John Gastil and John Wilkerson

There exist many successful examples of public deliberation engaging
groups of lay citizens, but questions remain about the extent to which deliberation can flourish online and how such discussions can be merged with
more traditional public meetings.[1] Previous deliberative efforts have built
online and face-to-face deliberative meetings in parallel, or they have integrated small-group deliberations into plenary sessions during a single-day
event.[2] The 2009 Australian Citizens' Parliament was the first event to
really make it possible to test those questions.

The deliberation process began in late 2008 with the Online Parliament (OP), which chapter 3 describes in more detail. The hundreds of
participants in the OP divided into groups that generated eleven discrete
proposals that then primed the face-to-face deliberations held in Canberra in February 2009. The Canberra face-to-face deliberations (hereafter called "F2F") included daily small-group discussions, which were
recorded and transcribed. These transcripts, combined with the digital
record of the OP's discussion threads, provide the first chance to track
issues over the course of both an online and a face-to-face deliberative
process. The aim of this chapter is to measure systematically the flow of
language and ideas from the OP to the F2F. This question is important
because it tests the viability of the Australian model for future public events
that hope to link a massive online process with a more focused and exclusive face-to-face deliberation.

Integrating Online and Face-to-Face Deliberation

In theory, the OP process should have aided the F2F deliberations by providing the face-to-face deliberators with a set of concrete proposals to consider, thereby saving them the considerable effort necessary to generate a robust set of initial proposals. This could help to focus their energy on the final, most challenging, deliberative task—namely, that of weighing the best solutions against one another and making a prioritized set of recommendations. The most basic question is, did this happen? This is important to know because the OP/ACP may become a model for organizing future deliberations.

Even with a well-designed process, there are forces at work that could undermine efforts to integrate online insights into the face-to-face discussions. In particular, prior research suggests the tendency of groups to converge on a shared identity that sets them apart from other groups.[3] Prior face-to-face deliberating groups, even larger ones such as the British Columbia Citizens' Assembly (see chapter 1), have engaged in precisely this kind of identity-building activity amidst their more rigorous deliberations. This process may make it less likely that those meeting face-to-face will incorporate the results of prior online deliberations into their own deliberations. From a broader social-identity perspective, the challenge is to either establish the online participants as part of the same citizen-deliberator "in-group" as their face-to-face peers, or to appeal to the face-to-face deliberators' superordinate social identity as "citizens" to take seriously the views of their online peers.[4] In sum, the ability of Australian organizers to integrate the identities of online and face-to-face deliberators may prove the key to determining the influence of the large-scale online discussions on the subsequent F2F deliberations.

The closest research program to the present study comes from the small-group literature—the research on decision development by communication scholar Marshall Scott Poole. He and his colleagues tried to develop a way to measure how small decision-making groups moved through different "phases" of discussion—from, say, the "orientation phase" (getting to know each other) to the "decision phase" (actually voting on a choice). The difference here is that we are trying to trace the flow of *topical* tracks, rather than broader categories of talk.[5] In this sense, our task is more akin to the identification of topics in legislative bills, proposals, or agendas.[6]

We aim to track the frequency with which different proposals get discussed in the OP and F2F sessions and combine that with additional data to answer a series of questions. We hope to learn the extent to which the F2F sessions took up the issues originally raised in the OP discussions, as opposed to dismissing them while moving on to other topics. Only half of the F2F participants also took part in OP discussions, so it was possible that those who eschewed the OP would have little patience for the ideas it had generated. A closely related question is whether the F2F sessions did, in fact, develop new discussion topic tracks of their own, as opposed to simply following those raised in the OP. If so, when—in the course of a four-day event—did these new issues arise?

In addition, the data we assemble show which F2F participants took part in which OP discussions, as well as where the F2F participants sat among the twenty-three tables recorded each day at the ACP. This information makes it possible to study the degree to which OP participants drove the F2F table discussions toward the topics of their choosing. In other words, did the authors of the online proposals influence the F2F deliberations by successfully promoting the topics they had championed during the OP?

Computer-Aided Content Analysis

Creating "Topic Dictionaries"

To answer these questions, we conducted a computer-aided textual analysis, which we describe briefly (and more completely in the endnotes).[7] Before we could conduct the main analyses, we extracted discussion data from the OP logs and F2F transcripts.[8] We then created a set of "topic dictionaries" to analyze those discussion data. In this study, a "dictionary" is a set of words and phrases whose appearance in a text indicates the likely presence of a topic. The ideal set of dictionaries identifies those words and phrases that uniquely identify a given topic.

To develop our dictionaries for studying the OP and F2F, we took advantage of the supplementary documents that described the relevant topics. Recalling that the ACP's focus was on reforming Australian politics, we began by reading the brief summaries of the OP proposals, as summarized in the ACP's *Final Report*, to identify "lexical markers" (i.e., words and phrases) suitable for each topic dictionary. For instance, we have italicized the key markers in the following proposal excerpt: "*Accountability* regarding *political promises*: Politicians should be made to deliver on their promises. An independent *auditor* could report on progress of implementing promised programs or policies."

These initial topic dictionaries then went through a series of tests and refinements, essentially testing the predictive accuracy of each dictionary on additional documents, such as the full-page summaries of proposals produced at the end of the OP and the longer list of fifty proposals generated at the F2F. These tests produced encouraging results, in that they yielded few false positives and suggested various improvements to better differentiate the dictionaries: root terms replaced keywords (e.g., "polit" in place of the more limited "politics"); linked pairs of words became more important than single words (e.g., one rule looked for "civic" within five words of "curricul[um/ar]"); and weights from 1–5 were assigned to dictionary entries based on the centrality of each lexical marker to its corresponding topic.[9] The final set of dictionaries included the following topics:

1. RIGHTS: establishing a Bill of Rights for Australia
2. DUPLICATION: removing redundancies across different levels of government
3. EMPOWER: civic education and citizen empowerment, particularly of youth
4. ELECTIONS: changing the electoral system, particularly replacing first-past-the-post
5. INDIGENOUS: more inclusion and recognition of Indigenous Australians in public life
6. ACCOUNTABLE: holding politicians and government more accountable for their actions
7. PARTISANSHIP: reducing the influence of polarizing partisanship in politics
8. REFERENDUM: establishing a national citizen initiative or referendum process
9. REPUBLIC: moving Australia from a constitutional monarchy to a republic
10. TERM/OFFICE: fixing the length of a term of office of elected officials, optionally including a presidential system of election

It is worth noting that one of those priorities—the one ranked fifth—did *not* appear in the OP. As we discuss later, this important topic was the clearest new topic to arise during F2F deliberation.

Assessing the Validity of the Final Dictionaries

Table 11.1 shows how well the topic dictionaries matched the text of the OP proposals. The expected matches appear in bold, and it is striking how few unexpected matches appeared—as evidenced by the empty cells in the table and the small scores for the topic mismatches.[10] The OP proposals sometimes do relate to more than one dictionary, and vice versa, but the overlaps are generally either sensible or negligible. The online proposals not associated with dictionaries are also what we would expect—the proposals that emerged later in the F2F and were not a focus of online discussions (i.e., Aboriginal concerns and making Australia a republic).

The texts of the OP discussions, which had not been used to create the dictionaries, offer a final "out of sample" validity check. ACP organizers rated each of these discussions on a scale from 1 to 10 for their "relevance" to the ACP main topic of "reforming Australian politics/government." In the current analysis, dictionaries vary in terms of their ability to predict topics, even if two topics are discussed for an equal length of time (i.e., in an equal number of words). Table 11.1 first identifies the maximum "match score" for each dictionary.[11] These maximums were then divided by 250 to create a range of weights from 1.0 (partisan politics) to .30 (Bill of Rights). The two dictionaries not in these proposals were given a default weighting of 1.0.

There should be a substantial correspondence between the expert ratings of the relevance of OP discussions and the ACP dictionary match scores. Moreover, because the OP forums were designed to generate independent proposals, there should be *only one or two* strong matches on those OP discussions. This is, essentially, a test of convergent validity. As predicted, for the vast majority of online discussion threads, there was only a *single* large category match.[12] Moreover, the OP discussions that had only weak category matches were the ones that experts scored as having little or no ACP relevance. Overall, there was a strong relationship between expert ratings and the total match score divided by total words ($r = .53$, $p = .001$).[13]

Topic Flow at the ACP

The primary questions examined in this study are descriptive. First, did the deliberative process effectively channel proposals developed in large-scale

Table 11.1 Match between final topic dictionaries and full-page Online Parliament proposals, plus dictionary weighting calculations

Dictionary category	Online Proposal											Max score (or avg.)	Category weight
	Bill of Rights	Fixed term	Refer-endum	Remove state govt	Party politics	First past post	Empower citizens	Account-ability	Unify state laws	Over-governed	Youth engage-ment		
Rights	**96**		10							19		96	0.3
Duplication				**22**					19	**44**		32	0.8
Empower	5		3	3			**46**	3	3			42	0.6
Elections			13		15	**30**					**38**	30	0.8
Indigenous												n/a	1.0
Accountable		5	5		5			**45**				45	0.6
Partisanship		5			24							24	1.0
Referendum		5	**46**									46	0.5
Republic	3							3				n/a	1.0
Term/Office		**47**					5					47	0.5

NOTE: Bold indicates a predicted category match.

online discussions into the final, smaller-scale face-to-face deliberations? Second, did the face-to-face deliberations also generate new proposals superseding those primed by online discussions?

The Influence of the Online Parliament Topics

To answer these questions, we began by assessing the relative frequency of topics during the F2F table discussions. Each day, the Citizen Parliamentarians (CPs) were seated randomly at one of twenty-three discussion tables, which included six or seven CPs plus a facilitator. Figure 11.1 provides a graphic summary of how frequently each topic came up at the various tables using "boxplots" and weighted frequencies to create a scale from 0 (not discussed) to 100 (discussed very frequently). For each topic on each day, the figure shows an average frequency (black bar), a typical range (the gray rectangle, which encompasses the middle 50 percent of discussion-table frequencies), and top and bottom lines (a.k.a. "whiskers") that encompass the full range of frequencies, minus the statistical outliers, which appear as circles and stars above the top whisker.

Above all else, what these data show is that yes, the F2F effectively channeled main areas of interest in the OP into the final proposals. Table 11.2 shows this in a side-by-side comparison. Most of the proposals from the OP ended up somewhere on that list, with the two exceptions being concerns about party politics and the length of term in office/fixed election cycles. Those issues received little discussion and fell away, replaced by concerns about Indigenous Australians, the one topic that clearly emerged in the discussions that was entirely absent from the OP discussions.

The Emergence of the Indigenous Australian Topic

The ascent of concerns about Indigenous Australians during the course of the F2F deliberations provides the clearest evidence of a newly emergent F2F issue. Discussion of this topic led to a top-ranked proposal, even though it had not been a part of the online deliberations. The results in figure 11.1 make precisely this finding clear: it was on the second day that concern about Aboriginal Australians surfaced as the top issue on Day 2 (see chapter 17). What was not expected, however, was the dramatically greater *variance* in the discussion of Indigenous Australians across the tables; its range (not counting outliers) extended from the floor to the ceiling of this frequency scale. Having said that, it was clearly among the most

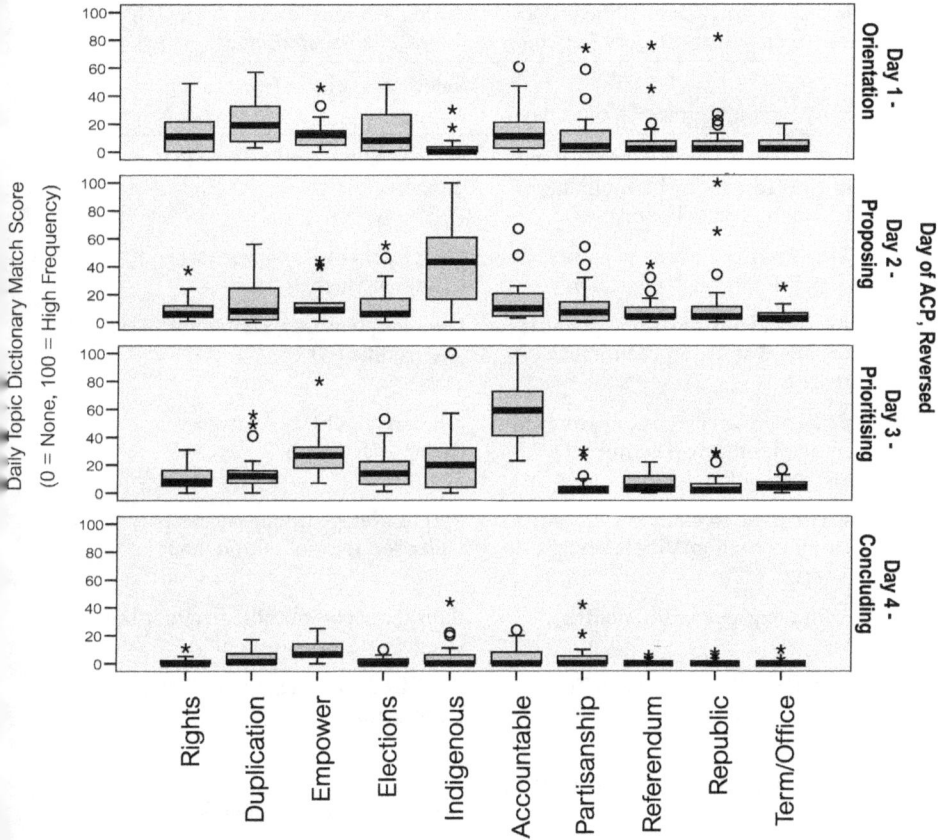

FIGURE II.I   Distribution of category dictionary matches at the ACP across the twenty-three table discussions across four days, adjusted for total words and category weightings

NOTE: Four outlier values above 100 were reduced to a score of 100 to change the boxplot scale and thereby better illustrate differences in the frequency of the ten categories.

frequent topics for most tables; after all, the bottom of its boxplot bar (the 25th–75th percentile) is near the top of most other bars.

Focusing specifically on the question of how a new proposal can supersede those fed into the F2F from the OP, note that the focus of talk on Day 1 was not a solid predictor of what would ultimately transpire. Though concerns about government duplication began and ended as the top priority, issues with the highest Day 3 (and even Day 4) frequencies climbed up the rankings, whereas the Aboriginal-recognition issue may have "peaked early," having its strongest showing on Day 2.

Table 11.2 Comparison of the proposal ideas highest-rated overall at the ACP and their corresponding category frequency in the ACP table discussions

Final ACP ranking (rank # and title)	Relevant results of from dictionary coding
1 Reduce duplication between levels of Government by harmonizing laws across state boundaries	"Duplication" most frequent Day 1 category
2 Empowering citizens to participate in politics through education	Most frequent Day 4 category ("Empowerment")
3 Accountability regarding political promises and a procedure for redress	Most frequent Day 3 category ("Accountable")
4 Empowering citizens to participate in politics through community engagement	Most frequent Day 4 category ("Empowerment")
5 Change the electoral system—Optional Preferential Voting	Part of average-frequency category ("Election reform") throughout
6 Youth engagement in politics	Subsidiary part of most frequent Day 4 category ("Empowerment")
7 Recognise Aboriginal and Torres Strait Island peoples in the Constitution	Most frequent category on Day 2 ("Indigenous")
8 Bill of Rights and Responsibilities	Prominent on Day 1 but average frequency category other days ("Rights")
9 Extend and fix the term of government	Low-frequency
10 Open and accessible government	Subsidiary part of most frequent Day 3 category ("Accountable")
11 Remove or Reduce State Level of Government	Subsidiary part of most frequent Day 1 category ("Duplication")
12 Resurrect the Republic debate and/or a Referendum	Low-frequency ("Republic")
13 Citizen Initiated Referendum	Low-frequency ("Referendum")
xx Term in office (not ranked)	Low-frequency ("Term")
xx Partisan politics (not ranked)	Low-frequency ("Partisan")

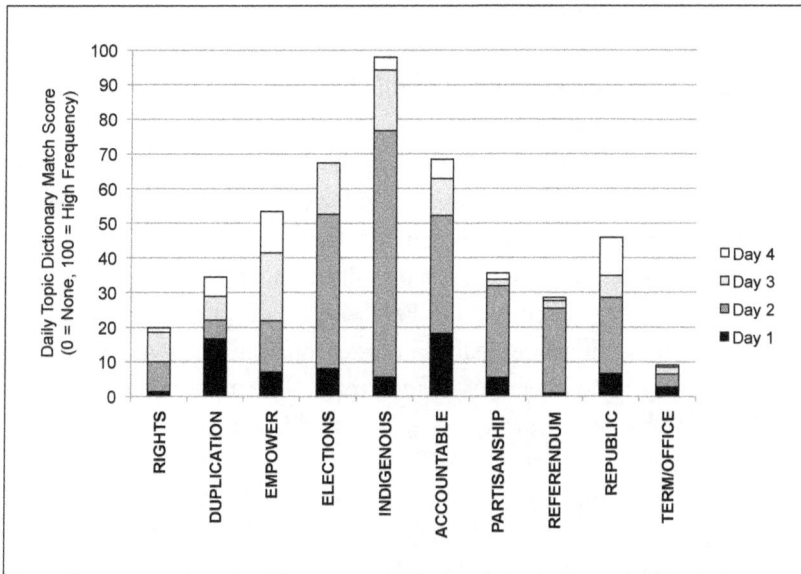

FIGURE II.2   Distribution of topic dictionary matches at the ACP plenary sessions across four days, adjusted for total words and category weightings

To see the role that plenary sessions played in changing the ACP's agenda, we turn to figure II.2, which provides similar data drawn exclusively from the plenary sessions. These large-scale sessions often featured selected participants or outside experts and advocates in panel discussions. This time, dictionary matching frequency is normalized across the full ACP (with the highest frequency set near 100), and each day's frequency is stacked on top of the previous one.

On Day 1, it is clear that government duplication and accountability get the most attention, with many topics (but not all) getting a robust hearing on Day 2. But the clearest feature is the dramatic spike in the frequency of discussion on Indigenous concerns on the second day. That day, the CPs heard from Mark Yettica-Paulson, who is a founding member of the National Indigenous Youth Movement of Australia. He raised explicitly concerns about how Indigenous Australians fit into the country's political system. Panelists also discussed the need for recognizing Aboriginal and Torres Strait Island peoples in the Australian Constitution, and comparisons were made to New Zealand.

The Rise of Youth Engagement

One post-hoc finding we wish to highlight is the ascendance of concern about citizen empowerment, particularly of youth. Though figure 11.1 does not break down empowerment scores by subcategory, it is clear that empowerment becomes the second most frequent topic on Day 3, where it begins to separate from the rest of the proposal categories.

It also is striking in figure 11.1 just how little topic-relevant talk there is on Day 4, the day that closed out the F2F with reflections, debriefings, and thank-you's. It is fair to say that the discussions on the final day did not address the key topic categories of the event. The empowerment category accounted for the most of any topic, by far, and this may well reflect the spirit of Day 4, which was about moving forward beyond the ACP. In that frame, an emphasis on empowerment—of both oneself and the wider society— makes sense.[14]

One possibility is that this kind of topic may frequently ascend during events like the ACP, which showcases precisely this kind of citizen empowerment. Had public engagement and youth participation *not* appeared during the OP, we suspect the experience of the F2F deliberations in Canberra might have prompted their emergence.

Summary

Once again, our purpose here is not to go further into the details of the talk. Rather, we have aimed to show simply overall patterns of talk as they relate to the topics and concerns addressed at the F2F. In sum, we found that the talk that occurred during the OP, as crystallized into specific proposals, powerfully shaped the F2F. At the same time, the face-to-face talk in Canberra had influence of its own on the ACP's *Final Report*.

Advocating for Online Proposals at the ACP

The final question addressed by this study concerns the importance of the OP participants in the F2F. Specifically, were the authors of the OP proposals the key conduits for promoting their ideas in the F2F deliberation? Answering this question required considerable data transposition and restructuring. A data set was created to juxtapose the topical foci of the OP discussions with those of the F2F. This meant identifying which individuals participated in which OP discussions and sat at which F2F tables, then aggregating their OP topical foci to create measures of the degree to which the people sitting at a given table on a given day had, in the recent past, focused on a particular issue while members of the OP. In other words, one table might have three people who had created a proposal to "reduce government duplication" during the OP, whereas another table might have no members who worked on that topic during the OP. Would the former table be more likely to discuss duplication, as a result of their members' focus on that topic back during the OP?

As it turns out, across the four days, what topics a table discussed were largely unrelated to what proposal categories its members had worked on previously during the OP. The lone exception was the "Bill of Rights" category, which correlated modestly between OP and F2F ($r = .21$, $p = .023$). In other words, tables that happened to have former OP participants who worked on the Bill of Rights proposal did make their tables more likely to discuss that particular proposal. This finding squares with the first author's direct observation of those particular individuals being uniquely passionate about their particular idea for Australian political reform.

A closer inspection broke these results down by F2F day on the chance that the OP history might be more important at one stage of the event versus another. All this did was clarify that those advocating the Bill of Rights in the OP were strongly influencing their respective ACP tables' discussion of that topic on Day 2 ($r = .61$) and Day 3 ($r = .37$), in particular. This same analytic method showed the largest of any day's correlation when it predicted, on Day 3, an emphasis on the "empowerment" topic ($r = .70$).

However, once again, those results were the exception to what generally amounted to weak and statistically nonsignificant relationships between the composition of CPs at a table and the topics it ended up discussing most frequently. In other words, though one or two topics' advocates did raise their preferred issues at a higher rate on one day or another, in general the discussion tables varied more idiosyncratically in what topics they discussed most often during their small-group deliberations.

This is only the beginning of what can be done with these data. In future research, it will be possible to add into the analysis other predictors from the surveys of the ACP participants to better learn what drove attention to one topic or another. For instance, the percentage of women at a table was predictive of concern with election reform ($r = .21$), and tables with higher average levels of education focused more on the Bill of Rights ($r = .15$) and less on duplication and empowerment ($r = .22$ for both).

Conclusion

We can summarize the surface results of these analyses in a straightforward manner: the OP had a clear and powerful effect on the content of discussions that occurred during the face-to-face discussions in Canberra. There was not a one-to-one correspondence between the OP's concerns and those addressed F2F, but it is fair to say that the agenda set by the OP dominated the F2F deliberations. That was due largely to an ACP-wide embrace of that agenda—at least as a basis for discussion. Only in selected cases did particular OP participants lobby more actively for their own preferred discussion topics, and only one of those proposals (Empowerment) cracked the top five proposals by the end of the F2F.

The clearest differences between the OP's priorities and those in the *Final Report* were the emergence of concerns about Indigenous Australians and the disappearance of fixed terms of office for elected officials and a concern with partisanship in Australian politics. Regarding the latter, those topics never had a high frequency at the table discussions, despite partisanship coming up for a fair bit of discussion during the Day 2 plenary. As discussed in detail above, the rise of concerns about Indigenous Australians could be seen both in the plenary and table discussions on Day 2.

In conclusion, it is possible to step back from these results and reflect on what kinds of topic flow and influence one might hope to find in a deliberative-democratic event such as this. In that spirit, it is heartening both to see that the ACP capitalized on the hard work that went on in the larger OP, because that signals that events like this can effectively combine large-scale online deliberation with more focused face-to-face events. Having some of the OP participants be part of the F2F probably helped make that connection strong. At the same time, one would hope that the F2F deliberators would do more than simply choose a ranking for the OP proposals, and they did precisely this—by adding and subtracting from the OP's menu of policy recommendations.

How one views the role of expert panels at a deliberative event likely shapes what one makes of the emergence of concerns about Indigenous Australians. On the one hand, those issues likely arose due to the participation of Aboriginal Australians both as members of the ACP itself and as one of the distinguished co-chairs, namely Lowitja O'Donoghue, a renowned civil rights leader who had twice won the preeminent national honor Australian of the Year. On the other, this issue only rose to prominence during Day 2, when it received considerable attention during the panel plenary sessions. This augurs well for deliberation, if one views it as an exercise in public learning whereby invited experts inform participants' judgment. It should give one pause, however, if adjustments in the composition of expert panels could yield dramatic differences in outcomes, as deliberation's critics have sometimes argued. In this particular case, the outcome was felicitous, but this issue warrants careful study in the context of future deliberative events.

NOTES

1. John Gastil and Peter Levine, eds., *The Deliberative Democracy Handbook: Strategies for Effective Civic Engagement in the Twenty-First Century* (San Francisco: Jossey-Bass, 2005); David M. Ryfe, "Does Deliberative Democracy Work?," *Annual Review of Political Science* 8 (2005): 49–71; Raphaël Kies, *Promises and Limits of Web-Deliberation* (New York: Palgrave Macmillan, 2010).

2. See, e.g., James S. Fishkin, "Strategies of Public Consultation," *Integrated Assessment Journal: Bridging Science and Policy* 6, no. 2 (2006): 57–71; Peter Muhlberger, "The Virtual Agora Project: A Research Design for Studying Democratic Deliberation," *Journal of Public Deliberation* 1, no. 1 (2005): art. 5, accessed January 16, 2012, http://services.bepress.com/jpd/vol1/iss1/art5; Carolyn J. Lukensmeyer, Joe Goldman, and Steven Brigham, "A Town Meeting for the Twenty-First Century," in Gastil and Levine, *Deliberative Democracy Handbook*, 154–63.

3. Ernest G. Bormann, John F. Cragan, and Donald C. Shields, "Three Decades of Developing, Grounding, and Using Symbolic Convergence Theory (SCT)," *Communication Yearbook* 25 (2001): 271–313. See also chapter 18 in this volume.

4. Dominic Abrams, Michael A. Hogg, Steve Hinkle, and Sabine Otten, "The Social Identity Perspective on Small Groups," in *Theories of Small Groups: Interdisciplinary Perspectives*, ed. Marshall Scott Poole and Andrea B. Hollingshead (Thousand Oaks, Calif.: Sage, 2005), 99–138; Sujin Lee, "Judgment of Ingroups and Outgroups in Intra- and Intercultural Negotiation: The Role of Interdependent Self-Construal in Judgment Timing," *Group Decision and Negotiation* 14 (2005): 43–62.

5. Poole and his colleagues were only able to categorize discussion using complicated manual coding procedures that have discouraged many other scholars from pursuing their line of research. Marshall Scott Poole and Jonelle Roth, "Decision Development in Small Groups V: Test of a Contingency Model," *Human Communication Research* 15 (1989): 549–89.

6. Dustin Hillard, Stephen Purpura, and John Wilkerson, "Computer Assisted Topic Classification for Mixed-Methods Social Science Research," *Journal of Information Technology and Politics* 4 (2008): 31–46.

7. We used two tools in the Provalis software package—QDA Miner and WordStat. The former is a program designed to parse and label text, whereas the latter software permits statistical analyses, only the simplest of which appear herein (principally cross-tabulations).

8. The OP discussions were trimmed using a feature in QDA Miner that began cases at the same point in each file—the start of discussion indicated by a common marking in each file. Each OP case was designated by a Discussion Number. The F2F discussions were similarly trimmed by using a transcription mark to denote the beginning of the relevant portion of each file. Each F2F case was also given two variable values, a Table Number and a Day Number.

9. At this stage, the preprocessing and lemmatization options in Provalis were turned off, as neither improved the dictionaries' performance.

10. Note that this particular test was less than ideal, since those proposals had been referenced previously in developing the categories themselves. The subsequent test using the OP transcripts (described below) provides an alternative validity test.

11. This required averaging the scores for the two categories (duplication, empowerment) that are the featured element of two online proposals.

12. The clearest exceptions all reflected the inclusion of two or three related topics in the discussion, such as when case 33 considered the danger of overgovernance ("duplication" category) to be a matter of basic human rights ("Bill of Rights" category).

13. The correlation between the unadjusted total match and relevance was 0.47 ($p = .003$). The correlation between the total number of words in a discussion and relevance score for that talk was .32 (two-tailed $p = .048$). There were two deliberation sessions (#867 and #870) that most clearly bucked these trends. Both received a 10 relevance score but had few if any category matches. In both cases, it turned out the discussions were simply too short, lasting a dozen turns or less.

14. Incidentally, removing the category-weighting adjustment does not substantially change the results. That is, boxplots with simple raw category scores (adjusted for total talk time at a time) look essentially the same as the weighted boxplots shown here.

12

EVIDENCE OF PEER INFLUENCE IN THE CITIZENS' PARLIAMENT

Luc Tucker and John Gastil

Deliberative democratic theory presumes that people influence one another through interaction. To move to the more nuanced questions addressed throughout this book, scholars generally take that presumption for granted. But the necessary assumptions underlying much of the work on deliberative democracy must, at some point, themselves be scrutinized, lest we build a tower of theory on a hollow foundation.

The Australian Citizens' Parliament (ACP) provides a special opportunity to examine this bedrock assumption of deliberative-democratic theory because of the richness of its data and the special properties of its design. Because the ACP organizers wanted the Citizen Parliamentarians (CPs) to get the benefit of hearing many different voices, each day CPs were assigned at random to one of the twenty-three different discussion tables. Though done to improve the quality of deliberation, that design choice also gave us the opportunity to look at the net influence of all those different pairings on CPs' attitudes.

Recall that the ACP asked its CPs to address a central question—namely, how best to reform the Australian political system. The CPs generated a number of proposals, even beyond the initial set drafted by the Online Parliament (see chapters 4 and 11). To winnow those down to a manageable number, the CPs came up with a set of judgment criteria, and on Day 3 they applied those to the proposals. They took a series of eleven votes (one for each criterion), and each time the CPs distributed one hundred weighting points across the different proposals, with a maximum weight of thirty for any single one. In essence, this chapter tests whether a given CP's weighting scores were influenced by his or her randomly assigned tablemates from the first three days of the ACP.

Theorizing Social Influence

When framed in broader terms, the assumption of influence occurring in small-group interaction has been challenged before. Communication theorist Dean Hewes has posited that group interaction may consist largely of solipsistic speech that follows interactional rules but constitutes little more than thinking out loud to oneself.[1] Hewes set up a strict standard for proving group influence, and although carefully designed studies have persuaded some scholars, others remain unconvinced.[2] The present study does not aim to resolve that debate, but we raise it simply to demonstrate that one cannot take for granted the existence of social influence.

In the particular case of public deliberation, few studies have had the ability to sort out the effects of group influence from other factors that might cause deliberators to change their minds. One of the exceptions is a study of a Deliberative Poll, which showed that the direction of individual attitude change had a slight but significant tendency to follow the shift in attitudes within the particular small group to which they were assigned.[3] Likewise, a study using brief laboratory discussions found group composition influences: groups with a higher proportion of politically liberal members tended to cause political moderates to drift toward the left. That same study, however, found that conservative discussants tended to react against liberal group members by shifting further to the right.[4] An earlier analysis of National Issues Forums also found a tendency for deliberation to yield more coherent and distinct liberal and conservative viewpoints, rather than a moderation of preexisting views.[5] In sum, there exists some evidence of group-level effects in political deliberation, but the research to date on this question is quite limited.

For the purpose of the present study, we start with the assumption that no peer influence occurred. In this view, whom CPs happened to sit next to on the first three days of the ACP had no influence on what they ultimately came to believe about Australian politics when they did their Day 3 policy rankings. We will look for evidence of social influence against the "null hypothesis" that what CPs said during the first three days of the ACP had no effect on their peers. Note that in doing so, we say nothing about the other potential influences on CP attitudes, such as the experts and advocates who testified during plenary sessions (see chapter 16) or the proposals developed in the Online Parliament (see chapters 4 and 11), both of which clearly shaped the course of the ACP meetings in Canberra.

There are many alternatives to the "no influence" hypothesis. One common sense possibility is that the CPs persuaded those CPs who happened to sit by them to move toward their own preferred weighting choices. Let's call that an "attraction" effect and leave aside questions of whether it reflects mindless conformity toward one's neighbor or constitutes evidence of persuasion based on the merits of arguments. Both effects have long histories in the small group literature,[6] and the analysis we do herein remains neutral on what "attracts" a person toward the views of his or her neighbors.

That said, it is also possible that CPs could have the opposite effect on each other—something like the "repulsion" effect described in a previous study.[7] If CPs are particularly ineffective in negotiations, they could actually push their table mates (hereafter called "neighbors") away from their own preferred choices. An alternative explanation holds that CPs behave tactically, engaging in what political scientists have called "strategic voting."[8] The CPs likely understood that their weighting choices were being combined to express the opinion of the group as a whole. If they knew that their neighbors were likely to rank choices in a certain way, they might, in response, choose to assign more extreme counterweights (than they would have otherwise) to redress the balance in the group judgment. Such behavior would result in a wider gap between the choices of two neighbors when compared against two CPs not seated at the same table, assuming (quite reasonably) that CPs find it easier to observe the voting choices of those on their table.

In sum, we start with the assumption that CP neighbors did not influence one another, and we test that null hypothesis against plausible hypotheses of attraction and repulsion. (The statistically inclined will note that these bidirectional hypotheses necessitate the two-tailed significance tests that we employ.)

Randomized Communication Networks at the ACP

To identify the set of neighbors that each CP had, we begin by excluding Day 4. Because we seek to account for the prioritizing decisions CPs made

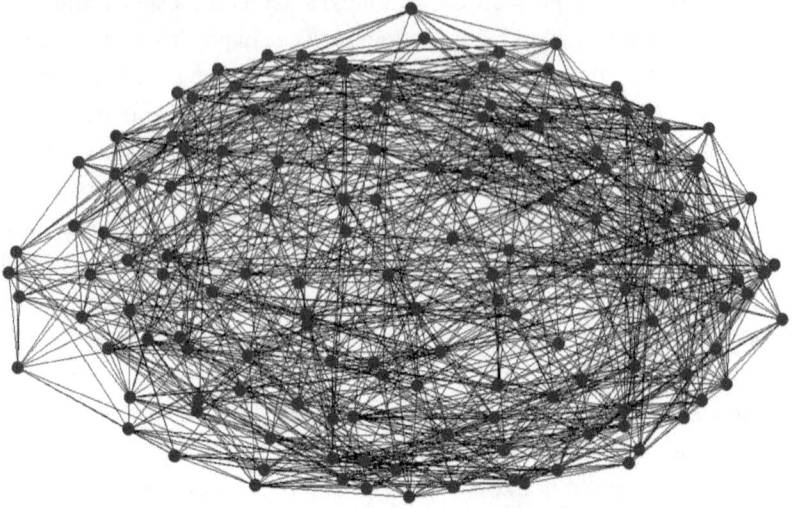

FIGURE 12.1   Links among the CPs seated together on Days 1–3 of the ACP

during the third day of the ACP, seating arrangements on the fourth day can be ignored. That day set aside, we drew a line to connect any two CPs who were assigned to the same table on at least one of the first three days of the ACP. That analysis yielded the network diagram shown in figure 12.1. A handful of CPs on the outside of the diagram had only a dozen neighbors, but most had substantially more connections over the course of the ACP's first three days.

It is relatively easy, in this age of online interaction and data archiving, to find peer networks much larger than the one shown in figure 12.1, but two aspects of its randomness make this ACP data set special. First, the CPs were chosen using stratified sampling to ensure a representative sample of the Australian population (see chapter 3), and that makes this network more ideologically diverse than usual. Without a special impetus like attending the ACP, people tend to huddle with like-mindeds when discussing politics.[9]

For the same reason, studies like ours generally face the problem of "homophily" (literally "love of the same") in the discussion network. In particular, if discussants had chosen their own table allocations, one might expect that like-minded CPs would have tended to sit together and, therefore, rank policy choices in similar ways, even in the absence of any genuine peer influence. Thus, the ACP data set offers a rare opportunity to check for the presence of peer-influence effects, while exploiting the randomized table allocations to rule out the possibility of homophily in the network.

Statistical Modeling of Peer Influence

The next steps in our analysis necessarily take us into mathematical and statistical details, the most daunting of which we've placed in the endnotes. For those less inclined or equipped to peruse such details, the basic summary is this: we use analytic techniques to compare the weighting choices between pairs of CPs allocated to the same tables with pairings who were never allocated to the same table.

The estimation method used here involves dyadic regression analysis in which the basic unit of analysis is a dyad—each possible pairing of CPs in the network. Through regression, we learn whether those CPs who shared a table on at least one of the first three days of the ACP showed a degree of similarity or divergence in their weighting choices that was *not* seen among those CP pairings that never sat at the same table during this period.

More specifically, the dependent variable in these regressions was the total difference in the weighting choices across all eleven evaluative criteria between each CP pairing. In other words, within each possible CP pairing, we compared every individual rating score that a CP gave and calculated the absolute difference, resulting in a number from 0 to 30 (the maximum rating allowed). We then summed those differences to get a total, and the lower that number, the greater the match (or "closeness") of the pair's ratings.[10]

We then used regression to predict the closeness of a pair depending on whether CPs were neighbors (i.e., via the dichotomous coding of "neighbor" = 1 vs. "not neighbor" = 0).[11] It was also possible to examine—or at least control for—other characteristics of the CPs that made up the various pairings. To do this, we used survey data collected on each CP member, including gender, age, income, education level, home Internet access, and Aboriginal background, as well as cultural and political orientations.[12] Thus, the differences in each of these characteristics within each CP pair became additional predictors, such that we could investigate questions such as whether CPs more similar in age who sat together ended up closer on their policy ratings than were those neighbors without the age similarity. For each pairing of CPs, we also controlled for the *sum* of these characteristics (e.g., the pair's "total age").[13]

The attitudinal control measures merit more description. The measures of cultural orientation came from a long line of research on "cultural cognition."[14] To assess the individualist (vs. collectivist) cultural orientation, six survey items asked CPs the extent to which they agreed or disagreed with statements such as "The government should stop telling people how to live their lives." To measure hierarchical (vs. egalitarian) orientations, we used a separate set of six items, such as "We have gone too far in pushing equal rights in this country."[15]

The other attitudinal variable controlled for left-right political leaning using a single survey item that asked CPs to assign themselves to a position on the political spectrum, with higher values corresponding to more right-wing responses.[16] A minority labeled themselves as "strongly left" (5 percent) or "somewhat left" (16 percent), a greater number saw themselves as "somewhat" (32 percent) or "strongly" right (5 percent), with the remaining 41 percent identifying as in the political "centre."

The cultural and political variables were related but distinct. Because of how we measured the cultural orientations,[17] the two dimensions were uncorrelated. Both, however, had significant associations with left-right orientation. Hierarchism scores correlated negatively with left-wing political orientation ($r = -.44$, $p < .001$), and individualism had a smaller, nonsignificant association in the same direction ($r = -.16$, $p = .105$).

For the attitudinal variables, as well as selected demographics, we also tested whether they moderated the size of the peer-influence effect. For example, we could test not only whether the age difference or total age of a pair of CPs affected the closeness of their policy ratings but also whether age differences changed the magnitude of peer influence. If CPs tended to influence one another, was that influence greater when they had a large or a small age gap? Likewise, how did other demographics and attitudes affect the size of the peer-influence effect? To answer those questions, we entered interaction terms into our regression analyses.[18]

Finally, as a result of combining separate observations to form each data point, it was not appropriate to assume that data points are independent and identically distributed. Traditional methods for calculating standard errors and significance levels require making that assumption, but we were able to use an alternative method for making those calculations called the Quadratic Assignment Procedure.[19] In a nutshell, the procedure required running simulations to estimate significance levels directly, and the results presented below reflect the best estimates yielded after running one million simulations.

Results

The Net Effect of Peer Social Influence

Table 12.1 shows the results of our regression analyses to estimate the power of peer social influence at the ACP.[20] The first column in table 12.1 looks at the peer effect by itself—the net impact of a CP sitting beside another CP at the same table on one of the first three days of the ACP, without controlling for any other variables. The negative coefficient (−1.4) in table 12.1 shows that on average, those CP pairings who were neighbors at least once assigned weights to their Day 3 policy choices that were a total of 1.4 weighting points closer together than they would have been had they never been table mates. The second column in table 12.1 shows that after entering a series of control variables, peer effect increases slightly and crosses a conventional threshold for statistical significance ($p = .04$).

Table 12.1 Regression equations estimating the difference in policy weighting scores for Citizen Parliamentarians

Predictor variable	Model 1	Model 2	Model 3	Model 4
Peer effect	− 1.403	− 1.503	− 2.912	− 3.013
	(0.057)	(0.042)	(0.011)	(0.009)
One male one female		− 0.439	2.723	2.711
		(0.869)	(0.325)	(0.327)
Both female		− 0.427	0.529	0.533
		(0.702)	(0.696)	(0.694)
Age category closeness		− 0.223	0.543	0.576
		(0.726)	(0.578)	(0.554)
Age category sum		0.224	0.730	0.715
		(0.768)	(0.487)	(0.496)
Education category closeness		− 0.787	− 0.601	− 0.591
		(0.279)	(0.456)	(0.463)
Education category sum		− 0.577	− 0.845	− 0.856
		(0.512)	(0.447)	(0.441)
One home Internet		1.155	2.515	2.400
		(0.662)	(0.465)	(0.484)
Neither home Internet		0.529	1.270	1.229
		(0.694)	(0.437)	(0.452)
One Aboriginal		16.143	15.007	14.994
		(0.072)	(0.157)	(0.157)
Both Aboriginal		7.507	0.282	0.353
		(0.152)	(0.953)	(0.945)
Individual closeness			− 3.404	− 3.424
			(0.043)	(0.043)
Individual total			− 2.574	− 2.610
			(0.070)	(0.067)

Table 12.1   *(continued)*

Predictor variable	Model 1	Model 2	Model 3	Model 4
Hierarchy closeness			−0.729	−0.482
			(0.575)	(0.704)
Hierarchy total			−0.596	−0.763
			(0.707)	(0.632)
Right-left self-reported closeness			−0.767	−1.250
			(0.584)	(0.392)
Right-left self-reported sum			0.546	0.778
			(0.748)	(0.650)
Individual closeness * peer effect				0.141
				(0.925)
Individual total * peer effect				0.155
				(0.864)
Hierarchy closeness * peer effect				−2.208
				(0.156)
Hierarchy total * peer effect				1.439
				(0.121)
Right-left self-reported closeness * peer effect				4.239
				(0.006)
Right-left self-reported sum * peer effect				−2.063
				(0.048)
Total observations (N)	21,462	21,462	9,900	9,900

NOTE: Figures shown are unstandardized coefficients, with *p*-values shown in parentheses. The dependent variable in these equations was the total difference in weighting choices between each possible CP pairing across all 11 criteria.

To provide some context, the average closeness score across the ACP was 97.1 units of distance, with a standard deviation of 28.3. Though it is not possible to sum the size of these effects, as they relate to pairings as opposed to individuals, over the first three days a typical CP shared tables with sixteen different people. It therefore seems plausible that the cumulative effect of all these interactions is, in fact, much larger, suggesting in turn that the three days of table discussions brought the CPs substantially closer together in their ultimate ratings.

Additional Effects and Moderating Variables

Looking more closely at the second column in table 12.1, one other result merits interpretation. Pairings that included only one CP with an Aboriginal background were found to have, on average, weighting choices that were a total of sixteen points further apart (compared to those pairings made up of two CPs where neither had an aboriginal background).

In addition, we tested the potential for age and educational differences to moderate the size of the peer social influence effect. Regressions including those interaction terms showed no significant moderating effect.

The third column of table 12.1 adds the attitudinal control variables— cultural orientation and left-right political self-identification. These results are based on the subsample of the population (roughly 110 CPs) for which cultural and self-reported political leaning indicators are available, which reduces the sample size of CP pairings from 21,462 to 9,900.

Before turning to the results for the new variables, one should note that in this smaller sample, the size of the peer influence effect has doubled, from roughly −1.5 to −3.0. This unexpected result appears with this smaller sample regardless of whether the control variables are entered into the regression equation.

The cultural variables came from a follow-up survey conducted a full year after the ACP, and though that survey had an excellent response rate, roughly one-quarter of the ACP participants declined to take part or could not be reached. It therefore seems reasonable to suggest that this smaller sample excluded many of those who had a less involving and important experience of deliberation in Canberra, based on the assumption that these CPs would be the least likely to complete a follow-up questionnaire. This hypothesis could explain why those who declined to stay involved in the follow-up research experienced significantly less peer influence during the ACP. Put another way, it appears that we found strong evidence that the subset of CPs who had a substantially lower peer influence impact were those who did not, overall, feel a strong sense of connection (and long-term obligation) to the ACP itself.

Having discussed the peculiar features of this subsample, we return our attention to the new variables in the regression equation. The two measures of individualism (both the closeness of a CP pair's individualism scores and their combined individualism) significantly predicted the closeness of their ratings. The first effect shows that CPs who shared a more individualistic or collectivist orientation tended to have more similar rankings—regardless of whether they were ever paired up at a table together. The second effect is different and suggests that those CP pairings consisting of strong individualists had more similar weightings than pairs of more collectivist CPs— again, regardless of whether the pairs ever interacted. Adding these effects together, it is fair to say that the individualist dimension of culture had a significant role in shaping how CPs viewed Australian politics and, consequently, how they rated different policy options.

But the more interesting question is whether the CPs' cultural orientations shaped the pattern of peer influence. That is, was one more subject to
influence from one's neighbors if they were culturally like-minded? The
fourth column in table 12.1 suggests that the answer to this question is no,
based on the available data. Whether one's table mates were similar or dis-
similar in their cultural worldviews did not change the tendency for CPs to
grow closer in their views as a result of talking with one another.[21]

Of the other moderator variables, the only significant result suggests
that for those pairings made up of CPs who assigned themselves positions
that were closer together on the left-right political scale, the effect of being
assigned to the same table is to push their weighting choices further apart.
This result is surprising, but could be a result of CPs inaccurately reporting
their true political positioning, with many reporting centrist views. Repeating the analysis with an alternative measure of political leaning supports
this claim, although neither scale can claim to be completely accurate.

Conclusion

Main Findings and Implications

Using dyadic regression analysis, we have shown that those CP pairings that
were assigned to the same table on any of the first three days of the ACP
expressed policy attitudes on Day 3 that were, on average, closer together
than among those CP pairings that never sat at the same table. Even after
controlling for gender, age, education levels, and political and cultural attitudes, this result remains statistically significant.

If one of the aims of deliberation is to discover common ground, our
results suggest that the odds of such a discovery increase with a denser network of connections among deliberators. In this case, the random rotation
of seating assignment plays a key role, because such an arrangement distrib-
utes the various patterns of influence more evenly across the deliberative
body. After all, the main finding in our study was a tendency toward convergence of judgments. The interpretation of this effect may depend, in part,
on one's degree of optimism that meaningful common ground exists on
issues such as political reform, as well as the desirability of arriving at consensus, versus clarifying and sharpening legitimate differences of political
perspective.[22]

A surprising finding that arose from the realities of post-deliberation response rates showed that the peer-influence effect was stronger for a subset of the ACP attendees. Specifically, those who felt involved enough in the project to participate in the follow-up research experienced significantly greater peer influence during their deliberations in Canberra. This should not surprise those who have convened such events, as it squares with the common observation that some participants connect with deliberative processes more strongly than others. Nonetheless, it underscores the fact that any visible signs of participant detachment or withdrawal likely indicate a real separation of those individuals from the strong peer-influence processes underway during a deliberative event.

Finally, this study showed a fascinating interplay of political and cultural orientations. Each pairing's identity on the individualism-collectivism spectrum had a significant effect on the differences in their attitudes toward Australian political reform, but cultural differences were not found to affect the flow of peer influence. By contrast, left-right partisanship had no meaningful direct connection to policy preferences.

Put in stronger terms, this study confirms past research showing that one's deeper cultural convictions shape policy attitudes, but it offers hope that those convictions do not forestall the tendency of robust deliberation to bring cultural opposites closer together even on issues where they disagree.

Future Research

Findings such as these show the importance of further research with other deliberative events and topics. At the same time, more remains to be done even with the data presented herein. One possible extension to the analysis in this chapter would be to run regressions that aim to capture the effect on a CP's weighting choice of a change in their neighbors' weighting choices, in a specific effort to capture the direction of influence.

With this objective in mind, an alternative method would be to estimate a model that considers each CP as a separate data point and specifies a model with weighting choices as the dependent variable and the average weighting choice of all neighbors as the explanatory variable of interest, with appropriate controls also included.[23] One obstacle to this type of analysis is the need to instrument the explanatory variable of interest, in order to address the problem of reverse causality, and thereby identify the influence of a change in the average neighbor weighting choice on a CP's weighting choice itself. This means that an appropriate instrumental variable is required, but it is possible to find such a variable by exploiting the shape of the network. This will be the focus of future work on this data set.

A further possible extension to this analysis would be to consider a more detailed breakdown of seating allocations and weighting choices, for example to determine whether peer effects are stronger depending on the day at which two CPs were matched to the same table, or how the weight of preferences around a table influences CP choices. This will be also be a topic for future research.

NOTES

1. Dean E. Hewes, "The Influence of Communication Processes on Group Outcomes: Antithesis and Thesis," *Human Communication Research* 35 (2009): 249–71, presents the most recent formulation of the "socioegocentric theory," which first appeared in the 1980s.

2. Marshall Scott Poole, Robert D. McPhee, and David R. Seibold, "A Comparison of Normative and Interactional Explanations of Group Decision-Making: Social Decision Schemes Versus Valence Distributions," *Communication Monographs* 49 (1982): 1–19, and Steven R. Corman and Timothy Kuhn, "The Detectability of Socio-egocentric Group Speech: A Quasi-Turing Test," *Communication Monographs* 72 (2005): 117–43, provide evidence of interaction's influence.

3. Robert C. Luskin, James S. Fishkin, and Roger Jowell, "Considered Opinions: Deliberative Polling in Britain," *British Journal of Political Science* 32 (2002): 455–87.

4. John Gastil, Laura Black, and Kara Moscovitz, "Ideology, Attitude Change, and Deliberation in Small Face-to-Face Groups," *Political Communication* 25 (2008): 36–37.

5. John Gastil and James Price Dillard, "Increasing Political Sophistication Through Public Deliberation," *Political Communication* 16 (1999): 3–23.

6. For a classic study on this issue, see Renee A. Meyers, "Persuasive Arguments Theory: A Test of Assumptions," *Human Communication Research* 15 (1989): 357–81.

7. Gastil, Black, and Moscovitz, "Ideology, Attitude Change, and Deliberation," 36–37.

8. Todd L. Cherry and Stephan Kroll, "Crashing the Party: An Experimental Investigation of Strategic Voting in Primary Elections," *Public Choice* 114 (2003): 387–420, show, for instance, that open primaries result in modest rates of strategic voting, whereby members of one party might participate in their opposing party's primary to elect the most extreme (i.e., undesirable) opponent, who will then serve as a weak challenger in the general election.

9. Diana C. Mutz, *Hearing the Other Side: Deliberative Versus Participatory Democracy* (Cambridge: Cambridge University Press, 2006).

10. More specifically, letting $c = 1, \ldots, 11$ represent the set of criteria to which weights must be assigned, CP_i's weighting choice for some criterion c can be written as w_i^c.

11. After forming the dependent variable in this way, it is possible to form a model with explanatory variables that include a dummy variable which specifies whether the CPs were matched to the same table. In particular, if t_i^d represents the table assignment of CP_i on day $d = 1, 2, 3$, you have:

$$x_{ij} = \begin{cases} 1 \; if \, t_i^1 = t_j^1, t_i^2 = t_j^2, \; or \; t_i^2 = t_j^2 \\ 0 \; otherwise \end{cases}$$

12. By defining z_i as a vector of background characteristics for CP_i, it is possible to adapt the model of Marcel Fafchamps and Flore Gubert, "The Formation of Risk-Sharing

Networks," *Journal of Development Economics* 83 (2007): 326–50, by using the following specification:

$$\sum_{c=1}^{11} \left| w_i^c - w_j^c \right| = \alpha + \beta_1 x_{ij} + \beta_2 |z_i - z_j| + \beta_3 (z_i + z_j) + u_{ij}$$

In the case of scale variables, ea ch of these variables is undirectional, in that they are related to the pairing itself, rather than one CP or the other. Therefore, by expressing the model in this way, β_2 represents the effect of the difference in characteristics between the two CPs that make up each pairing, and β_3 represents the combined effect of the characteristics of the two CPs. In particular, the "age" variable used here is a categorical variable, where each CP is allocated to a particular age bracket (ten years in most cases). Taking this information on each CP, and following the specification outlined above, it is possible to calculate the difference between the age categories of each CP, to control for the effect of the difference in age between two CPs that make up a pairing on their weighting choices. This age difference is then subtracted from the highest-possible difference to get an indication of the "closeness" of the ages of the two CPs in a pairing. It is also possible to control for the sum of these age categories, to capture the effect of having two CPs in a pairing with a higher combined age. Similarly, the "education" variable used here assigns each member of the ACP to one of four categories of education level (0 = low, 3 = high). Once again, it is possible to control for the difference between the education levels of the two CPs who make up a pairing (again reversing the indicator to measure education "closeness"), as well as the combined education levels, by summing the two values.

13. It was also possible to include binary variables in the specification above. In particular, three dummy variables are available for all individual CPs, one indicating whether that CP was female, one indicating if they had Internet access at home, and another indicating whether they had an Aboriginal background. Exactly as before with scale variables, it is possible to control for both the difference and the sum of these variables for each CP pairing. In this case, however, interpretation of the coefficients is slightly different, with $\beta_2 + \beta_3$ giving the effect of a (1, 0) or a (0, 1) configuration, and $\beta_3/_2$ giving the effect of a (1, 0) configuration. Such adjustments have been accounted for in the results tables that follow.

14. For a comprehensive list of publications and current research, see "The Cultural Cognition Project at Yale Law School," accessed January 9, 2012, http://www.culturalcognition .net. For a demonstration of the power of cultural orientation on a wide range of policy attitudes, see John Gastil, Don Braman, Dan Kahan, and Paul Slovic, "The Cultural Orientation of Mass Political Opinion," *PS: Political Science and Politics* 44 (2011): 711–14.

15. With minor textual adaptations for the Australian cultural context, both scales achieved respectable levels of reliability (alpha = .74 for individualism and .71 for hierarchism).

16. The item read, "In political matters, people talk about the 'left' and the 'right' in Australia. Please use the response scale provided to say if you are to the left, the centre, or to the right?"

17. The scores used in these analyses were orthogonal factor scores for the two separate cultural dimensions, as extracted from a confirmatory factor analysis using all of the cultural items.

18. In all cases, the scale variables are rescaled to ensure that they have mean zero. By doing so, the coefficient on the explanatory variable relating to the "peer effect" (x_{ij}) can be interpreted as the effect of being allocated to the same table when all the scale variables included in interaction terms take their mean values.

19. See Lawrence J. Hubert and James Schultz, "Quadratic Assignment as a General Data Analysis Strategy," *British Journal of Mathematical and Statistical Psychology* 29 (1976): 190– 241, and David Krackhardt, "QAP Partialling as a Test of Spuriousness," *Social Networks* 9 (1987): 171–86. After estimating the model using ordinary least squares, to determine whether the observed coefficients are beyond what could be expected under the null hypothesis (that table matching has no influence on weighting choices), CPs can be randomly reassigned to

different positions in the observed network, before running the estimation process in exactly the same way. By repeating this process many times, it is possible to infer the distribution of the coefficients if table allocations indeed played no role in the weighting choices of CPs.

20. As in all the regressions that follow, a constant term was included, but this term has been omitted from the results tables for the sake of brevity.

21. The interaction effects for cultural orientation fail to reach significance even when the other interaction effects are excluded from the regression equation.

22. For a classic work on the value of consensus versus conflict in democracy, see Jane J. Mansbridge, *Beyond Adversary Democracy* (Chicago: University of Chicago Press, 1983). See also Simon Niemeyer and John S. Dryzek, "The Ends of Deliberation: Meta-consensus and Inter-subjective Rationality as Ideal Outcomes," *Swiss Political Science Review* 13 (2007): 497–526, on meta-consensus in deliberation, as well as their chapter 10 in this volume.

23. See Yann Bramoullé, Habiba Djebbari, and Bernard Fortin, "Identification of Peer Effects Through Social Networks," *Journal of Econometrics* 150 (2009): 41–55.

PART IV

FACILITATION AND ORGANIZER EFFECTS

Well-structured deliberative processes involve considerable design and coordination, and the ACP relied extensively on a team of professional event organizers and process facilitators. The chapters in this section take a more interpretive approach to understand the influence that facilitators, plenary-session speakers, and key pieces of information had on the ACP. Chapter 13, "The Unsung Heroes of a Deliberative Process: Reflections on the Role of Facilitators at the Citizens' Parliament," by Max Hardy and Kath Fisher with Janette Hartz-Karp, looks at the process from the perspective of the event's lead facilitators. A more critical view comes from the lead authors of chapter 14, "Are They Doing What They Are Supposed to Do? Assessing the Facilitating Process of the Australian Citizens' Parliament," by Li Li, Fletcher Ziwoya, Laura W. Black, and Hartz-Karp.

Ian Marsh and Lyn Carson contribute a reflective chapter 15 that looks at the authoritative role of experts and knowledge in the ACP, stretching back to its inception, in "Supporting the Citizen Parliamentarians: Mobilizing Perspectives and Informing Discussion." The framing influence of the organizers is brought into sharp relief in chapter 16, "Investigation of (and Introspection on) Organizer Bias," in which Carson reflects on some of the tensest moments during the ACP—aided by reflections from others who were present for those events.

13

THE UNSUNG HEROES OF A DELIBERATIVE PROCESS:
REFLECTIONS ON THE ROLE OF FACILITATORS AT THE
CITIZENS' PARLIAMENT

Max Hardy and Kath Fisher, with Janette Hartz-Karp

Facilitation is regularly explained in group-dynamic training sessions and guidebooks, but for experienced practitioners it is often as much an art as a craft. It is one thing to know what a facilitator should do, that is, remain independent while balancing equally important elements: the group process, the task at hand, and the individuals involved. However, knowing what one should do cannot capture the social intelligence and quick wit needed when actually facilitating. The following conversation between one of the lead facilitators (Max Hardy) and the coordinating facilitator (Kath Fisher), with final comments from the other lead facilitator (Janette Hartz-Karp), captures elements of the experience of facilitating at a relatively large-scale and logistically complex process—the Australian Citizens' Parliament (ACP).

The Ecology of the Facilitation System at the Citizens' Parliament

MAX: There are many different facets of facilitation we could explore. Let's start with the layers or structure of the facilitation "system", necessary in a large deliberative process with 150 participants in one room, seated at twenty-three tables of six to seven people each.

KATH: As I saw it, there were four layers of facilitation: (1) the *lead facilitators* (Janette and you); (2) my role: the *coordinating facilitator*; (3) the *floor walkers*, who listened to what was going on at the tables and reported to me what they were noticing, which I would then report to you or Janette; and (4) the *table facilitators* who worked with the participants. There was another layer or process, *the debrief,* which I facilitated, when the table facilitators came together and reflected at the end of each day. You came to most of those debriefs, didn't you?

MAX: I did, and then often took messages to Janette, Carson, and others if the table facilitators felt something needed to be changed or an action needed to be taken. How did we come up with that system?

KATH: Janette had suggested the system of lead, coordinator, and table facilitators, from her experience with other 21st Century Town Meetings. I think I decided that floor walkers would be important because it was going to be too hard for me to cover the entire floor alone. So we had two, sometimes three other facilitators who observed the tables. They were responsible for eight to eleven tables each. The floor walkers communicated to me through walkie-talkies, much more efficient than physically crossing the room to talk. Messages included issues like tables not being able to hear at the back of the room or needing more time for their conversations. I would then speak with the person who could resolve those issues.

MAX: How do you think that overall system worked throughout those challenging few days?

KATH: Really well, I think, in large part because of the table facilitators. We had a lot of experienced people who mentored those who were inexperienced. They came to the daily debriefs with very clear and thoughtful reports and reflections on what was happening at their tables, which helped us understand the issues arising. I found it was better to communicate those issues directly to you rather than Janette, who needed to maintain the overview of the whole process and not be caught up with too much detail. Can you think of an example where that information helped the system of co-leadership?

MAX: Yes. Janette always knew what had to be done by when, and even though we were referred to as co-lead facilitators, I think we had very different roles. Janette kept everything on track, with an eye on the end point of the process as it was designed. You and I were more involved at the table level, and I think we both sensed that we needed to look after the table facilitators as well as the participants. We needed to honor what the citizens were saying because we wanted that experience to be rich and worthwhile for them. I remember there were a few occasions when the design changed as a result of the feedback. We had to be selective, and make a decision to respond when an issue seemed to be just too important to ignore.

MAX: One of those occasions happened towards the end of the process, when some of the table facilitators reported that the citizens were very concerned that they didn't have the opportunity to select who would represent them to present their recommendations to the government representative in the House of Representatives chamber of Old Parliament House on the following morning. These citizen representatives had been selected by one of the chairs, who was very concerned that the chosen citizens should represent everybody well and be polished communicators. Participants felt their input hadn't been acknowledged. After the table facilitators talked with us about this, and we recognized it was important, I raised it with Janette and she discussed it with the chair. The chair appreciated that viewpoint and there was a change in the selection process. There was no point following an agenda perfectly if people were left feeling unheard.

KATH: Yes, in my view, the task and maintenance roles both need to be operating for the group to be effective. By "maintenance" I mean the group climate and how people are being supported in the process. Janette's role was very much about the task. Much of your focus was on making sure that people were comfortable. You put them at ease, especially with your use of humor, which really helped to demystify the process in the context of a tight, task-focused schedule.

KATH: One example that stands out was when we were in the middle of those terrible fires in Victoria, and there were participants who were directly affected. One young person lost a friend in the fires. Here was a significant event, outside what we were doing in Old Parliament House, which was having a huge impact on people in the room, and it needed to be acknowledged. I think you and Janette handled this very well and was an example of you both attending to group maintenance, acknowledging the significance of the unfolding disaster.

MAX: It's interesting to recall times of real bonding, and this was one of them. It was almost a spiritual recognition of something else occurring out there. It was absolutely critical that we respected that, not just because participants knew people who were being directly affected, but because something really major was happening in the country. I remember how significant it was that one of the volunteers, Wendy, took on the role of giving regular updates about the fires throughout Saturday and Sunday. This was an example of what can happen in these processes when something unexpected happens. Flexibility is essential. We need to respect what's happening outside and how people are being affected on the inside while staying focused on the important task we have to do. I suspect that making space for those things helped people to bond much more strongly.

MAX: Another occasion where this dynamic occurred was the incident of bias described in chapter 16. I think it showed everybody that the integrity of the process mattered to people. It really mattered to the organizers and it was very real. I think these more emergent moments take people from "Oh, this is just an exercise and doesn't really matter that much" to "Wow, people really seem to care about this process and each other."

KATH: I agree, and I would say it often comes down to sensitive facilitation. The participants themselves can usually only express what they're feeling at the small tables or in their informal conversations. The table facilitators were very sensitive to what participants were expressing in their table discussions. There was a whole ecology within the facilitation team that ensured that participant concerns were taken seriously and addressed. Of course, it's inevitable with 150 very diverse people in a room that there's going to be a lot going on that can't be addressed. But in terms of the key concerns that affected the whole group, the sensitivity of the facilitators and their ability to raise these issues at the debrief, meant that not much fell through the cracks. I think that was a success of the whole facilitation system.

Empowerment Through Facilitation

MAX: Yes. And we found that by the end of the process the citizens themselves felt confident enough to influence the whole system by going directly to me or you. By then, they didn't feel like they had to always go through the table facilitators; that this was their space. I think that was indicative of success.

MAX: One example of this was some participants saying they wanted to see the youngest citizen at the Citizens' Parliament, Skye, who was eighteen years old, up on the stage because they felt she really had a story to tell. (See chapter 5 for more of Skye's story.) And she did tell her story about how she didn't feel like she had anything to contribute the first day, completely overwhelmed by all the talk about politics that she didn't understand. The second day she began asking questions and by the third day they couldn't shut her up! When she did tell her story in front of the whole Citizens' Parliament she finished by saying she was thinking of taking up a career in politics as a result of her experience.

MAX: But it wasn't just her up there on the stage. By then other citizens had said, "Hang on, if you get the youngest person up there, why not get the oldest person up there as well?" So we had Elizabeth at ninety years and Skye at eighteen years telling their stories and Elizabeth encouraging Skye to go for it and act in the world and make a difference. This spontaneous moment was allowed for in the design of the final day, and this really demonstrated how the citizens had come to feel, "This is our space; this is for us," which wouldn't have happened on the first day. The citizens had influenced the process in a significant way and produced what for many was the highlight of the four days.

The Range of Experience and Styles of Facilitation

KATH: I do think that empowerment is much more likely to be realized at that face-to-face, more intimate level in the small group. When people are in a large group, especially one that size, it can be fairly intimidating and people are likely to feel more anonymous. In a small group, when there's a sense of working together with a facilitator who is responding to what's important to people rather than focusing on completing the task, participants feel more confident to speak up. That does come down to different styles of facilitation, the extent to which facilitators are more task-focused or more maintenance-focused or whether they're directive or nondirective. Experienced facilitators usually have the capacity to do both and know when the task should be the main focus and when attention needs to be paid to group dynamics. I think we were fortunate that even the less-experienced facilitators had an intuition about what was required in those circumstances. [See chapters 5 and 14 for more on the significance of facilitator skill differences.]

MAX: We haven't talked about how people were recruited. All the facilitators were volunteers, including us. Many people, including very experienced professional facilitators, donated a fairly serious chunk of time. They also paid their own way to Canberra. We were selective, but we did end up with a mix of people in terms of their experience and style. How did you experience the different facilitation styles?

KATH: I didn't actually sit with anyone at the table. However, I had an overview, and I noticed things. For example, I noticed one of the more flamboyant facilitators who would get people out of their chairs to do physical exercises during the discussions, which most groups weren't doing; it was very obvious this was an experienced facilitator with a particular style, who felt confident he could do that. Then there were others who were really struggling because they were very new to it and needed more support and encouragement. There was a huge range. But I'd say the majority were experienced and very skilled. We had a couple of PhD students who were clearly very new to it but were young, smart, and just brilliant in the role. So experience is not necessarily the only criterion for being able to sit with a group of people and allow them to be part of a process where they had to think about politics in a way that they hadn't done before.

KATH: I understood what was happening at the tables through the debriefs, when we heard what was really going on; for example, the stories of people shifting their positions on particular issues. The one that comes most clearly to mind was the story of a particular Parliamentarian shifting his position on whether Aboriginal people should be mentioned in the Constitution. At the beginning, this man was absolutely adamant that they should not be. Over the period of days people listened to him and gave him the space to talk and were respectful and he didn't get into fights with people. By the end of the fourth day he had completely shifted to where he recognized his own blind spots and was advocating for Aboriginal people's rights to be included. I don't think we would have heard this powerful story if the facilitator hadn't told us in the final debrief.

MAX: Yes, there were so many stories like that and so much energy in those debriefs. I remember some facilitators being quite emotional or concerned and others that were absolutely exhilarated about something that had happened. There were facilitators who were quiet and unconfident; making space for them to express themselves was important. And of course there was the dynamic of a number of facilitators who really needed to talk; others who probably had a similar need to be heard but came in exhausted. It could have been quite intimidating for the inexperienced people because of the level of experience of other facilitators.

KATH: It was so important that everybody was heard, which was why we did a go-round at the beginning to make sure that people did have a chance to speak, even though there were twenty-three people. Because we had limited time, sometimes only half an hour, we had to be very efficient and capture as much as we could, focusing primarily on any burning issues we needed to be aware of for the next day. Those debriefs also gave us a sense of the different facilitation styles. What did you see, Max?

MAX: Well, like you, I was limited by how many different tables I could visit or observe. I had more of a visual view, rather than an auditory appreciation of it. In contrast to the energetic facilitator you mentioned earlier, there were others who were just very, very steady. They were quiet, but they were quite confident and composed. Those facilitators weren't immediately obvious, apart from their colored tags. They created a space for people to talk and were actively listening. They didn't feel the need to impose techniques on the group. I also noticed some facilitators who were new to the role feeling more anxious and wondering if they were doing the right thing; they were looking over their shoulder a bit, almost saying, "I might need a bit of help here." After all, the task was very challenging even for the most experienced facilitators. We had that system of different-colored cards that facilitators could hold up—a green card if they needed help with an information question or a question about the process, and a red card if there were problems with the computer—which I think was very helpful.

Any further thoughts on this, Kath?

The Impact of the Pressures of Time and Technology/Technique on Facilitation

KATH: I think we really need to remember the context and feedback we received both in the debriefs and since the Parliament, that facilitators experienced a lot of pressure, particularly around feeding responses into the table computers by the end of each session. I observed a few times that when the facilitator was focused on helping the participant who was inputting information into the computer, the group would break into small conversations. The facilitator's role is critical in holding the group process. As soon as that person leaves or is distracted from the task of facilitation, people default into conversation. They'll talk to the person next to them rather than wait for the facilitator's attention to return the group.

KATH: When there's a task to do, that loss of focus actually makes things very difficult. I suppose I have a question about whether it would be better to have an assigned person to do the inputting, who isn't one of the participants, which can free the facilitator up to stay with the facilitation role.

MAX: Reflecting on what you said about how the groups moved into side conversations, from reading some of the transcripts it was clear that the citizens had to absorb a lot of information, a lot of people talking who had interesting things to say, and then there was time pressure to record their responses. So there wasn't really time for everybody to get their thoughts out. Maybe there was pressure for people to have those side conversations because of a need to process information.

MAX: There was a buildup of time pressure to absorb new information and to formulate suggestions or make judgments about preferences or priorities for improving our democracy. I remember on the third day, when the Citizen Parliamentarians were about to rank their recommendations, people needed time to process and think. We suggested people "take some free time, go for a walk and come back to it."

KATH: It was very hard for facilitators to maintain that balance between allowing people to converse and the requirement to get things documented and into the computer. When people are rolling along with their conversation, they're really listening to each other, they're moving towards some sort of understanding of each other, and there's so much richness in that conversation that they are reluctant to stop. And then they have to stop because of the demands of time and the process. I understand from Ron Lubensky, who studied all the table conversational records, that facilitators did not get enough opportunity to help participants explore the values underlying particular concepts, such as what underpinned a statement like "need more education." So I think there are lessons to be learned about how to best manage these 21st Century Town Meeting processes in terms of people having the kind of meaningful dialogue they want given the time limits imposed in order to provide prompt, whole-of-room feedback.

Are Facilitators Necessary?

MAX: It seemed that facilitation worked better for those facilitators who were giving participants the message "This is about you and we're here to help you do your thinking." Do you think it would have been very different had there not been table facilitators, Kath? I know that some are experimenting with asking participants to organize themselves, either because of budget constraints or lack of volunteers.

KATH: Personally, I can't imagine a process where people have to do something as complex as listen to information that they haven't heard before, which they have to integrate and then come up with a recommendation or work toward a consensus, without someone thinking about the process. In my experience, without a facilitator who is focused purely on the process, who is making sure that those who are not used to communicating in this way have the opportunity to speak, there is a danger that the articulate people or those with strong agendas will dominate the dialogue. People who are middle-class and educated generally speak more than those who aren't used to articulating particular ideas or who haven't formed strong opinions. It might be men speaking more than women, English-speaking people being more talkative than those from non–English-speaking backgrounds, and so on.

KATH: In a deliberative process in particular, someone needs to ask questions like "Does someone have a different perspective? Is there someone we haven't heard from yet?" One of the primary roles of a facilitator in a deliberative process is to seek a diversity of views to ensure a robust consensus and to have confidence in the decision that participants are being asked to make. Without hearing that diversity, the loudest voice can be the one that defines the group's response, which can happen without skilled facilitation.

KATH: That doesn't mean that people can't self-organize. But I believe you would only get a robust outcome if such a group consisted of people with similar levels of education and communicative competence, so they could each assume leadership for the group. Even then I would caution about making assumptions about the levels of equality and capacity in the group, and how well the minority voice would be heard.

Is Neutral Facilitation Possible?

MAX: You'd like to think that the facilitators at the ACP were able to help the group at the table become more democratic, to enable dialogue to support deliberation. [See chapter 7 for an analysis of democratic deliberation vs. democratic social relationships.] Some participants might experience a facilitator as controlling what is okay to be expressed and what is not okay. Their own particular views or biases might in fact have an effect, and they may well be representing again a more middle-class, educated value system that may or may not honor those minority voices you're speaking about. [See chapter 5 for how participants dealt with these differences.]

KATH: I guess I'm talking about the ideal facilitator, and you could argue that facilitators will inevitably bring their own biases and values to the role. Is there such a thing as neutrality in facilitation? What we're trying to achieve with our facilitation training and reflection is getting to that neutral place that ensures the voices get heard. While it might never be possible to achieve neutrality consistently, there's a continuum. I think the more experienced the facilitator, the more likely they are to be able to maintain that neutral space. These are skills that have to be learnt. I don't think I'm always able to be neutral, especially when I have strong opinions. I think I succeed in being neutral in contexts where I don't have any opinions or I'm not invested in the outcomes.

MAX: How many of the facilitators at the ACP were there because they had a real interest in politics or democracy? I think we did have some who had strong views about the content, and I imagine it could have been difficult at times to maintain neutrality, or at least not to engage in the content in some way.

KATH: From the recorded conversations, there was very little evidence of that. If the facilitators did offer some clarifying information, they would preface it with a comment such as "taking off my facilitator's hat for a moment." The majority of the facilitators who volunteered were professionals, who would have had a very clear understanding of what their role required, even if they had an interest in the topic. I suspect we would have had a lot more complaints from citizens if the facilitator was attempting to influence them with their own opinions. I do remember one of the facilitators saying in the debrief that the participants really wanted to know what she thought about a particular issue, and she would just remind them of her role and that this was about their views.

MAX: The facilitators were heroes in terms of holding it together. I can't remember a citizen expressing any frustration that they weren't given a fair go by the facilitators or were overly managed, even those who came in with strong views about politics. I remember the man who felt very strongly about a Bill of Rights for Australia, which didn't in the end come up in the top ten recommendations. He wasn't able to persuade other people, yet I had no sense from him that he didn't get a fair hearing.

The Role of "Rules of Engagement" in Facilitation

KATH: Another aspect of the facilitation that we haven't really talked about is the role of making explicit the participation guidelines for participants to adhere to and for facilitators to hold.[1] They are the "rules of engagement," and the citizens were introduced to them at the regional meetings leading up to the main event. The goal is for everyone to have a common understanding of how to communicate in discussions and that was made very clear at the lead-facilitator level and the table-facilitator level. It's about treating people with respect and making sure that everyone stays on track and has a chance to be heard. Facilitators can use the guidelines to remind people about not interrupting or giving others a chance to be heard. They are simple rules, but not always easy to remember, especially in the heat of discussion, because they require people to step aside from the way they normally communicate. People are usually very relieved to have someone remind them of the rules so they can have a different type of conversation.

Reflections on Influence

KATH: An interesting feature about this particular process was the issue of who owned it. Because no government had convened this process, the recommendations were unlikely to directly influence policy or produce system change. However, one of the key aspects of a deliberative process is that of "influence," where citizens believe their recommendations will be acted upon, at least to some extent. Although government representatives did play a role in the official opening and closing of proceedings, there was no direct route to influence. [See chapters 19 and 20 for the wider political context.] Also, the ACP had another purpose, as a research process and a showcase for deliberative democracy. I think it succeeded in terms of the latter goals, but less in terms of influence. Having said that, it was certainly about giving the citizens a sense of empowerment by being part of a large-scale process where they could come to Canberra and engage in the kind of political conversations they would never have had before. In that way, possibly, what they were putting forward was not so important. They still engaged.

MAX: Indeed, and given that it wasn't sponsored or invited by government, in a way it's remarkable how much people did commit to the process. I think that one of the moments where there was a strong sense of being empowered was when those who were selected to represent the citizens had their say and delivered their recommendations to the government representative in the House of Representatives chamber.

KATH: It was the parliamentary secretary, because the prime minister couldn't be there because of the Victorian bushfires.

MAX: Yes, and when he received and acknowledged what they had done and recognised it as an important and historic event, I think that was quite encouraging to the Citizen Parliamentarians. While they were rightly skeptical about how much of their recommendations would be taken on, they nevertheless still appreciated the fact that the government was there to listen and receive the report. That was very important. It would have fallen quite flat without that, and the thank you for the work they had done.

Summary

MAX: Overall it was a fascinating experience and one that I am really glad to have been involved in.

KATH: I agree, it was an unforgettable experience. We all worked incredibly hard and achieved something remarkable—bringing together a group of diverse citizens from all over the country and enabling them to talk about politics in a way most of them had never before experienced. The fact that so many went back to their electorates and talked to their local members of Parliament and people in their communities about how Australia's democracy could be improved says a lot.

MAX: Janette, as the other lead facilitator, do you have any final thoughts?

JANETTE: I, too, found the experience fascinating, not only intellectually but also emotionally. At times, it felt like being on a roller-coaster ride without knowing if there would be a safe landing.

One example of this was when the computer software failed during the first prioritization count, and everyone within reach was co-opted to sit on the floor and count the priorities, virtually in "real time." The initial feeling of exhilaration that we had safely negotiated that obstacle was short-lived when two intrepid members of the "theme team" did a recount that evening, only to find that there had been a miscount and the lower priorities were wrong. However, we had done a whole afternoon's work on those priorities, and we were nearing the end of the Parliament, so there was no time to repeat the process. What to do? Pretend it never happened, or confess and try to find a way to end the ACP with a final report? We did confess, and it was resolved with an overwhelming participant vote to proceed with what we had already achieved. It was such a good reminder of leaving the wisdom to the group rather than trying to find the "right" answers oneself.

This consistently occurred during the facilitator debriefs, when facilitators found wise and often innovative ways around problems and opportunities. The load was shared. We all took responsibility for making the process work. In so many ways, the facilitators displayed the very characteristics we are all seeking in deliberative processes—finding ways to ensure the intelligence of the group far exceeds that of the individuals involved, with each person feeling empowered to bring out the best in themselves and others in reaching a common goal. I was so fortunate to be part of this.

NOTES

1. These were the guidelines for the Citizens' Parliament: speak openly and honestly, listen carefully, treat everyone with respect, keep comments brief, keep on track, and take a break if necessary.

14

ARE THEY DOING WHAT THEY ARE SUPPOSED TO DO?
ASSESSING THE FACILITATING PROCESS OF THE
AUSTRALIAN CITIZENS' PARLIAMENT

Li Li, Fletcher Ziwoya, Laura W. Black, and Janette Hartz-Karp

The use of facilitators is often a taken-for-granted aspect of deliberation, enabling groups to work through public problems in a way that embodies deliberative ideals.[1] Facilitators help frame the issues being discussed, set ground rules for the discussion, encourage equity and respect, and help groups analyze issues and make decisions. In short, it is assumed that facilitators are an important part of what makes public-participation events deliberative (see chapter 13).

Yet some scholars have raised concerns about the facilitator's role in the deliberative process.[2] Facilitators have power in the group and can influence group interactions by shaping which topics are discussed, who speaks, and how issues are framed. In other words, facilitators have a great deal of responsibility because they can shape both *how groups analyze problems* and *the overall quality of their social interactions*. It is with these concerns in mind that this chapter examines facilitation processes in the Australian Citizens' Parliament (ACP).

Conceptualizing and Studying the Facilitator

Whether in organizational, civic, or social-support settings, the general aim of facilitation is to guide a group through conversations that allow them to explore, learn, and act.[3] Toward this end, facilitators should be impartial, fair, and credible to all group members.[4] Though typically designed to serve as process guides, rather than decision makers, facilitators do retain the power to frame issues and discussion processes. Thus, to create an egalitarian atmosphere, facilitators need to create a neutral ground for discussion by demonstrating that they are open to and capable of encouraging varied perspectives and opinions from participants, creating an enabling atmosphere for free deliberation.[5]

In the context of deliberative events like the ACP, whether facilitators actually behave in a way consistent with these broad guidelines remains a subject of speculation. After all, several scholars have observed that actual communication during deliberative processes needs more systematic examination.[6]

We believe it is imperative to examine the dynamics between participants and their facilitator. One way to examine these dynamics is to adopt a framework that highlights both the *analytic* and *social* aspects of deliberation (see chapter 7).[7] Following this model, the analytic deliberative process affords participants a point of reference for well-informed decisions and solution identification. Good deliberative analysis comes from creating a solid base of information, clarifying key values, generating solutions, weighing solutions, and making a decision. Equally important to deliberation is a well-developed *social* process that provides participants equal and adequate speaking opportunities that can be regarded as a demonstration of mutual comprehension, respect, and appreciation of views of other participants and equality of influence.

Facilitators can have significant impact on both the analytic and social aspects of the deliberative process.[8] Regarding the former, researchers have observed the importance of the whole group being adequately informed about the issue so as to be able to analyze and examine relevant information and claims.[9] Facilitators can help participants critically evaluate the multiple information sources (booklets, plenary session presentations, personal stories, etc.) in a deliberative process.[10] Facilitators can also attend to ensure a more democratic social process by remaining neutral in showing their own viewpoints, leading the participants to critically evaluate different perspectives, and ensuring equal participation among participants.[11] Likewise, an overly directive style can make the facilitator too visible and is likely to shut the participants out of the deliberation processes.[12]

In this study, we aim to discern overall patterns in facilitator communication that can help in assessing the facilitators' role in deliberative analytic and social processes. Specifically, our research investigates three questions. First, what aspects of facilitators' communication demonstrate analytic and social processes of deliberation? Second, how did facilitators' communication change over time throughout the Australian Citizens' Parliament deliberation process? And finally, how did the facilitator input affect the deliberation process?

Research Method

To answer these questions, we investigated patterns in facilitators' comments during the first and last days of the ACP. Day 1 was when the Citizen Parliamentarians (CPs) were introduced to the topics of the event and its goal-setting process. Day 4 aimed at consolidating and delivering the recommendations agreed to by all participants. We chose to focus on these two days since they represented the initial phase and the product of the public deliberation process, which would help us address our research questions regarding changing facilitator behaviors over time.

Sample and Unit of Analysis

We systematically selected six facilitators who worked on both days. This gave us a total of twelve table discussions to analyze.[13] We chose each of the facilitators' speaking turns as our basic unit of analysis because the turn constitutes a *speech act,* "an uninterrupted utterance of a single group member which is perceived to perform a specific function (or action) within the group interaction process."[14] We assume that each speaking turn can be performing multiple functions, and thus coding in this way allows us to capture more information about the social and analytic tasks accomplished by facilitators. This unit of analysis allowed coders to interpret the overall intended meaning of the facilitators and minimized potential misinterpretation.[15] Two of the authors went through the transcripts included in this study and identified a total of 2101 speaking turns in our data.

Coding Scheme Construction

We conducted a content analysis using a coding scheme with two major categories, *analytic processes* and *social processes.*[16] The former includes subcategories, such as *creating information base, prioritizing key values, identifying solutions, weighing solutions,* and *making best decisions.* The social category includes *speaking opportunities, mutual comprehension, consideration,* and *respect*. These key features are consistent with the ACP framework (see the introduction and chapter 8).

Using this framework, a content-analysis codebook was developed that defined and exemplified each variable.[17] Each speaking turn was assigned a specific number based on the facilitator, the day, and the order of the speaking turn. Each speaking turn was then coded on the nine variables of the codebook. The nine variables were not mutually exclusive; one speaking turn could present qualities of several variables.

Analytic-process variables. For each of the analytic variables we noted the source of the information prioritized by the facilitator. The analytic variables had four nominal-level categories: facilitator, participant(s), other, and absent. For example, the variable *creating information base* meant anything that the facilitator said to acquaint the CPs with the targeted issue; for example, they could discuss personal and emotional experiences, as well as facts. In one speaking turn, if the information base was created by using the facilitator's knowledge or experience, the speaking turn would be coded as "facilitator." If the facilitator was encouraging the participant(s) to use their own knowledge to build the information base, the speaking turn would be coded as "participant(s)." If the facilitator was using other things (e.g., conference materials, etc.) to create the information base, the speaking turn would be coded as "other." If there was nothing present in the speaking turn about such information building, we would code it as "absent." We followed this same coding format for each of the analytic measures. The variable *prioritizing key values* measured whose values were highlighted in the facilitator's comments. *Identifying possible solutions* measured how facilitators encouraged brainstorming and other talk about different solutions, and *weighing solutions* dealt with the facilitator's discussion of which and whose solution should be prioritized and emphasized. Finally, *making decisions* measured whether and how the facilitator described the decision that had been reached.

Social-process variables. For the social variables we only used two nominal-level categories: present and absent. Our assumption was that these corresponding categories could provide enough categories to detect possible facilitator bias or facilitators' interpersonal communication. The first social variable, *speaking opportunities*, was coded as "present" if the speaking turn indicated that the facilitator was creating speaking opportunities for the CPs by, for example, structuring the discussion, encouraging CPs to speak, and ensuring that more talkative CPs did not dominate discussion. *Mutual comprehension* was noted as "present" if the facilitator attempted to make sure the CPs understood each other, asked the CPs to use plain language, or asked for clarification when confused.

Consideration was coded as "present" if the facilitator provided encouragement or appreciated CPs' contributions. *Respect* was coded as "present" if the facilitator treated the CPs respectfully. Respect is difficult to see in transcripts, but we coded for indications of respect such as greeting CPs warmly, showing respect for different views, and acknowledging their unique experience and perspective.

Coder Training and Intercoder Reliability

The first two authors went through three rounds of training and thoroughly discussed each variable in the codebook. We used a sample data set (5.24 percent of the total) to calculate *Scott's Pi* value for intercoder reliability and obtained these results: *creating information base* = .83; *prioritizing key value* = .74; *identifying solutions* = .86; *weighing solutions* = 1.00; *making decisions* = .90; *speaking opportunities* = .82; *mutual comprehension* = .66; *consideration* = .65; *respect* = .73. Even our comparatively lower *Scott's Pi* values are still acceptable due to the conservative nature of the test and the exploratory nature of the study,[18] so once the acceptable intercoder reliability was achieved, the first two authors coded the remaining data independently.

Results

Question 1: What Aspects of Facilitators' Communication Demonstrate Analytic and Social Processes of Deliberation?

We investigated the key features that characterized the analytic and social facilitation (see table 14.1). For the analytic facilitation, the simple frequency counts indicated that overall on both days *prioritizing key values* (1073 units, 54 percent) and *creating information base* (798 units, 40 percent) were the top two most-used analytical processes. That was still the trend in each day, even though there were some order changes on two days: *creating information base* (Day 1: 515 units, 48 percent; Day 4: 283 units; 30 percent) became the priority on Day 1, and *prioritizing key values* (Day 1: 468 units, 44 percent; Day 4: 605 units, 65 percent) was the most frequently used on Day 4. For the social facilitation, the results showed that facilitators created abundant opportunities for the CPs to speak (1205 units, 60 percent), and they constantly showed respect towards the CPs (1076 units, 54 percent). The priority of *speaking opportunities* was still the case on each day (Day 1: 679 units, 64 percent; Day 4: 526 units; 57 percent). Explicit signs of respect towards the deliberative abilities of the CPs dropped on Day 4. However, *respect* still ranked second on Day 4 (Day 1: 687 units, 64 percent; Day 4: 389 units; 42 percent).

In sum, the key features of analytic facilitation were *prioritizing key values* and *creating information base,* though on Day 4 *creating information base* was not a priority. The key features of social facilitation were participant *speaking opportunities* and constantly showing *respect* for CPs, though the latter dropped slightly by Day 4.

Question 2: How Did Facilitators' Communication Change over Time Throughout the ACP Deliberation Process?

The frequencies of each analytic and social variable were used to explain the time influence on the facilitation processes. Even though not comprising a major percentage of the analytic-facilitation processes, there were some trends that were interesting.

Most analytical variables such as *prioritizing key values, identifying solutions, weighing solutions,* and *decision-making* processes were used more frequently on Day 4 than on Day 1. The only analytical variable that we observed more on Day 1 than Day 4 is *creating information base.* A Pearson correlation test analyzing all the analytic-facilitation variables obtained from the current data set showed that the frequencies of each analytic-facilitation variable were significantly related to the day of the facilitation: $r = .843, p < .05$.

To understand how the analytic process differed across two days, we used crosstabs to compare the frequencies of each category (facilitator, participant, other, absent) of each analytical variable. Crosstabs showed that there were significant differences in each analytic-facilitation process between Day 1 and Day 4.[19] A closer look at the results revealed that both days involved facilitators promoting higher levels of analytic tasks than would be expected by random chance. On Day 1, facilitators used CPs' and the facilitators' experiences to create an information base, identify possible solutions, and weigh the solutions. On Day 4, facilitators emphasized forum resources to accomplish these tasks. Day 4 also involved higher levels of value prioritization and decision making. However, both facilitators and CPs showed more signs of prioritizing their values and making decisions than expected by chance on Day 4.

Table 14.1   The frequency and percentage of each variable and its category

Variables	Categories	Day 1		Day 4		
		Count	%	Count	%	Total
Creating information base	Facilitator	52	94.5	3	5.5	55
	Participant	287	91.4	27	8.6	314
	Other	176	41.0	253	59	429
	Total	515	64.5	283	35.5	798
Prioritizing key values	Facilitator	17	35.4	31	64.6	48
	Participant	352	46.8	400	53.2	752
	Other	99	36.3	174	63.7	273
	Total	468	43.7	604	56.3	1072
Identifying possible solutions	Facilitator	5	.83	1	16.7	6
	Participant	104	59.8	70	40.2	174
	Other	11	12.6	76	87.4	87
	Total	120	44.9	147	55.1	267
Weighing solutions	Facilitator	1	100	0	0	1
	Participant	26	56.5	20	43.5	46
	Other	10	19.2	42	80.8	52
	Total	37	37.4	62	62.6	99
Making decisions	Facilitator	0	0	0	0	0
	Participant	19	17.1	92	82.9	111
	Other	6	27.3	16	72.7	22
	Total	25	18.8	108	81.2	133
Speaking opportunities	Present	679	56.3	526	43.7	1205
Mutual comprehension	Present	398	74.0	140	26.0	538
Consideration	Present	133	53.4	116	46.6	249
Respect	Present	687	63.8	389	36.2	1076
Facilitator asked the CPs to respect each other	Present	6	85.7	1	14.3	7
Facilitator asked the CPs to show consideration of others	Present	1	1	0	0	1

Another Pearson correlation test analyzing all the social-facilitation variables derived from the current data set indicated that the frequencies of each social-facilitation process dropped significantly on Day 4: $r = .945$, $p < .05$. More specifically, crosstabs showed significant differences in each social-facilitation process between the two days for three variables: *speaking opportunities, mutual comprehension,* and *respect.*[20]

In sum, it appears that the facilitators' communication did change over time: they tended to focus more on task communication on Day 4 than Day 1 and they emphasized social communication instead of task communication on Day 1. Interestingly, for the task communication on Day 4, the facilitators emphasized more of the ACP's resources to identify and to weigh solutions, yet they prioritized more of their own and the CPs' values and relied on those opinions to make decisions. Prominently on Day 1, facilitators created more speaking opportunities, enhanced mutual comprehension among CPs, and showed respect towards the CPs during the facilitating processes.

Question 3: How Did the Facilitator Input Affect the Deliberation Process?

As mentioned, we deliberately put a "facilitator" category for each analytical facilitation variable to detect the possible facilitator bias. Even though an ANOVA procedure indicated that there was no significant difference between the three factors: $F(2) = 2.271$, $p > .05$, it turned out that on both Day 1 and Day 4 the facilitators exerted a minimal influence on influencing the CPs' discussions (*creating information:* 55 units, 2.8 percent; *prioritizing key values:* 48 units, 2.4 percent; *identifying solutions:* 6 units, 0.3 percent; *weighing solutions:* 1 unit, 0.1 percent; and *making decisions:* 0 units, 0 percent). Meanwhile, the analysis results indicated that the CPs' opinion was instead valued the most in the facilitators' speaking turns (*creating information:* 314 units, 20 percent; *prioritizing key values:* 752 units, 36 percent; *identifying solutions:* 174 units, 8 percent; *weighing solutions:* 46 units, 2 percent; and *making decisions:* 111 units, 6 percent). Another noticeable phenomenon was that facilitators also appeared to pay a lot of attention to emphasizing the forum resources (*creating information:* 429 units, 15 percent; *prioritizing key values:* 273 units, 13 percent; *identifying solutions:* 87 units, 4 percent; *weighing solutions:* 52 units, 3 percent; and *making decisions:* 22 units, 1 percent). Hence, as shown in table 14.1, there was little evidence of facilitators' bias in this case study, nor of undue influence on discussions either by the facilitator or by allowing a participant to dominate.

On review, the table discussions yield some surprising places where facilitators' comments could have detracted from the social processes of deliberation. There were some times on the first day when facilitators joked around with CPs by, for example, prompting them to speak by asking, "At the moment, what are [you] thinking about? Going home? . . . what's for lunch?" Another example comes from a facilitator who told a story about one of the CPs falling asleep at the table the day before and then receiving advice about how to pretend to have been listening. Presumably these comments are meant to build relationships with the CPs, but we caution that they could easily lead CPs to feel discouraged or singled out in a negative way, especially if they are occurring on the first day of the session.

Discussion

In the plenary session of the ACP, organizers stated that the facilitators' job "is to get out of your [the CPs'] way, so they [the facilitators] see what they're doing is to define an agenda, a schedule, so that you can work through what you need to work through, but it's about you finding your way to where you need to go. They are not going to lead you."[21] Overall, our analysis reveals that these facilitators successfully accomplished this charge. They guided the groups' deliberations by helping CPs create an information base, prioritizing key values, creating speaking opportunities, and asking CPs to show respect towards one another. In terms of the analytic process, facilitators encouraged CPs to create mutual understanding by freely and honestly expressing their own opinions and perspectives, and to transcend their differences productively with key values in mind. Regarding the social aspect of deliberation, the CPs were not only given abundant chances to contribute to the discussion; they were also led to actively listen to and respect one another's viewpoints. Thus, the facilitators encouraged CPs to engage in well-informed, respectful, egalitarian deliberation. In all, our analysis shows that the facilitation was effective in putting the CPs at the locus of control, thus creating an enabling atmosphere for public input.

A closer look at the results provides a more nuanced view of facilitation. Although facilitators had varied styles, our analyses show some general tendencies of the analytic process. On Day 1, facilitators created an information base primarily through asking for participant input, and on Day 4 they relied more on ACP resources. Facilitators prioritized both CPs' and the forum's values on Day 4 despite the fact that neither set of values was privileged on Day 1. At the beginning of the ACP, facilitators used CPs' experiences to identify the possible solutions, and by Day 4 they relied more on the forum resources. Similarly, facilitators encouraged the group to weigh the solutions more from the perspectives of the CPs on Day 1 and more from the ACP's objectives on Day 4. Finally, facilitators used both the CPs' opinions and the ACP's solutions to make decisions on Day 4.

These results are not surprising given the stated aims of the agenda each day. On Day 1, the stated aim was to "understand what we want to achieve together." On Day 4, the stated aim was "consolidating and delivering our recommendations." Hence, the focus moved from what each person wanted to achieve at the outset, to the collective views of the whole forum by Day 4. The set of forum values was not known on Day 1, whereas both personal and collective values defined how the options would be prioritized by Day 4.

We noted many comments from facilitators about the lack of time. This is mentioned here even though it was a variable that was largely out of the control of the individual table facilitators. Facilitators encouraged CPs to summarize and move on in order to meet the time constraints of the session. The first day included several facilitator comments such as "I'm conscious of the time, we're running out here" and "we're about to get the buzzer." There were similar comments on Day 4 including, "All right, so we've got two minutes and we can still talk about other [things], but we need to figure out what we're going to put on these cards. So, what do you reckon were the two best parts?"

This sense of time pressure can have a negative impact on the social dynamics of deliberation because it may prevent people from feeling that they have equal and adequate speaking opportunities or ample time to comprehend and consider all the views presented. Moreover, time pressure can lead groups to quickly label something as a minority view rather than making an effort to fully analyze the varying positions and come to a more thoroughly reasoned judgment. For example, one facilitator on Day 1 stated, "There's an option we have with this system in that we can put marginal opinions in because we don't have very long to discuss that. Did you want to put that comment in and it can go in as a marginal opinion because it hasn't been discussed by us? Is that okay?" Although we overall find that facilitators did a good job of promoting the analytic and social aspects of deliberation, their concerns about time seemed quite noticeable and potentially problematic.

Conclusion

Reflecting on the patterns in the analytical process, we see that facilitators made use of both the participants' and the ACP's resources to keep the deliberation processes on task. They generally tended to privilege participants' experiences early in the process and move toward more policy-oriented discussions later in the event. Although the ACP's main goal was to solicit public input, the facilitators still informed the participants about Australia's political system. In this sense, ACP facilitators tried to balance between expert knowledge and lay knowledge throughout the process.

On Day 1, the facilitators asked the CPs to talk, promoted mutual comprehension, and made explicit statements of respect towards the CPs more often than they did on Day 4. This set of behaviors early in the process indicates that the facilitators worked hard in the beginning to socialize the CPs and familiarize them with the deliberation processes. The lack of significant difference and the low frequencies on the cell of presence in the left three variables (*showing consideration, asking the participants to show respect*, and *asking the participants to show consideration towards each other*) on the two days seem to indicate that, at least in the discussions we examined, facilitators did not see a need to reinforce ground rules for courtesy. Presumably this indicates that the facilitators found CPs to be respectful and considerate.

In all, the results showed that the ACP facilitators used what David Ryfe would characterize as a "weak" style of facilitation.[22] After setting initial norms of equality and respect, the facilitators generally took a more hands-off approach to the social aspects of deliberation. The facilitators were more active in guiding the analytic tasks. They often provided procedural guidance to lead the CPs' discussion on task. They provided forum-related information or other background information to the CPs and then encouraged each table's CPs to freely express their various views, to exchange different information, and to collaborate on making decisions. The facilitators' minimal speaking turns in terms of weighing solutions or making decisions further confirmed that CPs were led to voice their own concerns and perform their own citizenship. Moreover, even though there was variation in terms of the facilitators' input due to the time influence, we did not see evidence of facilitator bias in our investigation.

The strength of a content-analytic method is that it can provide insights into the general trends throughout the forum, and overall our findings are positive, with ACP facilitators successfully guiding groups' deliberative discussions. However, further qualitative work would be useful to explore how the issues of time and relationship-building influence the CPs' experiences of ACP facilitation.

At times the analytic and social needs of deliberative groups may be at odds with one another, and a facilitator can help groups balance these opposing needs and accomplish their goals within the logistical framework available. However, this is a great deal to ask a facilitator to do. Further research is needed to determine the elements for an effective balancing of facilitator tasks.

This detailed analysis of group discussion mediated by six selected facilitators over a two-day period indicated that the facilitators performed remarkably consistently and well in terms of the "ideal" role of the facilitator: being impartial, creating neutral ground and an egalitarian atmosphere that enables free discussion, listening, and guiding the conversation without too many interventions or forcing agreement. In some instances, such as occasionally using questionable humor and being constrained by the logistical framework in terms of time limits, the effectiveness of facilitators could well have been impacted, though this needs further investigation.

In terms of the first two questions this research addressed—the aspects of analytic and social processes of deliberation that came to the fore, and whether they changed over time—our discourse analysis showed a clear alignment with the aims of the agenda for each day researched. In terms of the third question—how the facilitator input affected the deliberation process—it was apparent that facilitator bias was not a factor, that analytic elements aligned with the aims of the agenda, and that social elements enabled egalitarian, respectful discourse. This research supports the value of facilitators to deliberation. Further research is needed to investigate even more nuanced elements of facilitation to develop a more in-depth understanding of the factors that might impact effective deliberation, and potentially, what might differentiate a "masterful" facilitator from one who is merely competent.

NOTES

1. See John Gastil and Peter Levine, eds., *The Deliberative Democracy Handbook: Strategies for Effective Civic Engagement in the Twenty-First Century* (San Francisco: Jossey-Bass, 2005); Nurit Guttman, "Bringing the Mountain to the Public: Dilemmas and Contradictions in the Procedures of Public Deliberation Initiatives That Aim to Get 'Ordinary Citizens' to Deliberate Policy Issues," *Communication Theory* 17 (2007): 411–38; Jane Mansbridge, Janette Hartz-Karp, Matthew Amengual, and John Gastil, "Norms of Deliberation: An Inductive Study,"

Journal of Public Deliberation 2, no. 1 (2006): art. 7, accessed January 13, 2012, http://services
.bepress.com/jpd/vol2/iss1/art7; David Matthews and Noëlle McAfee, *Making Choices Together:
The Power of Public Deliberation* (Dayton, Ohio: Charles F. Kettering Foundation, 2003); David
M. Ryfe, "Narrative and Deliberation in Small Group Forums," *Journal of Applied Communication Research* 34 (2006): 72–93, on the importance of facilitators for deliberative events.

2. Guttman, "Bringing the Mountain to the Public"; Ryfe, "Narrative and Deliberation";
Shawn Spano, "Theory and Practice in Public Dialogue: A Case Study in Facilitating Community Transformation," in *Facilitating Group Communication in Context: Innovations and
Applications with Natural Groups*, ed. Lawrence Frey (Creskill, N.J.: Hampton Press, 2006),
271–89.

3. Frey, *Facilitating Group Communication in Context*.

4. Gregg Walker, Steven Daniels, and Anthony Cheng, "Facilitating Dialogue and Deliberation in Environmental Conflict: The Use of Groups in Collaborative Learning," in Frey,
Facilitating Group Communication in Context, 218.

5. Spano, "Theory and Practice in Public Dialogue."

6. Laura Black, "How People Communicate During Deliberative Events," in *Democracy
in Motion: Evaluating the Practice and Impact of Deliberative Civic Engagement*, ed. Tina Nabat-
chi, John Gastil, Matt Leighninger, and G. Michael Weiksner (New York: Oxford University
Press, 2012), 59–82; Laura Black, "Listening to the City: Difference, Identity, and Storytelling
in Online Deliberative Groups," *Journal of Public Deliberation* 5, no. 1 (2009): art. 4, accessed
January 13, 2012, http://services.bepress.com/jpd/vol5/iss1/art4; see also Mark Button and
Kevin Mattson, "Deliberative Democracy in Practice: Challenges and Prospects for Civic
Deliberation," *Polity* 3 (1999): 609–37.

7. John Gastil, *Political Communication and Deliberation* (Thousand Oaks, Calif.: Sage,
2008). On applying this framework, see John Gastil, Katie Knobloch, and Meghan Kelly,
"Evaluating Deliberative Public Events and Projects," in Nabatchi et al., *Democracy in Motion*,
205–30; Laura W. Black, Howard T. Welser, Dan Cosley, and Jocelyn DeGroot, "Self-Governance Through Group Discussion in Wikipedia: Measuring Deliberation in Online Groups,"
Small Group Research 42 (2011): 595–634.

8. Peter B. Edwards, Richard Hindmarsh, Holly Mercer, Meghan Bond, and Angela
Rowland, "A Three-Stage Evaluation of a Deliberative Event on Climate Change and Transforming Energy," *Journal of Public Deliberation* 4, no. 1 (2008): art. 6, accessed January 13, 2012,
http://services.bepress.com/jpd/vol4/iss1/art6.

9. Guttman, "Bringing the Mountain to the Public."

10. Francesca Polletta, Pang Ching Bobby Chen, and Christopher Anderson, "Is Information Good for Deliberation? Link-Posting in an Online Forum," *Journal of Public Deliberation* 5,
no. 1 (2009): art. 2, accessed January 13, 2012, http://services.bepress.com/jpd/vol5/iss1/art2.

11. Alice Siu and Dragon Stanisevski, "Deliberation in Multicultural Societies: Addressing
Inequality, Exclusion, and Marginalization," in Nabatchi et al., *Democracy in Motion*, 83–102.

12. Mansbridge et al., "Norms of Deliberation."

13. In the transcripts we had access to, there were nineteen facilitators moderating both
days' deliberation. To select a sample, we arranged Day 1's table minutes in order and selected
every fourth table from the beginning of the list. Our sample consists of six tables' minutes on
Day 1. We used the facilitators' names to select the tables that they facilitated on Day 4. In the
end, we got twelve tables' discussions (a total of ninety-two minutes) to code.

14. Randy Hirokawa, "Group Communication and Problem-Solving Effectiveness II: An
Exploratory Investigation of Procedural Functions," *Western Journal of Speech Communication*
47 (1983): 63.

15. Tamar Ginossar, "Online Participation: A Content Analysis of Differences in Utiliza-
tion of Two Online Cancer Communities by Men and Women, Patients and Family Members,"
Health Communication 23 (2008): 1–12.

16. Based on the "Key Features of Deliberative Conversation and Discussion" variables
developed by Gastil and Black. See John Gastil and Laura Black, "Public Deliberation as the

Organizing Principle of Political Communication Research," *Journal of Public Deliberation* 4, no. 1 (2008): art. 3, accessed January 13, 2012, http://services.bepress.com/jpd/vol4/iss1/art3.

17. Contact the first author for the codebook.

18. Guttman, "Bringing the Mountain to the Public."

19. Creating information base: $\chi^2 = 272.177$, df = 3, $p < .05$; prioritizing key values: $\chi^2 = 100.244$, df = 3, $p < .05$; identifying solutions: $\chi^2 = 64.334$, df = 3, $p < .05$; weighing solutions: $\chi^2 = 26.031$, df = 3, $p < .05$; and making decisions: $\chi^2 = 64.468$, df = 3, $p < .05$.

20. Speaking opportunities: $\chi^2 = 10.392$, df = 1, $p < .05$; mutual comprehension: $\chi^2 = 124.955$, df = 1, $p < .05$; and respect: $\chi^2 = 101.809$, df = 1, $p < .05$.

21. Cited from the transcript of Plenary Day 1.

22. Ryfe, "Narrative and Deliberation."

15

SUPPORTING THE CITIZEN PARLIAMENTARIANS: MOBILIZING PERSPECTIVES AND INFORMING DISCUSSION

Ian Marsh and Lyn Carson

From its inception, the organizers of the Australian Citizens' Parliament (ACP) were conscious of the need to support participants as they explored a complex subject, but in ways that responded to their expressed needs. This was the essence of the project: to analyze the capacity of ordinary citizens to consider a many-sided issue. Too much direction, denying the norm of independent judgment, would have been contrary to the spirit of the project. On the other hand, no access to resources would have hampered deliberation. Thus, one part of this chapter is a descriptive account of how this was done.

But a deeper question may also be relevant concerning the uses and limits of the deliberative approach. Firstly, are there limitations circumscribing the utility of deliberative processes, at least in the case of complex systemic issues? Secondly, would a different evaluative standard apply to a deliberative activity that is advisory or not convened by government, in contrast with one in which conclusions carried authoritative or even binding standing? The ACP's handbook opts for the former: "Deliberative processes are not meant to replace representative or direct democracy but to support it."

Thirdly, deliberative events do not happen in isolation. If the political system as currently structured is corrupted by systemic or structural deficiencies, then problems will arise.[1] In such a context, it may be easy to misuse deliberative processes to legitimize a compromised system. It seems difficult to make a judgment about the efficacy of deliberative activity without some larger judgment about the efficacy of the system within which it is contained.

These broader evaluative issues arose from a consideration of support arrangements and how they should be judged. An ideal measure might be direct references by the deliberating participants. Although discussions were recorded, there is little specific indication, apart from passing references, of the contribution or influence of the resources provided to Parliamentarians. So we need to look elsewhere. One possibility would be to assess the final outcomes of the ACP against the perspectives that might have been derived from the various resources that were made available to participants. This, admittedly more speculative, route is the one pursued here.

But how is the "quality" of the final outcomes to be assessed? The imposed agenda shaped the discussions. Some of that agenda, but not all, was shaped by participants via the prior online activity. Linking outcomes directly to the support arrangements is tentative at best.

At least three questions are relevant. Were the recommendations normatively defensible—at least from a liberal-democratic perspective? Were they practical—in the sense that they could actually be implemented? And were they sufficiently informed and/or comprehensive—in the sense that they involved logically distinct changes which together formed a (broadly) coherent agenda, one which was sufficiently comprehensive to ensure particular purposes could not be thwarted by the Machiavellian manipulation of seasoned partisans?

But there are further threshold considerations. What is to count as "the" outcome? Stretching over four days, the Citizen Parliamentarians (CPs) identified fifty-one separate suggestions for reform of the system and eleven characteristics of a healthy democratic political system. As deliberations advanced, these latter were ranked and the top five were used to evaluate the leading proposals. This occurred through six iterations: an assessment based on an overall judgment of the individual outcomes, then successively based on their impacts on freedom, transparency, innovation, ease of implementation, and long-term significance. Against these tests four outcomes scored at least three positive assessments and one scored two. But an overall vote resulted in six proposals being selected. There was of course consistency between these final six, the five that emerged from the democratic-rankings exercise and the thirteen that were selected in the first evaluative round of voting. These variations arose as CPs sought to reduce the long list of ideas to manageable numbers and then, within this, to identify the most favored changes. For present purposes we focus on the outcomes that emerged from the initial meetings and online deliberation and the final thirteen. This is illustrated in table 15.1, which displays the priority outcomes that emerged at each major stage of this exercise.

Moreover, the question that the CPs were tackling in a brief three-day period—how to strengthen our political system—is many-layered and faceted. There are many obscure but important aspects arising from both its formal and informal features. In addition, there were particular features associated with the evolution of broader norms of democratic liberalism—for example, protecting minority rights in a context of majority rule, or determining the balance between efficiency (e.g., uniformity of legislation or rules, unified versus decentralized government), equality, and citizen choice and freedom—whose rationale was interred in long-forgotten historic conflicts. Their relevance and significance might not be alive for present-day citizens.

Other considerations concerned the dynamics of change. For example, an important if less widely appreciated feature of Australia's representational political system is how the formal structure of power is determined. Short of a completely rewritten Constitution, this understanding is absolutely fundamental to any possibility of radical or substantial systemic change. Unlike the U.S. Constitution, the Australian Constitution is silent about the representative structure of power. This is determined by three conventions—confidence, ministerial responsibility, and cabinet responsibility—that are decided by votes on the floor of Parliament. All these conventions have been interpreted differently in earlier phases in Australian political development, and they are currently interpreted differently in multiparty New Zealand or (formerly multiparty) Scotland in comparison with two-party Australia. This creates a repertoire of democratic forms within the representational system, any one of which could in principle be applied in Australia. This is also a critical factor in any consideration of the potential to amplify and deepen citizen engagement through a routine use of deliberative or other political models that involve selection mechanisms other than voting.

Hence there were many complex questions associated with seeking to build the information base and perspectives of participants. Assembling a team which could, if necessary, explain these aspects of the political system was one step. Others included structuring prior deliberation and organizing sessions at the subsequent assembly to allow discussion to be informed by specialist liberal-democratic and other considerations. This design and

Table 15.1 Pre-ACP and final recommendations from Citizen Parliamentarians

Scope	Recommendations from pre-ACP deliberations	Recommendations from ACP
Structural	Unify laws across state boundaries	Reduce duplication between levels of government by harmonizing laws
	Accountability regarding political promises	Accountability regarding political promises and procedures
		Open and accessible government
	Extend and fix the term of government	Extend and fix the term of government
	Remove state level of government	Remove or reduce state level of government
Substantive		Resurrect Republic debate and referendum
		Recognize Aboriginal and TSI people in the Constitution
	Bill of Rights and Responsibilities	Institute a Bill of Rights and Responsibilities
Participation	Empowering citizens to participate in politics	Empower citizens to participate in politics through education
		Empower citizens to participate in politics through community engagement
	Youth engagement in politics	Youth engagement in politics
	Citizen initiated referenda	Citizen initiated referenda
Voting system	Change the electoral system first past the post	Change electoral system to optional preferential
	Change the electoral system proportional representation	
	Change the electoral system to a quota system	

planning task fell in the first instance to the newDemocracy Foundation's Research Committee. As planning for the ACP advanced, this group was substantially augmented.

The following sections explore these descriptive and normative issues. The descriptive account covers the steps that were involved in informing the work of the CPs. This involved two distinct phases, one covering the period *prior to* the ACP and the other support *at* the ACP. These two phases are briefly reviewed in succeeding sections. In a third section, the outcome of the ACP is assessed.

The Initial Phase: Supporting Prior Deliberations

Planning for the ACP started at least two years before the event (see the introduction and chapter 1). The idea of a "parliament" was developed initially in the newDemocracy Foundation's Research Committee. This involved a small group of six individuals who met on an irregular basis. All were united in agreeing that the political system as it currently operated failed both democratic and functional tests. From the outset the need for a central charge to frame discussion was recognized. It was also agreed that there should be prior opportunities for citizens to express their views whilst at the same time developing systemic understanding, and that there would need to be advisers and other sources both before and at the Parliament to respond to queries and to broaden perspectives.

Soon after the project received funding, a newDemocracy working group was established as a more broadly based reference panel. This was intended to involve people who would widen the available pool of experience and expertise. The reference group was intended to oversee both the coverage of issues and the overall design of the Parliament. In addition it was envisaged that at least some members of this group would be available to respond to any queries which the novice Parliamentarians might raise in their pre-assembly reflections. Some also participated in a similar role in the ACP itself.

Selection of participants and the approach to them was orchestrated through the co-chairs of newDemocracy, John Button and Fred Chaney. Both of these individuals had had many years' experience in opposite sides of federal government. Others who agreed to join this group included former government ministers, political advisers, NGO activists, and additional academics. This group met several times (both face-to-face and via teleconference) in the run-up to the ACP. It reviewed all aspects of the planning and timetabling of the event. Sadly, John Button died as these arrangements were being finalized.

In establishing the ACP, there were two prior tasks. One involved the establishment of advance meetings to explain both project and process to participants. Another involved the determination of a charge for the ACP. As a result of these discussions the basic question was phrased as, how can Australia's political system be strengthened to serve us better?

There was much discussion both in the newDemocracy research committee and in the reference panel about the resources that needed to be provided to participants *before* the Parliament. In retrospect, there were broadly two schools of thought. In one camp (mainly those with prior experience of deliberative events), confidence in the capacity of ordinary citizens to grasp and judge complex issues was high. In the other camp were those who felt that the specialist nature of the system required a substantial level of understanding if practical, radical suggestions were to emerge.

Information papers were assembled and made available online along with links to other resources. These covered brief descriptions of the Constitution, the Parliament, cabinet, the executive and administration, voting systems, and political parties. The Commonwealth Parliamentary Library was an important source of this material, as its briefings on the overall political system had been prepared with the general public in mind. Fortuitously, two parallel projects provided excellent materials on which participants could easily draw. One involved a "Democratic Audit of Australia," in which chief research investigator John Dryzek was also a principal.[2] Under the terms of this project, a number of papers on aspects of the system (e.g., voting systems, political parties, interest groups and social movements, etc.) had been commissioned, and these too were placed online. In addition, another member of the reference group, David Yencken, was chair of an umbrella think tank, the Australian Collaboration, which had recently published a comprehensive paper, *Democracy Under Siege*,[3] offering arguments about the condition of Australian democracy and some international comparisons.

The online discussion prior to the actual assembly sought to generate preliminary suggestions for systemic change. Participation was open to both the selected Parliamentarians and those who had indicated interest but had not been randomly selected.

Fifty-eight ideas were proposed, and twenty-five teams ultimately emerged to explore specific proposals. Of these, eleven proposals were completed, and these became the starting point for the ACP (see table 15.1). The actual proposals emerging from the online deliberations involved at least a page (and mostly more) of discussion, which included a problem statement, the detailed proposals, and an extended justification.

Here is the summary of the first three proposals:

1. *Proposal: Accountability regarding political promises.* Politicians should be made to deliver on their promises. An independent auditor could report on progress of implementing promised programs or policies. At the end of the term, the political party could report on implementation of promises and why promises which weren't kept were not implemented.

2. *Proposal: Bill of Rights and Responsibilities.* A Bill of Rights entrenches in law basic rights that citizens have in the society. It could include freedom of speech and assembly, separation of judiciary, religious institutions and government, presumption of innocence, and freedom from unwarranted search, seizure, and arrest. Some suggested rights may be contentious—e.g., right to life and freedom from unjust taxation—depending on interpretations. Proposed responsibilities include avoiding force or fraud in relations with others; taking responsibility for one's own behavior; raising children in a safe, happy, and healthy home; and caring for the environment.

3. *Proposal: Citizen-initiated referendum.* A citizen-initiated referendum (CIR) is a legislated provision to enable citizens to request a referendum (e.g., as in Switzerland, which has regular CIRs, and some states in the U.S.). To be put before the people, the proposal requires the signatures of a certain number of petitioners (e.g., 50,000 in Switzerland, where if the vote achieves over 50 percent it is successful).

Design of the ACP proceeded with the eleven proposals as the preliminary starting point. In addition, specialist presenters were selected to inform more intensive reflection on these or other topics. One presenter was specifically included to address an issue not covered in the preliminary list of topics. This concerned the political standing of Indigenous Australians.

The Second Phase: Advising the Assembled Parliament

Save for Indigenous issues, the eleven advance proposals provided the basis for the selection of topics to be addressed at the ACP. This covered, for example, the putative inefficiency of Australia's federal system, the need for a Bill of Rights, the need for more citizen participation and engagement, and the effectiveness of the voting system.

Apart from expert informants, the daily comments of the co-chairs, Fred Chaney and Lowitja O'Donoghue, also informed proceedings. The co-chairs spoke at the beginning and end of the Parliament as well as at the beginning and end of each day and, often, in the transition between sessions.

To ensure deliberations were informed at an appropriately early time, the expert presentations were organized in two sessions, both on Day Two. Each presentation involved three invited participants, who spoke for no more than ten minutes. A period of group discussion and deliberation followed. Then a further short plenary session was staged at which the three presenters were able to answer questions or comment on particular proposals. These presenters were all experienced platform speakers with proven abilities to explain arcane issues to lay audiences simply and succinctly.

Together with members of the reference panel they were available to answer questions that arose during the CP sessions. The conversational record shows that during most sessions assistance was requested, and during intense discussions some experts were run off their feet.

Assessing the Outcomes of the ACP

What was the overall effectiveness and impact of these support arrangements? If outcomes are to be used as a metric, their varied derivation needs to be noted. In table 15.1, the final thirteen proposals nominated by the ACP (from which a further six were selected as the most generally favored proposals) are compared with the eleven proposals that were advanced through the pre-ACP online activity. There is a surprising degree of congruence between these two streams of reflection. When the Parliament initially assembled, delegates were invited to nominate other changes, and a large list was framed. Thereafter the task became one of reducing, sifting, and assessing these various ideas. We would need a detailed analysis of the precise justifications that were offered to see if there was a significant development in argument or thinking as the ACP itself advanced. As it happened, there turned out to be relatively limited change between the original proposals and the final list—nine proposals were unchanged. Should we expect much change? Does this indicate that the deliberations had no impact on preexisting views? Or that they deepened and amplified preexisting views?

Or that there was a deeper failure of systemic imagination? More on this point later, but it is fair to say that the original eleven proposals were more fully developed and considered than those that were proposed spontaneously.

Taking the thirteen outcomes from the ACP, we can see that these might be subdivided into four categories: structural changes (5); changes involving participation (4); substantive changes (3); and voting-system changes (1). These can be considered in the context of the three criteria discussed at the outset—conformity to liberal-democratic norms, practicality, and coherence and comprehensiveness. An additional issue concerns the direct impact of the expert speakers at the ACP. Is there any evidence of this? These matters are briefly discussed in turn.

Conformity to Liberal-Democratic Norms

There is of course no settled theory of liberal democracy. There is only a spectrum of more or less conservative and radical possibilities.[4] Take one of the themes emphasized in the recommendations: participation. There were four recommendations in this category: empower citizens to participate in politics through community engagement; empower citizens to participate in politics through education; youth engagement in politics; and citizen-initiated referenda. This covers a spectrum of possibilities that generally fall within the broader norms of a representative parliamentary system and a further spectrum that might involve greater use of deliberative processes. As suggestions these four are all no doubt eminently attractive. But of course the detail is all-important.

The proposed structural changes all involved more unified and centralized government. The liberal norm of subsidiarity which was urged by several of the expert presenters appears to have counted less amongst the CPs than efficiency and uniformity. For example, Antony Green warned, "Fast quick efficient government doesn't necessarily make the right decisions and doesn't keep government accountable." He continued to describe the virtues of both federal systems and bicameral structures of government. Similarly, John Warhurst instanced the Australian Capital Territory (ACT) government, which often decides to do things in a different way from the rest of Australia. He warned that unified government would shrink this democratic right of choice.

In the event, such comments did not prove persuasive. The CPs opted for unified government rather than divided government and harmonized laws to more locally responsive rules (which could of course be more or less liberal). Uniformity can be interpreted as both an egalitarian virtue and an illiberal vice.

Although support for a Bill of Rights was sustained, its priority fell considerably in the course of the ACP, despite the advocacy of several CPs. This might suggest that the cautionary observations that were expressed were registered by participants. It could also indicate the impact of small-group deliberation. The merits and drawbacks of such measures were discussed by Martin Krygier, as were proposals for more uniform laws. Krygier observed that although these appeared to be different questions, what they shared was a concern to limit government. He invited participants to consider these ideas in the context of three larger questions: Do you have a clear definition of the problem that you're trying to solve? Is the proposal a plausible solution to this problem? And could there be unintended consequences worse than the initial condition?

Krygier also described the merits and drawbacks of the common law as an alternative to a more abstract statement of citizen rights. For example, should a putative bill cover civil, political, and socioeconomic rights and responsibilities or only some of these matters? Similarly, uniform laws may be more coercive than those that allow more freedom of choice to smaller groups of citizens.

In sum, although the CPs' decisions may not have conformed precisely to the more nuanced views that were put to them by the experts, the outcomes were nevertheless surely consistent with liberal-democratic norms. If some of the cautions expressed by the speakers did not prove persuasive, that is no criticism. Independent citizens have made their own judgments.

Practicality

Were the recommendations practical, in the sense that they could actually be implemented? Each recommendation was accompanied by a detailed discussion of scope and intent. However, in every case these remained closer to outlines of aspiration rather than fully developed proposals. Nor in the context of such a wide-ranging question is it clear what degree of detail may have been appropriate. Take the participatory recommendations again.

In drawing on her experience of large-scale deliberative consultations, Alannah MacTiernan stressed the merits of widespread citizen engagement: "[T]he more we have our population engaged and informed, then we believe that there is a way in which we can create a political culture which is less 'us and them' in terms of the public and their politicians and more one of engagement and sharing of these very real problems: global financial meltdown, climate change—huge challenges that we face and that we have to deal with." MacTiernan discussed the valuable contribution that deliberative forums had made to her role as planning minister in the Western Australian state government. But she cautioned against citizen referenda as involving an insufficiently informed or aware public, observations that were also generally reflected in the comments of other expert presenters and the chairs.

The two recommendations that involved extended use of deliberative processes were wholly in line with MacTiernan's reflections on her own experience. That such recommendations should have figured prominently is perhaps also not surprising given the nature of the event. And of course these recommendations were couched in quite general terms.

The attention to accountability and strict adherence to programmatic promises in the outcomes also implied that the comments of the two former practicing politicians had had little impact. Both sought to underline the difficulties they faced in reconciling negatively affected groups to difficult decisions and their need for flexibility and freedom of maneuver in solving these matters. For example, Alannah MacTiernan underlined the complex trade-offs that faced governments in practice: "It's important to stress that actually being in government is really quite hard. . . . It's quite hard to determine where you are going to draw the line. With all these competing interests that we have in society, each decision that you make has a positive impact on this group, a negative impact on that group. . . . Very rarely, but most beautifully when it happens, you can get a win-win." Amongst CPs, there was evidently substantial distrust of politicians and skepticism about their promises. The recommendations on structure and accountability clearly indicated that the CPs wanted politicians to offer clear promises and to be held responsible for their precise delivery.

In the case of practicality, judgment would seem to turn on whether the outcomes of deliberative assemblies are to be accorded more than advisory standing. In the latter case, a higher political authority would be the ultimate judge. Otherwise, the practicality of findings—for example, from the perspective of their capacity to attract broader public support—would seem to become much more significant considerations.

Coherence and Comprehensiveness

This last factor touches systemic questions. While individual parts of the political system can be considered discretely—for example, voting-system change or political-education programs for schools—there are wider issues both about the overall quality of the present political system and the spillover impacts of particular changes. How aware of the interconnection between recommendations or of the unintended consequences of particular recommendations could participants be expected to be?

In a representative political system, the defense against hasty or ill-considered decisions lies in a formal approval process with a variety of veto points—ideally enough to favor prudent outcomes but not too many to block needed social choices. Further, the political system is such an important structure for choice that attention to systemic considerations is unavoidable. If a deliberative engagement of randomly selected citizens is to be only one step in a wider process of choice, then of course their more ill-considered determinations can be readily overturned by more informed authorities. But if their findings are to be accorded more imperative standing, then the issue of systemic awareness becomes relevant.

In the case of more complex systemic issues, is their potential more circumscribed? This would cover large and uncertain strategic matters where systemic considerations are important. Examples include the New South Wales Climate Summit, the Queensland Youth Jury on political engagement, and Perth's Dialogue with the City concerning metropolitan planning.[5] Here deliberative processes could have an important role in signaling the potential for common ground at various steps in the resolution of issues, but this would be part of a wider and more protracted process, including other modes of engagement (e.g., representative processes) and other authoritative actors.[6]

Moreover, in the present case, hindsight might suggest more caution about how broad systemic deliberations are to be structured. The ACP occurred over a very short period—four days, although if regional and online discussion is included, the period is considerably longer. No doubt throughout this process of deliberations much was revealed to researchers about how preferences develop and the role of particular modes of interaction in facilitating this outcome. These are important and positive findings. But it also seems clear that the basic question was too large to be satisfactorily handled within this narrow time period. By contrast, despite considering a more restricted question, the British Columbia Citizens' Assembly concerned with a new voting system was held over eleven months.

It also seems clear that the decision of the organizers to include a persuasive Indigenous speaker, Mark Yettica-Paulson, had an impact. His radical reframing of possible perspectives challenged the dominant way of thinking about the positioning of Indigenous culture in Australian democracy. The attention to Indigenous issues was evidently reinforced in dialogue by Indigenous Parliamentarians and by the co-chair, Lowitja O'Donoghue. One of the few substantive items that was added to the list of recommendations as a result of the ACP involved Indigenous recognition.

However, some comments of participants on Indigenous issues also confirm the deep populist orientation that is present in Australia's particular version of a democratic political culture, an orientation which the deliberative setting did not transcend. David Marquand describes this exclusionary logic: "The people are a homogeneous monolith. . . . There is no need to protect minorities from the tyranny of the majority. Minorities are either part of the whole, in which case they need no protection, or self-excluded from it, in which case they do not deserve to be protected."[7] Sadly, on Indigenous issues at least, this logic seemed to have a deep hold on some ACP participants.

Conclusion

The commitment, engagement, and integrity evident amongst most participants was of a very high, indeed exemplary, order. At a time when there is almost universal concern about the gap between the formal political system and its publics,[8] the need for fresh and more innovative patterns of citizen engagement is surely urgent. Moreover, the prior online engagement suggests the many opportunities for much more substantive connection via this medium. How nonparticipant citizens might be persuaded to accord such decisions authoritative standing is another matter.

There is an urgent need to find new ways to link citizens to the formal policy-making and representational systems. Despite the many steps that remain to be navigated, this exercise convincingly displayed the potential of deliberative activity. In more or less pure forms, deliberative processes could make substantial contributions to a renewed political system. Change that stretches and deepens the practice of democratic citizenship will surely be the keystone of a robust twenty-first-century democracy.

NOTES

1. Ian Marsh and R. Miller, *Democratic Decline and Democratic Renewal: Political Change in Britain, Australia, and New Zealand* (Cambridge: Cambridge University Press, 2012).

2. Marian Sawer, Norman Abjorensen, and Philip Larkin, *Australia: The State of Democracy* (Annandale, NSW: Federation Press, 2009).

3. David Yencken and Nicola Henry, *Democracy Under Siege* (Albert Park, VIC: Australian Collaboration, 2008), accessed January 10, 2012, http://www.australiancollaboration.com.au.

4. See, e.g., James G. March and Johan P. Olsen, *Democratic Governance* (New York: Free Press, 1995); James G. March and Johan P. Olsen, "Elaborating the 'New Institutionalism,'" in *The Oxford Handbook of Political Institutions,* ed. R. A. W. Rhodes, Sarah A. Binder, and Bert A. Rockman (Oxford: Oxford University Press, 2006), 3–20; John S. Dryzek, *Deliberative Democracy and Beyond* (Oxford: Oxford University Press, 2002).

5. See the ACP handbook, *Australia's First Citizens' Parliament* (Royal Exchange, NSW: newDemocracy Foundation, 2009), 8–9, accessed January 14, 2012, http://www.newdemocracy.com.au.

6. One of the present authors (Marsh) also notes several other practical issues that need to be addressed if findings are to be more than recommendations to some higher authority or are to prove persuasive with such an authority. For example, is random selection likely to be accepted as a legitimate mode of representation by a broader public? During the 2010 election campaign, the (Labor) prime minister, Julia Gillard, proposed establishing a nonbinding Citizens' Assembly to deliberate a national response to climate change (see chapter 20). No doubt conceiving this as a political ploy to avoid a contentious issue, the media and the Opposition greeted it derisorily. But the response did underline the deeper issue of the legitimacy of random selection and of the degree of authority that could be carried by such events. Another issue concerns wider impacts on public opinion. How might the outcomes of such activity be communicated to a wider public so as to influence broader public opinion? This remains to be resolved. In an observation which has lost none of its force for contemporary democratic politics, Rousseau accorded to public opinion preeminent standing: "Opinion, queen of the world, is not subject to the power of kings. They are indeed its first slaves." Jean-Jacques Rousseau, "Lettre à M. d'Alembert sur les spectacles," in *Politics and the Arts: Letter to M. d'Alembert on the Theater,* trans. Allan Bloom (Glencoe, Ill.: Free Press, 1960). It is not clear how the deliberative processes favored by the ACP would be extended to influence the thinking of a broader public, or indeed how any of the above practical issues might be addressed.

7. David Marquand, *Decline of the Public: The Hollowing Out of Citizenship* (Oxford: Polity Press, 2004), 100–101.

8. See, e.g., John Faulkner, "The 2011 Wran Lecture," New South Wales Parliament House, Sydney, NSW, June 9, 2011, accessed December 9, 2011, http://www.nswalp.com/about/labor-history/speeches/john-faulkner—the-2011-wran-lecture/; Sawer, Abjorensen, and Larkin, *Australia: The State of Democracy*; Ian Marsh, "Fix the Economy, Destroy the Polity: Australia Since 1983," *Drum Opinion,* November 11, 2011, Australian Broadcasting Corporation, accessed December 9, 2011, http://www.abc.net.au/unleashed/3660706.html; Colin Hay, *Why We Hate Politics* (Cambridge: Polity Press, 2007); Gerry Stoker, *Why Politics Matters: Making Democracy Work* (New York: Palgrave Macmillan, 2006).

16

INVESTIGATION OF (AND INTROSPECTION ON) ORGANIZER BIAS

Lyn Carson

Writings on deliberative democracy usually attribute "bias" to poor population sampling, inappropriate framing of the topic being deliberated, or the omission of important perspectives within expert panels or background information.[1] Such situations can be categorized as exhibiting *organizer bias* since organizers must ultimately take responsibility for them.

This chapter examines a critical incident that occurred during the ACP when one of the organizers (the author) was privately accused of bias, which led to a public apology and retraction. Revisiting the incident provides an opportunity for reflection on organizer bias that might inform future deliberations.

Organizers' Commitment to Neutrality

A steering committee is typically convened to watch out for bias and to ensure neutrality. For the Australian Citizens' Parliament (ACP), the Research Committee played this role, under the auspices of newDemocracy Foundation (nDF), in conjunction with a team of researchers funded by the Australian Research Council.[2] The founder and director of nDF, Luca Belgiorno-Nettis, was named as one of the chief investigators, as were all members of the multi-university team.

Though the Research Committee had an oversight role, none of its members was an "organizer." The ACP organizers, who made most decisions and handled day-to-day operations, included a number of researchers, including myself, one of the co-chairs,[3] plus project officers from nDF and elsewhere. To help organizers scope and name the main subject for discussion, we convened eight World Cafés prior to the ACP.[4] In doing so, we were mindful that "organizing a deliberation is also an exercise in power."[5]

Prior to commencement, the organizers had several discussions that touched on objectivity or bias, and the team expressed a commitment to impartiality. However, there were potential conflicts even internal to the organizers. For instance, Belgiorno-Nettis insisted on the research being neutral but, for his own part, shared his low opinion of political parties— one of the key topics for the ACP to consider. I was also serving as both a director of nDF, responsible for advancing its mission, and a chief investigator committed to unbiased research.

This desire for a bias-free event was more than a private commitment among the organizers. At the opening session in the House of Representatives chamber in Old Parliament House, co-chair Fred Chaney assured participants that there would be no organizer bias towards the outcome of the ACP: "I've been asked by people, 'Well what's the end result?' And I say, 'I wouldn't have a clue. . . . That's in the hands of the people who are coming here, not in the hands of those of us who've been part of organizing it.'"

I elaborated on Chaney's comments when I outlined the role of the volunteer table facilitators. This public instruction was equally intended to set all organizers and the expert panel on their best behavior: "Their job is to get out of your way . . . so that you can work through what you need to work through. . . . If you get the sense that they are leading you . . . let them know."

Bias, Bias Everywhere

In spite of the aforementioned intentions and proclamations, when I read the transcripts of the recorded ACP sessions after the event had completed, I found bias *everywhere*. In his opening remarks, Chaney enumerated "the things I like about our democracy." He posed rhetorical questions such as "Do you want [minority views] to be trotted out as a means of destroying the government?" and "Do you want principled politicians or do you want politicians who do what the electorate of the moment wants?"

Chaney had been chosen for his political reputation of considerable integrity, which was needed to project *gravitas* during the proceedings. Chaney spoke glowingly about the historical system of government and nostalgically of a more satisfying political era: "When I was young, a much larger proportion of Australians participated through membership of political parties, and in a funny sort of way branch meetings were a bit like the sort of thing we were going to have here. . . . People . . . got together and talked to each other and had to . . . try to meld their views to understand each other's perspective."

Later, Belgiorno-Nettis made plain his opposing view when addressing remarks, in part, to the cabinet member who was present for the early proceedings—Senator John Faulkner. Belgiorno-Nettis began his speech by saying that he and other directors of nDF

> felt frustrated by how government seemed increasingly compromised by party politics. We believed that Australia had evolved as a society but that our political system held us back. . . . Too much [that] passes for elections these days is hoopla. Too often our parliaments are reduced to puerile debating and as a consequence the business of government is unduly compromised. . . . Governments are failing us. . . . I believe we can do better, better than these B-grade, high school debating societies. Sorry, Senator. [*laughter and applause*] . . . Deliberation, not debate, is the key. A dialogue aimed at sensible outcomes, not self-serving party politics. Carson convinced us that everyday Australians can address difficult issues, just give them a chance and provide them with the time, the space, and the tools.[6]

This speech was to have unexpected consequences. First, Belgiorno-Nettis named me as the driver behind the idea as a passionate advocate of deliberative democracy. Second, he implied that I shared his negative view about governments. Lastly, he put the senator off badly. In his earlier speech, the senator had said, "[T]he ideas that come from this Citizens' Parliament I can assure you will receive serious consideration from the government." However, an organizer was later told by a ministerial staff member that the senator "thought the forum was somewhat political rather than analytical." It was made clear that Belgiorno-Nettis's remarks had earned the rebuke.

In spite of such public expressions of political viewpoints on the part of key event organizers, toward the end of the ACP Chaney said, "I want to pay tribute to the extraordinary restraint of the specialists who've made up the panels. I know some of them quite well. I know they have passionate views, and I think their restraint has been in the best tradition of assisting impartially in the process."

That he said this is important in itself, but more noteworthy is the fact that no one challenged his claim. This problem would become most visible in the critical incident that is the focus of this chapter, but first, I offer one more illustration of bias at the ACP.

Typically, for public deliberations, it is not important that panelists be unbiased, simply transparent, because organizers are trying to canvass all aspects of the topic. But the ACP was different. Many panelists were invited to fulfill an educational role, in which they would provide general background information rather than advocating a position.

Nonetheless, one of the expert speakers used his time on the panel to decry "Mafia politics" and "secret committees" who govern "behind closed doors and there's really no public accountability." In a further example of inflammatory language, another speaker repeated the term "elected dictatorship."

There were also instances of advocacy and warnings. For example, one of the chief investigators, Ian Marsh, specifically advocated parliamentary committees: "These create a very powerful element of transparency upon executive government . . . . [T]he U.S. of course is a very powerful example. . . . [C]onvert the Senate into a committee house . . . I think would meet the problems, or some of the problems you're talking about." Further advocacy emerged when another speaker said, "I'm a bit of a fan of conscience votes in moderation," and then warned against devolving power: "To give local communities the right to do what they want to do even if what they want to do flies in the face of best practice or expert opinion."

Strong language, warnings, and advocacy permeated the expert panelists' statements, even when defending the status quo. For example, one speaker claimed, "Australia has been a world leader in trying to involve people in the processes of government," with reference to signing petitions, writing letters, etc. Another ostensibly neutral background speaker offered this perspective: "For Indigenous people . . . this is a system that we did not invite, that we did not welcome . . . . Are you talking about . . . those who continually feel like they're blocked out of the system. . . . We want Indigenous seats in Parliament. We want an Indigenous State."

These are hardly neutral utterances, but rather appeals for participants to consider particular points of view that deviate from popular opinion. But does the passionate advocacy of alternative frames constitute a kind of bias that could undermine the legitimacy of a deliberative process? This question would prove more than a philosophical puzzle in the case of the ACP, because an unusual chain of events led the parliament to a critical juncture where precisely this subject briefly became the focus of the event itself.

The Critical Incident

Near the end of Day 2, the ACP had to suddenly abandon its previously scheduled facilitated table discussions and return to the plenary chamber in Old Parliament House (due to an inadvertent double-booking at the venue). This upset the agenda, so a plenary session scheduled for later was brought forward. The lead facilitators made what they thought was only a slight schedule change, with no time to discuss this with other organizers. The original agenda showed the two academics (John Dryzek and me) reporting on how we thought everything was going so far. But with more time up his sleeve than originally planned, the session facilitator, Max Hardy, thought that he would "personalize" the session as "a chance just to kick back a bit and just think about how the whole process is going." Hardy suggested that "it might be quite useful to know a bit about this pair . . . because they've been part of the project team for quite a while."

Hardy started by asking, "Why does this stuff matter to you?" I described my experience of being elected to local government many years earlier, and then added,

> I've always felt that if you try to design the world's most inefficient form of decision making, you would devise local government in Australia [*laughter*], but I could be wrong on that one. And it led me to an exploration of how could you do this differently? I couldn't understand why I couldn't just go into a council chamber and say, "But shouldn't we ask the population what they think about this? You know if we're going to spend these millions of dollars and it's so contentious?" It just didn't make any sense to me why everyone didn't just say, "Yes, of course we should. We are the servants of the population." And I think my real interest in deliberative democracy sprang from that. . . . I never tire of this idea of actually allowing people to make their own decisions. It seems so perfectly obvious to me that I almost don't understand why everybody doesn't get this. That the more we own our own decisions the more likely that they're going to be enacted really well.

Hardy then asked a direct question, which related to an exercise that I did with university students when examining the word "democracy." I responded that I instructed students thus:

> Do not use that word unless we're actually agreed about what it is we're talking about, because I'm actually very uncomfortable with describing the Australian political system as a democracy. I do think it's an *oligarchy*. You know it's a select group of people who have oversight of the system. So we have representative government and it is a strong and robust form of government. . . . I tend to think if it's democracy it's certainly audience democracy, it's a very passive form of democracy. And I'd prefer that we agree on the terms in the tutorial room before we start using it. Because if we all start referring to this thing called democracy I know that one person will have a very different view of what that means compared to the way that I think about it, which is a much deeper, much stronger sense of joint decision making.

Hardy turned to Dryzek and asked him to explain his interest in deliberative democracy. Dryzek responded,

> I was working in the area of environmental politics and policy and just looking at the kinds of adversarial processes which prevailed and were producing extremely bad outcomes as far as I could see. And I tried to figure out . . . ways of doing this better. And that's really what led me I think to deliberation. . . . I do have, like Carson, a passion for democracy. . . . [A]s someone who has . . . delved into some of the history of democracy, thought about its complexities I've just become very interested in the different ways in which democracy can be deepened. . . . [T]his Citizens' Parliament is I think a kind of a pioneering effort to more effectively involve citizens to deepen the quality of our democracy. . . . This chamber is set up for debating, which implies that we are adversaries. . . . [W]e would sit or stand apart here so that we can't reach each other with our swords [*laughter*]. . . . [T]he idea of deliberation I think is in a sense is much more oriented to cooperative problem solving rather than adversarial debate.

For most of the remainder of this session, our comments praised the hard work of the ACP participants. We noted that people were working with good humor and showing genuine interest in what each other had to say. The facilitators were working hard, and panelists and experts interacted well together. The Citizen Parliamentarians were showing signs of concentration, creativity, and a growing appreciation of the complexity of the issues before them.

When the participants were then asked to talk in pairs about their experience so far, Dryzek and I were prompted by Belgiorno-Nettis to go to the foyer, where Chaney, the event co-chair, was furious and threatening to abandon the ACP. Chaney and fellow chief investigator Ian Marsh vented their fury for nine minutes, saying that all the organizers' good work had been undone by me, that I had ruined everything. It was quite unlike the respectful exchanges we had been observing amongst participants. Bystanders (Belgiorno-Nettis, Hardy, and lead facilitator Janette Hartz-Karp) occasionally tried to interject a comment to restore calm. I said little other than holding my own ground and insisting that I be given an opportunity to fix things. None of the bystanders saw the situation quite as starkly as Chaney and Marsh, who finally agreed that I could try to make it right, and we returned to the chamber.

We returned to the parliamentary chamber, where Hardy ended the animated paired conversations that were absorbing the Citizen Parliamentarians. He signaled a special announcement and explained that the two academics had something they wished to say.

Here is part of the apology offered by me when we returned to the chamber:

> This is actually quite difficult for me to say and it won't mean to you what I suspect it means to us and the organizers and that is when you create a deliberative space it's incredibly, incredibly important as we said at the very beginning that organizers don't bring their biases into the room and I think we've had two chairs who've been really restrained in terms of how they talk about, you know for Fred [Chaney] he's a member of a political party, he's exercised I think tremendous restraint when it comes to talking about issues, because he's very mindful of the importance of honoring that process and not expressing a bias. Now I would have to say that I have just upset Fred and I have upset him because I violated that very important rule and the reasons why that happened. We were sharing anecdotes about our life and when you do that inevitably you get into the things which you care about and are passionate about. . . . [I]f I may ask you to bear in mind that

that's what that is . . . it's my life. It's got nothing to do with what I want to advocate for you.

During this apology it was immensely quiet in the chamber. The assembly was listening closely. Chaney had come in to listen, then abruptly left, followed by Hartz-Karp. I was unaware of this as I continued with my heartfelt apology.

> I can't tell you how much I want to step outside the process and allow you to find your own way. John [Dryzek] and I spend our lives talking about this stuff, and so when we talk about our lives unfortunately it does start to sound like we're saying, "We want you to support this mission that we feel so strongly about." We don't. We honestly don't want you to support that mission. We want you to support whatever it is that you came in here wanting to advocate. . . . *We have people who feel incredibly strongly that we have a very robust system that needs only minor changes, and I absolutely respect their right to that opinion. And what's fantastic is that they haven't said that here. You know they're not coming in saying, "This is a fantastic system and we only need to tinker at the edges."*

The apology was *much* longer than this but I stop here to point out the transcribed words emphasized above. I said that others had *not* expressed their bias, but the evidence demonstrates this to be false.

Chaney later returned to the chamber and added a postscript, explaining that he had intervened to protect the integrity of the process. He made mention again of the "extraordinary restraint" of the expert panelists. He finished by saying, in relation to his continued involvement, "I will sleep on it."

Citizens Responding to the Incident

After Chaney's comments, ACP participants were invited to offer their own comments on the process thus far. Not surprisingly, some reflected on what had just transpired. One female ACP participant said, "First of all, on behalf of all the Citizens of Parliament, what we've just experienced actually tells me that there is integrity in this process and I congratulate the organization [*applause*] for that. I must say I did have doubts and what has occurred shows integrity of all the players."

Others came forward and spoke of the ACP as "the most exciting kind of political activity that I've ever been involved in," and "I reckon there is at least half of this nation that would be keen to be part of this kind of activity." Another noted, "[T]he respect that you see at the table for someone else's idea and passion even though you mightn't agree with it has been very, almost transformative in my understanding about how you would go about reaching a result." After many other speakers, Chaney made some final comments, shifting from "I will sleep on it" to "I feel very much better since I heard you come to the table and put those views, so thank you very much."

Many people spoke to me afterwards. The overwhelming reaction was one that echoed the words of the first female speaker: any lingering doubts about the integrity of the process had been dispelled by how that incident had been handled by the organizers.

The transcripts of subsequent table discussions recorded a wider range of reactions. For instance, one participant considered it a "storm in a teacup," with another adding that she did not hear "anything that was offensive." One participant thought that Chaney had "a bit of a hissy fit" and found it "really quite unbelievable how it got people stirred up." At another table, the group considered whether quelling the expression of opinion infantilized the participants, who were "all adults," capable of judging for themselves.

Some ACP participants struggled to understand the drama and saw nothing wrong in the original statement. As one participant mused, "[F]rom my recollection, [Carson] said, 'I have been involved in research on democracy for, like X number of decades,' I think. 'My personal view is I very strongly feel that citizens should be involved,' and whatever. . . . I thought it was maybe when she said, 'I don't believe we live in a democracy.'"

Many participants, though, appreciated Chaney's stepping in. "Ninety percent of us wouldn't have noticed what was said," the participant said, but Chaney "stood behind us." Another expressed gratitude that Chaney upheld "the rigor of the process. . . . For us as a group to be independent we have to be free from any influence at all."

Conclusion

Political scientist Elmer Schattschneider sees conflict as the key to politics, particularly the extent to which the audience becomes involved. Don't watch the key players, he advises: "If a fight starts, watch the crowd, because the crowd plays the decisive role."[7] Schattschneider also notes that "nothing attracts a crowd so quickly as a fight. Nothing is so contagious."[8] The fight has a few individuals at the center, but the spectators are an integral part of the situation, and they determine the outcome of the fight.

Applying this lesson to the ACP, the transcripts suggest that many "in the crowd" thought it was merely a distracting skirmish, but others saw it as a signal event in the parliament. Most of those who commented thought it was good that the critical incident occurred because it engendered trust in the organizers and the process.

In the end, the will of the crowd prevailed, in that Chaney dropped his threat to leave and publicly acknowledged "feeling better" about the incident, even paying "tribute" to the crowd and, later, the miscreant herself who started it all. As co-chair, Chaney held considerable formal authority and could have derailed the entire event. However, he allowed himself to be convinced by the crowd that no damage had been done, saying, "You have restored my sense of order and sense of value in the consulting of citizens, and I just want to pay tribute to you all."

As organizers, we had underestimated the consequences of convening a deliberative event in which *convening deliberative events* would be a topic of conversation. We should have anticipated that practicing deliberative democracy would lead to advocacy by the organizers for that model, both blatantly and in subtle ways. As a result, when the ACP participants called for more deliberative democracy in their final recommendations, we could not gauge the degree to which we influenced those recommendations.

More fundamentally, this experience opened my eyes to the impossibility of neutrality. I could discern no intentionally hidden biases at the ACP, but there were unacknowledged, unconscious expressions of genuinely held viewpoints by persons charged with playing neutral roles. I doubt that we can organize a completely neutral process in this sense, but it is not the expression of alternative frames, including emotionally charged expressions, that requires attention. Rather, the question is how we handle those expressions.

The organizers of deliberative events must meet bias head on—define it, own it, and decide how it will be addressed. Cultivating a critical stance is the most obvious and robust way of working with biases. This also requires that the word "bias" itself be unpacked: worldviews, hidden assumptions, values, beliefs, opinions, and perspectives. It's a collection that demands close scrutiny by deliberators. Organizers must work with participants to hone the critical faculties necessary for identifying and classifying this collection of biases.

The potential of participants in the ACP, and citizens generally, is under-estimated. Decision makers, unfamiliar with principles of adult learning, have a habit of employing the "banking" concept of education (which Paulo Freire wrote about in *Pedagogy of the Oppressed*).[9] Citizens are not empty vessels waiting to be filled with deposits of knowledge and/or biases that might, intentionally or unintentionally, come their way, only to regurgitate them in the form of recommendations.

Public deliberations should harvest citizens' existing knowledge and experiences. Instead of avoiding passion or bias, it is best to expose biases to considerable scrutiny, discussing the worldviews that are behind them, and generally understanding the lenses through which we each see and explain the world. With this skill at participants' disposal, deliberation becomes then a more lively, creative, exploratory, and critical pursuit.

In addition, organizers of public deliberations could spend more time foregrounding critical thinking. Working with the metaphor of the class-room, "What the student does is actually more important in determining what is learned than what the teacher does."[10] Inadvertent framing can arise in any public event, and it makes sense to alert participants to that likelihood. Participants can then play "spot the bias," a worthwhile exercise that enables further critical reflection.

Others needed to be alerted, of course. Participants attuned to the pres-ence of bias could benefit from trained facilitators who are able to expand their repertoire of skills to include critical analysis and self-reflection and an ability to share these skills with others. Also, expert speakers, alone or as part of a panel, should be made aware of the acceptable level of advocacy. Organizers can be prescriptive about this, depending upon the forum's pur-pose. At the ACP, speakers responded directly to questions from partici-pants at their tables, beyond the ears of others. Therefore, shared guidelines and transparency are important.

Analyzing and reflecting upon this critical incident has left me with a belief that diverse and strong opinions are to be valued and encouraged from speakers and organizers alike. However, such encouragement comes with a caveat: organizers of deliberative events should spend time in early discussion with participants about framing and bias. This shared critical stance at the start should then permeate the entire event as it unfolds. With-out this, organizers will always be open to accusations of inappropriate bias. A transparent, shared intention is consistent with an attitude of respect and equality between organizers and participants that is considered fundamental to deliberative democracy.

Commentaries from Key Players

Because this chapter offered a first-person account of an experience, I turned to the key players for their reactions. These are the reflections from other organizers who saw first-hand the events described in this chapter.

Luca Belgiorno-Nettis (Sponsor)

The conclusions make sense: it is difficult in practice to eliminate bias, and it would be better to allow the biases to be expressed while acknowledging them openly. I was not aware of my own bias, or of the negative impact my statements would have on how the government representative communicated the ACP to his colleagues. When I spoke, which was immediately after the senator's extensive speech, I was impassioned and thought the participants needed a wake-up call—that the current way of doing politics is puerile and exasperating. After all, those were my motivations for sponsoring the event. In hindsight, I was naïve, in that the government was likely to (and did) take offense.

Fred Chaney (the Chair)

Reading this has helped inform my understanding of the bias in all of us and how to deal with it in a deliberative forum. Transparency rather than suppression is the answer. My view remains that we did move from information giving to advocacy at a number of points, and the ministerial staffer's response shows that it mattered. As well, the account exposes a bias of mine that led me to give Luca latitude that I denied Carson. My own remarks supportive of Australian democracy were driven by my appreciation of the value and rarity of stable government that can be peacefully dismissed by the people. The powerful lessons in the chapter relate to the potential value in taking a different approach—of accepting and identifying bias to yield a more robust conversation. Taking that view from the outset would have changed how we planned for and conducted the deliberation.

John Dryzek (Chief Investigator)

I think the take-home message is right: at some level, it's impossible to avoid bias. The important thing is to make clear when people are expressing their own opinions, and in our case that was perfectly obvious. One must also ensure that participants are in a position where they can critically evaluate any normative claims that are made. Our familiarity with citizen forums helped us understand this, as well as the degree to which participants can exercise critical competence. It should not have shocked anyone that organizers of a deliberative process like the ACP advocate deliberative democracy! Part of the reason for that enthusiasm comes from a diagnosis of the limitations of existing parliamentary institutions and practices.

Max Hardy (Session Facilitator)

It was such a memorable experience to be caught in the middle of such powerful emotions and interpersonal dynamics. It was a pivotal moment in the Citizens' Parliament. Our Citizen Parliamentarians saw that this was serious business and applied themselves with a greater respect for the occasion. Apart from that, the main insight for me was that key players held different views about the best way to support citizen deliberation. Some believed in the ability of citizens to digest, critique, and make judgments having been exposed to many different perspectives. Others espoused the importance of protecting citizens from overt persuasive appeals, especially from the sponsors' perspective. It would have been interesting to have each of the key sponsors openly share their views at some point, as another input to the deliberation process. Given that diversity existed among the sponsors, it is hard to imagine how this would have been unhelpful or controversial.

NOTES

1. See, e.g., James Fishkin, *The Voice of the People: Public Opinion and Democracy* (New Haven: Yale University Press, 1995); Peter Levine and Rose Marie Nierras, "Activists' Views of Deliberation," *Journal of Public Deliberation* 3, no. 1 (2007): art. 4, p. 5, accessed January 19, 2012, http://services.bepress.com/jpd/vol3/iss1/art4/; Will Friedman, *Reframing "Framing,"* Center for Advances in Public Engagement Occasional Paper no. 1 (New York: Public Agenda, n.d.); Ellen Belcher et al., eds., *Framing Issues for Public Deliberation: A Curriculum Guide for Workshops* (Dayton, Ohio: Kettering Foundation, 2002).

2. The project ran under an ARC-Linkage grant from the Australian Research Council (ARC), co-managed by "chief investigators" and an "industry partner," in this case the newDemocracy Foundation (nDF).

3. As in most deliberative forums, the chair has overarching responsibility for keeping the process on track, and facilitators—in this case, two lead and twenty-three table facilitators—work directly with the citizen participants (see chapters 13–14).

4. Despite this, the charge for the ACP was altered at the insistence of a team member from "How do we improve Australia's political system . . . ?" to "How do we *strengthen* Australia's political system . . . ?" The team member considered that "improve" had negative connotations, suggesting that the current system was broken.

5. Levine and Nierras, "Activists' Views of Deliberation," 1.

6. The reader will note several references to "Carson" rather than "Lyn" because Carson is the name I prefer. The speaker is being friendly!

7. Elmer E. Schattschneider, *The Semisovereign People: A Realist's View of Democracy in America*, 2nd ed. (Hinsdale, Ill.: Dryden Press, 1975), 3.

8. Ibid., 1.

9. Paulo Freire, *Pedagogy of the Oppressed*, 30th anniversary ed. (New York: Continuum, 2000).

10. Thomas J. Shuell, "Cognitive Conceptions of Learning," *Review of Educational Research* 56 (1986): 429.

PART V

IMPACTS AND REFLECTIONS

The value of large-scale deliberative events like the ACP depends partly on their longer-term impacts, beyond the more narrow purpose of prioritizing reforms to the Australian political process. Did the ACP change its participants, popular opinion, public officials, or the prospects for a more deliberative Australian democracy?

Using follow-up survey data collected a year afterward, in "Participant Accounts of Political Transformation" (chapter 17), Katherine R. Knobloch and Gastil find that the CPs still believe their experienced changed much of how they think and act in public life. In chapter 18, "Becoming Australian: Forging a National Identity Through Deliberation," Janette Hartz-Karp, Patrick Anderson, Gastil, and Andrea Felicetti provide evidence that through their deliberations participants increasingly identified as working in the national interest.

Less encouraging findings come from chapter 19, "Mediated Meta-deliberation: Making Sense of the Australian Citizens' Parliament," by Eike Mark Rinke, Knobloch, Gastil, and Lyn Carson. That chapter shows that contrary to aspirations, the media did not pick up the larger themes of the ACP and thus failed to engage the wider public in reflection on Australian politics and deliberation itself. Carson also delivers critical reflections on the echoing influence of the ACP in Australian politics in chapter 20, "How *Not* to Introduce Deliberative Democracy: The 2010 Citizens' Assembly on Climate Change Proposal."

In the conclusion, "Theoretical and Practical Implications of the Citizens' Parliament Experience," the four editors revisit core concerns about deliberative design, quality, and social change to reassess the place of the ACP in the larger movement toward deliberative democracy. We also pick up some of the threads that pull through numerous chapters, including the role of professional facilitators and organizer effects. Most of all, we offer critical reflections that stress things missing from the ACP, such as early skill development for the citizen participants.

17

PARTICIPANT ACCOUNTS OF POLITICAL TRANSFORMATION

Katherine R. Knobloch and John Gastil

Political theorist Mark Warren once asked whether participation in democracy can make us "better" citizens. His "self-transformation thesis" pulled together writings by philosophers from John Stuart Mill and Jean-Jacques Rousseau to modern theorists such as Carole Pateman and Benjamin Barber. All of these writers pointed to the same basic idea—that democracy is a complex social process that requires civic attitudes and habits best developed through equally complex experiences.[1]

We now know from a growing body of research that participation in public life can, under the right circumstances, inspire people to return to help tackle future problems in their community or nation. We also know that this does *not* always occur, and its effect depends on the quality of the experience someone has. Research on the jury system in the United States, for instance, shows that serving on a deliberative jury even just for a couple of days can inspire people to become more regular voters, get more active in public affairs, and come to view themselves and their society differently. That same study, however, shows that these civic transformations are less likely for those already active in public life, and the quality of the deliberation with fellow jurors can influence the degree of attitude and behavior change.[2]

This leads us to ask, did the participants in the Australian Citizens' Parliament (ACP) and Online Parliament (OP) experience this kind of self-transformation? We cannot take for granted that they had such an impact, but there was good reason to expect one. After looking at the past research briefly, we will show how we helped participants assess the effect of the ACP and OP on their political and community lives. We will then show that when surveyed a year later, participants reported profound changes in how they viewed themselves, politics, and public life, as well as how they participated in the latter. The transformation appeared to stop, however, when it came to the most institutionalized kinds of politics. But we get ahead of ourselves.

Do Public Forums Really Change People?

One of the principal aims of deliberative democracy is to transform the deliberators themselves, making them more politically efficacious and public-spirited.[3] And while a growing literature has begun to gauge the degree to which deliberative participation fulfills these goals,[4] questions still linger about how different processes affect people differently as well as the long-term effects of participation. Moreover, the introduction of online deliberation raises further lines of inquiry about the difference between online and face-to-face deliberation and their effects on the political actions and attitudes of participants.

In part because participants must think deliberative processes work and have a purpose in order to gain the civic benefits associated with participation, carefully designed forums conducted in real-world settings are likely the best means to answer these questions.[5] Scholars have paid particular attention to forums such as the Deliberative Poll and National Issues Forums (NIF) for just this reason, and their findings suggest that theoretical predictions about how deliberation could change citizens are often verified in practice. Moreover, a growing literature on online forums suggests that computer-mediated deliberation can have benefits similar to those stemming from face-to-face interaction. Below, we discuss a few of these forums and how they inform what effects we may expect for both ACP and OP participants.[6]

Deliberative Polls are particularly suited for comparison with the ACP because of the large-scale and highly structured design of the events. Like the ACP, Deliberative Polls gather hundreds of individuals together to learn about and deliberate on local, real-world issues in a face-to-face setting. Several of these events have been shown to increase participants' external efficacy, or their faith that governing officials are attentive to the will of the public, as well as their internal efficacy, or individuals' faith in their capability for governance. Further, participating in Deliberative Polls seems to lead to greater discursive and electoral engagement.[7] Smaller-scale and less highly structured events, however, have also proved to foster positive democratic norms. NIF participation has been linked to greater internal efficacy and deliberative discursive practices, though results concerning external or group efficacy are mixed.[8]

Findings from these forums suggest that face-to-face deliberation can foster greater faith in oneself and the political process and promote increased political and discursive engagement, though results vary from forum to forum. But what happens for those who never meet face-to-face and only deliberate online, such as our OP participants? Online processes can foster larger-scale deliberation, owing both to the efficiency of online social networking and to the logistical ease and cost-effectiveness of online deliberative formats,[9] but we're still rather uncertain about whether these events can produce the same benefits as face-to-face forums. Recent work suggests that online discursive participation can foster greater efficacy, though it does not necessarily lead to greater engagement, whereas more formal forms of online-deliberative engagement have produced increases in efficacy and a desire for further participation.[10] This line of inquiry, however, is relatively new, and still requires further examination.

The presence of the OP provides a comparison group to the ACP that can help sort out these inconsistencies. Both of these parliaments have unique design features and distinct roles in the larger process. Further, these very differences might well come to represent the prototypical difference of the online versus face-to-face experiences in future mixed-medium deliberative processes. Thus, it is important to learn whether the online role afforded Australian participants yields attitudinal and behavioral shifts comparable to those resulting from their face-to-face counterparts.

Measuring a Sense of Political Transformation

To assess these changes, we started by distinguishing two types of participants: those who took part in the face-to-face meetings in Canberra in February 2009 (the "ACP participants") versus those who only took part in the Online Parliament that preceded the Canberra meetings (the "OP participants").

For each of these populations, the research team conducted a pair of surveys—one that occurred months before the OP/ACP and another that occurred a full year after the conclusion of deliberations in Canberra.[11] The pre-event survey reached 91 of the 158 persons who attended regional pre-ACP meetings, for a 58 percent response rate. The follow-up obtained surveys from 71 percent (N = 115) of the ACP attendees, compared to just 35 percent (N = 63) of the active OP-only participants.[12]

This difference in follow-up survey response rate has both a mundane and a meaningful explanation. We contacted the OP sample by e-mail only, and that limited our ability to catch their attention.[13] The more interesting likelihood is that the OP participants also made less effort to respond *because they had less to say to the researchers.* As recounted in chapters 4 and 11, the OP played an important role in the Canberra meetings, but many of the most active participants in the online component are in our ACP sample. By contrast, those who only took part in the OP include many who said relatively little in their online topic groups. More than a quarter (29 percent) of those responding to the follow-up survey acknowledged that they "did not participate actively in the Online Parliament" (and were consequently of little use in the present analysis). The OP groups included many silent partners or "lurkers," people who showed up online and said little or nothing beyond a "hello." Surely, many in this situation eschewed an invitation to reflect back on their OP experience and its impact because the experience was forgettable.

We approached the survey assessments themselves in a distinct manner, owing to the circumstances of this research. When the University of Washington research team joined this project, the ACP had already conducted its preliminary surveys, which included only a pair of questions we could use as baseline measures in our research. Thus, to detect *change over time,* we would have to rely principally on participants' own subjective sense of political transformation.

For those who might only feel persuaded by before-and-after survey measures, we offer two notes. Much of the research cited in the previous section of this essay uses such a longitudinal design and has certainly provided evidence that deliberation can yield significant changes in such measures.[14] Or viewed another way, this study complements past research by measuring systematically participants' subjective sense of change in terms of a wide range of beliefs and behaviors. It is with precisely that point in mind that we gave this chapter its title.

Changing Political Attitudes and Behaviors

To assess change, we used inferential statistics appropriate to each of the corresponding survey items. In the body of the text, we convey these results through response frequencies—how often ACP and OP participants gave different answers to our different questions. In the endnotes, the more statistically inclined can see what tests we ran to identify the statistically significant patterns in these data—i.e., those results that cannot be explained by "mere chance." For those who eschew endnotes but remain curious, we principally used binomial nonparametric tests (a "coin-flipping" test to see if one result is more common than its opposite) and paired-sample *t*-tests comparisons (to see if the average response to a single question changed from one survey period to the next).

Attitudes

Our results suggest that ACP participation had a significant impact on many of the political attitudes for those involved in the face-to-face meetings in Canberra. Those who participated only in the Online Parliament, however, saw fewer changes to their attitudes. The lower levels of attitudinal and behavioral changes among online participants versus face-to-face participants may be due, in part, to our decreased sample size for online participants, which increases the difficulty of reaching significance, though as you will see, face-to-face deliberation generally created larger, and sometimes different, changes than online deliberation.

Table 17.1 summarizes our results, showing that face-to-face participants felt a significant increase in their political self-confidence and deliberative faith and increased their faith in government on some, but not all, items. Online participants, however, believed that they had increased their political self-confidence along only one measure, saw no significant changes to their deliberative faith, and had mixed results regarding political faith, gaining faith along one measure while losing faith along another.

Although our review of the existent literature suggested that deliberative participation may not significantly change participants' internal efficacy, our results suggest that the ACP did lead to significant increases in political self-confidence, particularly for those who participated in the face-to-face meeting held in Canberra. ACP participants reported increases in their feelings of being better informed than others and being qualified to participate in politics and community affairs, with over half saying they felt more qualified after participation, as well as in their sense that they understood the important issues facing Australia.[15] OP participants only increased along one measure, understanding the important issues facing Australia,

Table 17.1   Self-reported changes in political and deliberative attitudes after participating in ACP or Online Parliament

	Face-to-face ACP (N = 115)			Online Parliament (N = 38)		
	Agree less	No change	Agree more	Agree less	No change	Agree more
Political self-confidence						
I think I am better informed about politics and government than most people	7.9%	35.1%	57.0%***	5.4%	70.3%	24.3%
I have a pretty good understanding of the important issues facing this country	0.9%	29.2%	69.9%***	0.0%	73.0%	27.0%**
I consider myself well-qualified to participate in politics and community affairs	9.6%	56.1%	34.2%***	13.5%	67.6%	18.9%
Deliberative faith						
The first step in solving our common problems is to discuss them together	0.0%	17.0%	82.1%***	13.9%	52.8%	33.3%
Even people who strongly disagree can make decisions if they sit down and talk	1.8%	16.7%	80.7%***	16.2%	51.4%	32.4%
Everyday people from different political parties can have civil, respectful conversations about politics	3.5%	19.5%	77.0%***	20.0%	54.3%	26.7%
Political faith						
Under our form of government, the people have the final say about how the country is run, no matter who is in office	27.2%	49.1%	23.7%	37.8%	54.1%	8.1%*
People like me don't have any say about what the government does	52.6%	33.3%	14.0%***	32.4%	48.6%	18.9%
There are many legal ways for citizens to successfully influence what government does	3.5%	29.8%	66.7%***	5.3%	63.2%	31.6%*

NOTE: * $p < .05$, ** $p < .01$, and *** $p < .001$.

though the majority of online participants did not change their views regarding any of the measures of political self-confidence.

We found similar results regarding participants' faith in the deliberative process. After participating in an intensive and highly structured deliberation for four days, over three-fourths of the participants at the General Meeting gained greater faith in the deliberative process, indicating a significant increase in deliberative faith. OP participants, however, did not significantly change their attitudes toward deliberation, and though more OP participants increased their faith in deliberation than decreased their faith in the deliberative process, as many as 20 percent lost their faith along at least one measure.

Changes in participants' external efficacy were a bit more complicated, with ACP participants showing significant increases in political faith along two measures, but split in their belief that the public has the final say in government, with more losing faith along this measure than gaining faith. And while about 30 percent of OP participants increased their faith that there are legal ways for the public to influence decision making, about 40 percent decreased their belief that the public has the final say no matter who is in office, indicating that deliberative participation may increase participants' faith in themselves and the deliberative process but not necessarily in contemporary political actors and institutions.

Behavior

As with our results regarding changing attitudes, table 17.2 shows that ACP and OP participation led to increased engagement along some, but not all, measures, and face-to-face participants increased their engagement along more measures than online-only participants. Those who met at the General Meeting significantly increased their communicative engagement, both in person and through the media, as well as their local engagement, while OP participants only saw significant increases in mediated engagement. Neither group increased their engagement in institutionalized electoral activities, perhaps stemming from mixed changes regarding their external efficacy.

Institutionalized engagement, or engagement directly tied to large-scale political organizations and structures, is perhaps the most difficult form of political behavior to change, and our results suggest that simply participating in a deliberative process has limited impact on individuals' electoral activity, though it may increase participation in non-governmental forms of

Table 17.2   Self-reported changes in political and deliberative behavior after participating in ACP or Online Parliament

	Face-to-face ACP (N = 115)			Online Parliament (N = 38)		
	Engage less	No change	Engage more	Engage less	No change	Engage more
Conversation						
Talking to people to learn more about a political issue or a candidate	2.6%	48.2%	49.1%***	5.3%	68.4%	26.3%*
Talking to other people to show them why they should vote for one of the parties or candidates	1.8%	79.8%	18.4%***	2.6%	89.5%	7.9%
Media use						
Paying attention to news about government, politics, or community while watching TV	0.9%	31.6%	67.5%***	0%	68.4%	31.6%***
Paying attention to news about government, politics, or community affairs while reading the newspaper	1.8%	39.5%	58.8%***	0%	73.7%	26.3%**
Local engagement						
Voluntarily working or co-operating with others in your local community to try to solve some of the community's problems	1.8%	78.9%	19.3%***	7.9%	84.2%	7.9%
Discussing local community affairs with other members of your community	3.5%	49.1%	47.4%***	7.9%	76.3%	15.85%
Institutional engagement						
Going to political meetings, demonstrations, fund raising dinners or things like that	1.8%	88.6%	9.6%*	5.3%	94.7%	0%
Doing volunteer work for one of the parties or candidates, for example, making a speech, putting up posters, or working in a candidate's office	1.8%	95.5%	2.7%	5.4%	91.9%	2.7%

NOTE: $* p < .05$, $** p < .01$, and $*** p < .001$.

institutionalized engagement. Though a small number of respondents indicated that they had increased their involvement in electoral activities, such as volunteering or attending meetings or fundraisers for a party or candidate, about 90 percent of both ACP and OP participants said they had engaged in these activities neither more nor less frequently since their deliberative experience. In addition, only two of the ACP participants joined a political party after their experience, though fourteen joined at least one activist or advocacy organization, indicating that while ACP participation did not foster party membership, it did produce a statistically significant increase in other types of organizational involvement.[16]

Our findings regarding political faith may explain these mixed results. As previously mentioned, out of all the attitudes measured, participants were least likely to increase their faith in the political process, particularly regarding their faith that politicians listened to the public, though ACP participants did have more faith in their own power to affect government decision making. In line with this, participants were not more likely to join party organizations or work to elect specific candidates, though they were more likely to join activist organizations. These results indicate that deliberative processes may actually decrease participants' faith in and engagement with traditional political institutions while spurring their faith and engagement in more citizen-centered institutions.

Our results regarding local engagement further verify this hypothesis. Face-to-face participants reported significant increases in working or volunteering in their local communities and almost 50 percent said they at least discussed local affairs with members of their community more often after their ACP experience. Again, however, OP-only participants did not report such changes, with no significant increases in either form of engagement.

At this point, we can see that ACP participation has mixed effects regarding traditional political engagement. Face-to-face participants increased their local engagement and citizen-centered engagement but not their partisan engagement, and online participants saw no significant changes in either form of engagement. Because deliberative participation is a communicative act, however, and provides participants with deliberative experience and skills,[17] its behavioral effects will likely be greatest for communicative forms of engagement. Our results verify this assumption. Forty of the 115 face-to-face participants surveyed a year later said they had written a letter to an editor or performed some similar form of public comment, a statistically significant increase.[18] Moreover, both ACP and OP participants reported paying more attention to public affairs while watching TV and reading newspapers, with over 50 percent of ACP participants saying they engaged in this activity more often after their experience. Similarly, face-to-face participants reported significant increases in both talking with others about political issues or candidates and about voting, though OP participants only reported increasing their frequency of talking with others about issues or candidates but not about how to vote.

Finally, though most of our measures of attitudinal and behavioral change relied on post-only measures, we did ask two before-and-after questions to some face-to-face participants. The first found that participants were significantly more likely to agree that their friends and family knew their political views after participation.[19] This measure is an indication of the amount of communicative engagement and signals that participants were more prone to express their political views in informal conversation after their deliberative experience.

The second pre- and post-deliberation measure asked participants how compelled they felt to defend their political views, measured along a five-point scale from "strongly disagree" to "strongly agree." Although without some treatment we would expect responses to this item to regress toward the scale midpoint, "neutral," in the post-test we hypothesized that a greater percentage would move towards agreement, indicating that they felt the need to defend their political views but not to the extent that they were not open to updating those views. Figure 17.1 shows the distribution of responses in both the pre- and post-tests. Our results confirm our hypothesis, with a greater percentage of participants moving towards agreement than towards the scale midpoint for those who indicated they were either timid or defensive in the pre-deliberation survey.[20] Along with the other results presented here, this indicates that ACP participation appeared to be particularly influential in spurring more communicative and deliberative forms of engagement.

Conclusion

Returning to our original question, we can now conclude that the Australian Citizens' Parliament—particularly the highly structured, face-to-face General Meeting—did have an effect on participants' cognitions and behaviors, often fostering greater faith in the political process and oneself as well as increased communicative and community engagement. These effects, however, are not universal, and less structured forms of deliberative communication, such as online-forum participation, may not have the

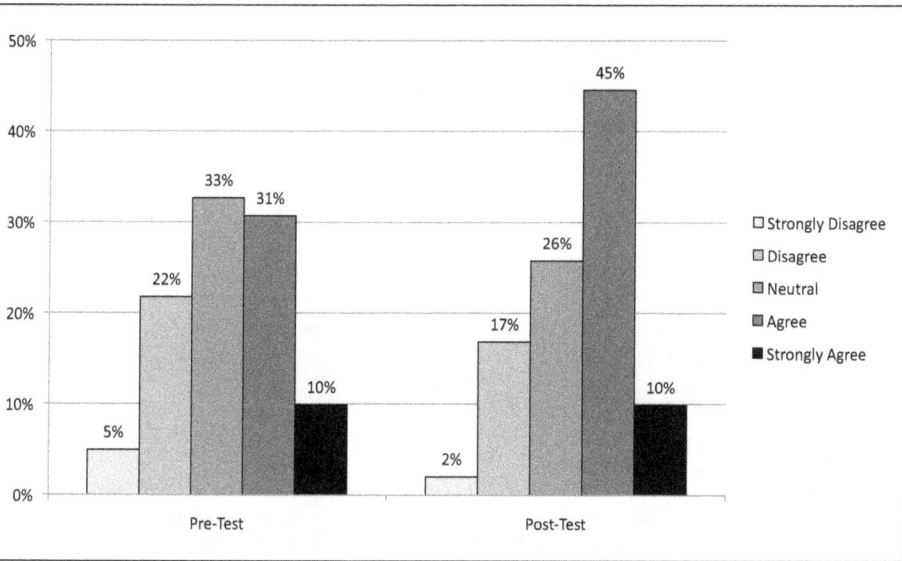

FIGURE 17.1   Percentage of respondents who felt "compelled to defend their views"

same power for fostering democratic faith and participation. Further, participation in such events may even have a dampening effect on some participants' external efficacy, translating to limited, if any, changes in institutionalized forms of participation.

And while not explored in detail here, our results suggest that changes in attitudes are likely related to changes in behavior. More research needs to be done parceling out these links, particularly the connection between external efficacy and behavioral changes. Though we traditionally measure external efficacy along a scale, our results suggest that these items may have discrete meanings as participants distinguish between their ability to utilize the political system for change and their faith in individuals' and institutions' willingness to listen to the public. ACP, and to some extent OP, participants appeared to gain faith in the former while losing faith in the latter, and their behavioral changes may be a result of these mixed cognitions.

In addition, researchers should continue to explore how different deliberative structures affect which cognitive and behavioral changes participants experience. Although ACP and OP participants paralleled each other in some cognitive and behavioral effects, particularly in increases to communicative engagement, similar mixed-media events structured in different ways or which integrate online and face-to-face experiences differently may result in different effects. Future studies could advance our understanding of how deliberative participation affects individuals across contexts by applying the same measures used here to different deliberative forums, exploring whether participants with different deliberative experiences undergo the same cognitive and behavioral changes.

NOTES

1. Mark E. Warren, "Can Participatory Democracy Produce Better Selves? Psychological Dimensions of Habermas's Discursive Model of Democracy," *Political Psychology* 14 (1993): 209–34.

2. John Gastil, E. Pierre Deess, Philip J. Weiser, and Cindy Simmons, *The Jury and Democracy: How Jury Deliberation Promotes Civic Engagement and Political Participation* (New York: Oxford University Press, 2010).

3. Stephanie Burkhalter, John Gastil, and Todd Kelshaw, "A Conceptual Definition and Theoretical Model of Public Deliberation in Small Face-to-Face Groups," *Communication Theory* 12 (2002): 398–422; Amy Gutmann and Dennis Thompson, *Why Deliberative Democracy?* (Princeton: Princeton University Press, 2004); Warren, "Can Participatory Democracy Produce Better Selves?"

4. For an overview of the existent literature, see Heather Pincock, "Does Deliberation Make Better Citizens?," in *Democracy in Motion: Evaluating the Practice and Impact of Deliberative Civic Engagement,* ed. Tina Nabatchi, John Gastil, Matt Leighninger, and G. Michael Weiksner (Oxford: Oxford University Press, 2012), 135–62.

5. Jennifer Stromer-Galley and Peter Muhlberger, "Agreement and Disagreement in Group Deliberation: Effects on Deliberation, Satisfaction, Future Engagement, and Decision Legitimacy," *Political Communication* 26 (2009): 173–92; Archon Fung, "Survey Article: Recipes for Public Spheres: Eight Institutional Design Choices and Their Consequences," *Journal of Political Philosophy* 11 (2003): 338–67; Peter Levine, Archon Fung, and John Gastil, "Future Directions for Public Deliberation," in *The Deliberative Democracy Handbook: Strategies for Effective Civic Engagement in the 21st Century,* ed. John Gastil and Peter Levine (San Francisco: Jossey-Bass, 2005), 271–88.

6. For the purposes of brevity, we have focused on the effects of two specific deliberative events, Deliberative Polls and National Issues Forums. For similar results stemming from participation in other formal deliberative events, see Gastil et al., *The Jury and Democracy;* Michael E. Morrell, "Deliberation, Democratic Decision-Making, and Internal Political Efficacy," *Political Behavior* 27 (2005): 49–70. For a discussion of the effects of less formal discursive participation, see Lawrence R. Jacobs, Fay Lomax Cook, and Michael X. Delli Carpini, *Talking Together: Public Deliberation and Political Participation in America* (Chicago: University of Chicago Press, 2009); Tina Nabatchi, "Deliberative Democracy and Citizenship: In Search of the Efficacy Effect," *Journal of Public Deliberation* 6, no. 2 (2010): art. 8, accessed January 19, 2012, http://services.bepress.com/jpd/vol6/iss2/art8.

7. James S. Fishkin, *When the People Speak: Deliberative Democracy and Public Consultation* (New York: Oxford University Press, 2009).

8. John Gastil, "Adult Civic Education Through the National Issues Forums: Developing Democratic Habits and Dispositions Through Public Deliberation," *Adult Education Quarterly* 54 (2004): 308–28; John Gastil and James P. Dillard, "The Aims, Methods, and Effects of Deliberative Civic Education Through the National Issues Forums," *Communication Education* 48 (1999): 1–14.

9. For example, Vincent Price and Joseph N. Capella, "Online Deliberation and Its Influence: The Electronic Dialogue Project in Campaign 2000," *IT and Society* 1 (2002): 303–28.

10. Jacobs, Cook, and Delli Carpini, *Talking Together*; Seong-Jae Min, "Online vs. Face-to-Face Deliberation: Effects on Civic Engagement," *Journal of Computer-Mediated Communication* 12 (2007): 1369–87.

11. The authors of this essay were not involved in the earliest survey of ACP/OP participants.

12. This percentage excludes those for whom we no longer had a valid e-mail address.

13. A basic principle of survey research is to do multiple contacts with, when possible, multiple modes, so the e-mail-only approach invariably reduces one's response rate. Moreover, e-mail itself does not grab attention the way postal mail can, particularly in an era where mail has become rarer and e-mail prodigious. See Don A. Dillman, *Mail and Internet Surveys: The Tailored Design Method*, 2nd ed. (New York: Wiley, 2006).

14. See, for instance, Gastil et al., *The Jury and Democracy*, which tracked changes in juror behavior before, shortly after, and months or even years after deliberating on juries.

15. These results, along with the other attitudinal and behavioral changes reported in tables 17.1 and 17.2, were found using a binomial nonparametric test, which measures the likelihood that participants would agree more or less with statements regarding their attitudes and behaviors after participating in the ACP, either through the Online Parliament or at the General Meeting in Canberra.

16. These results were found using a one-sample t-test, and the results concerning increased membership in an activist or advocacy organization, $p < .001$.

17. Burkhalter, Gastil, and Kelshaw, "A Conceptual Definition."

18. One-sample t-test, $p < .001$.

19. Paired-sample t-test, $p = .005$.

20. These results were found using a paired-sample t-test, $p = .011$, with responses recoded into their absolute distance from the most deliberative answer, "agreed."

18

BECOMING AUSTRALIAN: FORGING A NATIONAL IDENTITY THROUGH DELIBERATION

Janette Hartz-Karp, Patrick Anderson, John Gastil, and Andrea Felicetti

One of the unexpected outcomes of the ACP was the emergence of a robust sense of shared identity among the deliberators. Research has shown Australians to be ambivalent about their national identity, making the spontaneous emergence of a common sense of identity unlikely in an Australian setting.[1] Other factors augured against this: the ACP discussion topic was about politics, something Australians generally dislike;[2] there were limited external rewards, such as remuneration and official recognition; and discourse between diverse others was routinely maximized (see the introduction and chapter 2).

Since the ACP's primary research team had no a priori expectation of emergent collective identity, a relevant methodology to track it had to be designed retrospectively. This was made possible through the copious data available, including surveys before, during, and after the ACP, daily feedback notes and daily preliminary reports documenting each day's outcomes, notes from researchers who each observed a number of tables, table inputs to the computer, transcriptions of discussions at each table, online social networking sites following the ACP, and a follow-up survey to all participants one year after the main event.[3] All these data sources were drawn upon to explore how this shared identity emerged and its potential role in the final agreed outcomes reflecting the "common good."

Emergence of Identity

It became apparent from the outset that unlike most community engagement initiatives, the ACP tapped into a sense of excitement and pride.

Rather than responding to the written invitations by e-mail, many participants phoned to express how "excited," "privileged," and "honored" they felt at receiving invitations. As one CP noted, "I thought it was a chance of a lifetime." This was exemplified at the regional meetings through an exchange between an organizer and a CP who requested permission to leave her cell phone on so she could hear from her son, who was in a debating competition state finals. When asked why she was not with him, she replied, "My country has called. I had to be here. My son understood." It was also evident in the online deliberations, with participants talking publicly about the time, effort, and learning that had gone into their proposals, and their pride in the outcomes. One online participant spoke of the "importance of being part of something bigger" than herself.

On the first day of the ACP in Canberra in the historical House of Representatives chamber of Old Parliament House, a number of CPs spoke of how extraordinarily proud they felt to be "part of history" and to have their views taken seriously. For instance, "We have the [chance] to say something. . . . It's going to give awareness to the individual Australian people . . . about our democracy." At the closing session, one CP said the lesson she believed participants had learnt during the process was "We're lucky we live in Australia. . . . We need to take responsibility to participate, protect, and enhance our system and democracy." Another said, "I heard about a 'we' and an 'us.' If I'm sitting here, which I am, then I think I'm becoming a part of the 'us.' . . . I hope that we can take this new approach back to our communities."

The results of a pre-deliberation survey completed by CPs complemented these qualitative findings.[4] Participants were asked whether they "felt like an outsider here at the Citizens Parliament," and 87 percent reported that they did not. Only 5.6 percent reported feeling like an "outsider." Additionally, in the one-year follow-up survey asking, "How important is 'being Australian' in describing who you are?," only 9 percent said it was "not too important" or "not at all important" to them, with 23 percent saying it was "fairly important," 35 percent viewing it as "very important to them" and the remaining 33 percent reporting that "being Australian" had become an "extremely important" part of how they describe themselves.[5] Over two-thirds of CPs had woven Australian national identity into their core conception of themselves—even a full year after the ACP. Notably, a strong national identity is rarely reported as part of the makeup of Australians.[6]

Convergent and Divergent Identities

Viewed in the larger context of deliberative democracy, CPs faced similar challenges as in other deliberative processes, including that of working with the conflicting cultural and political vantage points inherent in any pluralistic society.[7] By degrees, deliberation seeks to advance towards a "reasoned consensus," or at least the more modest kinds of agreement possible in political reality.[8] Deep and stable cleavages often form between diverse sub-publics, political cultures, and political partisans, with Australia being no exception.[9] Given the distorting effects these divides can have on information processing and discussion,[10] designers of deliberative democratic processes face a significant obstacle when seeking to help "the public" find anything like a singular voice.

Social groupings of all sizes often seek to secure their relationships and self-understandings through creating a social identity, "that part of an individual's self-concept" derived from his or her social group membership, "together with the value and emotional significance attached to that membership."[11] "Social identity theory" helps us understand the formation of collective identifications,[12] where people constantly make social comparisons to establish their placement within in-groups, as contrasted with out-groups. Such social identities are deployed to accumulate status, strengthen self-concept, and coordinate actions with others. Which of our many identities becomes salient in a given context depends on the objective features of that context and how it is framed. Having settled on an in-group identity, people move quickly to develop prejudices against out-groups and resist any influence from outsiders. Meta-analyses of these effects show them to be both strong and pervasive across a wide range of cultural settings.[13] Experimental studies repeatedly show how difficult it is for people of a given social identity to weigh information and argument equally across lines of social difference.[14]

How one judges the social value or harm of such identification processes depends, in part, on the particular behavioral norm to which in-group members become habituated as a result. Consider the case of "superordinate identity," which is an overarching social identification that reaches across more particularistic social divides to unify a social group.[15] Making salient a superordinate identification, such as nationality, can result in pro-social cooperative behavior that overrides regional or personal self-interest— potentially (though not necessarily) for the betterment of all. Forging a superordinate identity, however, constitutes a remarkable achievement, given the difficulty of arriving at any universally shared perceptions or judgments in even the smallest social groups.[16]

Challenges to Shared Identity

If there exists a generic difficulty in achieving superordinate identification, the particular case of Australian identity constitutes a particular challenge. Commentators on Australian identity have suggested that since the "birth" of the modern Australian nation, Australians have perceived themselves with a sense of ambivalence.[17] From early national identification in terms of "Britishness"[18] came uncertainty with the increasingly diverse ethnic and cultural populace and the embrace of multiculturalism.[19] Heated debates about the nature of Australian identity persist.[20]

This ambivalence is augmented by attitudes towards Aboriginal Australians. Historical discrimination and marginalization of Aborigines has resulted in institutionalized racism and a legacy of psychological trauma and entrenched socioeconomic disadvantage.[21] Empirical studies suggest that underlying racist attitudes towards Aboriginal Australians persist in both direct and more subtle forms, particularly among older respondents and those with less formal education.[22] This prejudice is often based on false assumptions about the behavior of Aboriginal people and their treatment by government, and it is frequently reflected in common discourse that discounts the prevalence of discrimination and racism and emphasizes the need for a collective identification as Australians without affording special privilege to any one group.[23]

These attitudes were reflected in CP deliberations, particularly at the outset, with comments such as "talking about Australians" is like talking about "a bag of licorice all-sorts" and "I'm not very sympathetic to Indigenous peoples." Others argued that Aboriginal people have no claim to any "special treatment," and "no Australians should have a status" different from any other. One CP asked, "Is there an Indigenous American Day? Is there Indigenous Inca Day? . . . I mean, nearly every single continent on this earth was invaded at some stage." Another said, "There shouldn't be different groups of people. We should be put as Australian, as a group, and that should . . . encompass everyone no matter where you come from," receiving the response "Well, for me, the 'we' as Australians has to include recognition of Indigenous people as the First People of Australia and I don't think Australia can move ahead without that occurring."

The influx of ethnic groups was also perceived by some to be a threat to a common Australia. As one CP remarked, "So Australians generally feel that they are under threat of losing their identity." Another said, "I fear for some other cultures that are coming into the country now, they will never integrate, even the second or third generation."

The question for deliberative theorists is whether being involved in deliberation changed the sense of "us" and "them" sufficiently to enable a convergence on a coherent set of outcomes that encompassed all Australians.

Consensus Outcomes and Shared Identity

Some critics of deliberation have raised legitimate concerns about the power dynamics likely to occur in deliberations that privilege one legitimate mode of discourse over another.[24] Even when deliberation embraces divergent styles and perspectives, the fear persists that minority voices will be outvoted by emergent majorities.[25] Recent evidence, however, suggests that women and minorities participate as actively and with at least equal enthusiasm to their counterparts in well-structured deliberative settings.[26] This was reflected in many CP comments: "We could say what we think" and "We could speak out without worrying what others thought." Notably, there were two ombudsmen, though CPs never called for their intervention.

The final list of proposals submitted to the federal government was almost as surprising as the development of shared identity. Although ACP organizers hoped by the end of the deliberations to reach consensus-based, well-reasoned proposals, there were no expectations about the content of the proposals. Hence, it was unexpected that the final priority list also reflected an apparent understanding of and commitment to the common good (i.e., the proposals were seen to benefit all Australians), with four reflecting an apparent attitudinal shift on Indigenous people, affording them a unique place in the institutions of government.[27] Comments supported this stance: "[T]he [prime minister's] apology was wonderful . . . but until that recognition comes [at the constitutional level] we don't move forward at all as a country." The final comment of one Aboriginal participant was particularly moving: "For a rare moment in my life I actually felt part of the majority and not the minority." Whereas the inclusion of an Aboriginal co-chair and an Aboriginal presenter could have influenced the participants' perception of their role as representing all Australians, it is an inadequate explanation. The consensus that emerged during the ACP did so organically, as a result of the deliberative process itself. As one facilitator noted, "One of the CPs had a profound discovery, which I feel was one of the many achievements that came out of the forum. Through dialogue, this CP learned more about the Indigenous plight, mainly through discussion with one of the Aboriginal participants and his mind-set shifted through this dialogue.... He discussed this shift as being one of the poignant experiences for him personally." At the ACP close, an Aboriginal CP, one of those selected to present the final report to government, commenced his talk by extending his arms outwards to all present and saying solemnly, "Australia . . . ," as if *all of Australia* were sitting in the Chamber. This gesture resonated with CPs and was discussed as a symbolic moment.

The apparent shift in attitude towards the common good was also reflected in the final CP proposals about how the federation could better function. The question of state rights versus centralization at the federal level has long been a contentious issue in Australia.[28] Many CPs had come to the event with local identities foremost in their minds: "I identify as being Tasmanian first, Australian second." Later conversations reflected a significant change: "You're changing my mind now, I was thinking we should have gone with states but now I'm listening to your point of view, I'm seeing something I didn't see before. . . . [W]e also need to have different states with different ideas but as a basic umbrella we need certain things coming as one to unify the country." This was reflected in the final policy list, with the top-ranked proposal recommending the harmonization of laws across the states and the eleventh-ranked proposal recommending a significantly reduced state focus.[29]

Precursors to Shared Identity

Since the emergence of a superordinate identity appeared to be a precursor of a singular voice that enhanced understanding of the common good, discerning the factors that could have led to this outcome is important. The following themes often interweave:

The sense of integrity and legitimacy. This was reiterated though diverse comments, including how random selection gave "everyone a chance to participate," how "respected Australian universities" convened the process rather than government, how the process was "unbiased," and how Old Parliament House gave legitimacy: "The thing is, we've all become a part of the history of this building now." CPs often described the process as "open and honest," supporting "respectful conversations," for example: "I loved the group discussion . . . no one was attacked"; "I strongly disagree, but I'm trying to be tolerant"; or "I'm worried I might be speaking over people." At the closing session, one CP commented: "The other reflection that I've had just in talking with different people is just the power that comes from being heard, being understood, not judged and not criticized and that is a very, very powerful dynamic." Surprisingly, several unscripted incidents reaffirmed the integrity of the process. When the ACP chair raised his concern in the Assembly about potential bias being introduced in a prior session, and at another point, when the lead facilitator openly confessed to a prioritization miscount, these potentially damaging admissions resulted in CPs publicly announcing that this honesty had allayed their earlier cynicism about the process.

Mutual trust and bridging capital. Trust was typified by comments such as "I found myself speaking . . . in front of total strangers, which I would ordinarily not do. The fact that everyone listened, without making rude comments or interrupting me most of the time, even agreeing with what I said, was very reassuring." CPs described how it was all right to "not know" and to "speak out" without "feeling silly." They talked about developing firm friendships over a short time, often with people very different from them. One CP wrote after the event of "being so much at ease with 150 strangers, who weren't strangers any more at the end of it. . . . Watching my narrow focus and intense passion broadening and strengthening after listening and learning. . . . Feeling so involved with the process and feeling we could bring change for our children's future." What was being described was bridging capital, where diverse groups with weak connections develop generalized trust and mutuality,[30] key to a sense of social cohesion and inclusion.[31]

Facing adversity together. This emerged partially from the grueling four-day program of intense discussion and learning, alien to many and devoid of obvious personal gain, but mostly was due to enduring together one of Canberra's most intense heat waves, suffering sweltering evenings without air-conditioning, and daily facing a national tragedy—the raging Victorian fires. CPs and support team members from fire-affected areas agonized about whether to leave the ACP, but in the end stayed. One CP who had lost her best friend to the fires decided that her friend would have wanted her to stay—to "make the most of this opportunity to make a difference"; another CP who stayed said, "this is a once-in-a-lifetime opportunity." Observations on Australian identity are rife with images of Australians pulling together in the face of hardship, supported by mateship and wry humor[32] also epito-mized through sport.[33] It logically follows that a nation brought together—even in the form of a deliberative microcosm—could experience a rising national identification.

Achieving a satisfying result. The usual Australian cynicism about public consultation being "talkfests" that yield little action was replaced by satis-faction and pride in the ACP's collaborative outcomes. CPs selected by their fellow participants to present the ACP findings to the prime minister's rep-resentative spoke poignantly about the responsibility they felt for "getting it right" on behalf of "all Australians." A listening CP commented, "Our rep-resentatives speak with clarity and passion, emphasizing . . . our conviction that a group of ordinary citizens can make a significant contribution to the political debate—if only given the opportunity. We are simultaneously exhausted and proud of what we achieved."[34] This finding supports the theory about the interplay of group achievement and identity, of a clear relationship between members' perceptions of their effectiveness and their willingness to trust and identify themselves with their group. While this may be expected in the case of team building,[35] it also appears to be true of a mini-public.

The ACP experience provides further evidence that social identity forms through communication and interaction,[36] and more specifically, as posited by deliberative theory, that the process of carefully working through issues together fosters a recognition of shared values, an appreciation of the moral justifications underlying different views, and the discovery of common ground—all factors that contribute to a sense of common identity that transcends conventional self-interest.[37]

Conclusion

The emergence of a common identity of "being Australian" was surprising given Australians' ambivalence about their national identity. Attributes tra-ditionally linked to Australianness—mateship, the belief in a "fair go" for all, and determination in the face of adversity—were all evident as the CPs readily embraced each other as friends and colleagues irrespective of their background. Even more profound was the organic emergence of shared identity, predicated not just upon tolerance and acceptance, but on a true embracing of all participants as bona fide Australians, whose values, opin-ions, and aspirations carried equal importance in both the deliberative process itself and within the context of the broader task of strengthening Australia's political system.

The collective repositioning that resulted from being asked to take responsibility for formulating effective reforms for the future on behalf of all Australians, and to do so through an egalitarian process with ethnically and attitudinally diverse others, proved to be critical in the emergence of identity at the ACP. To effectively address the question assigned to them, participants created a microcosm of an informed, empowered, and egalitarian Australian society, revealing what Australians might sound like if they were to take responsibility for their political system while ensuring an equal voice for all, regardless of ethnic or cultural heritage. Not only did the CPs unintentionally map out new territory of Australian identity, but their experience also brought to the fore new insights into deliberative democratic theory and practice.

Given the importance of forging shared identity in deliberating across political and cultural differences,[38] the ACP findings are intriguing in terms of the potential to enhance participants' understanding of the common good. Given the heterogeneous nature of the Australian electorate and the challenges inherent in the country's federal governance structure, the findings have significant implications for policy makers in similar constituencies, notably the United States and particularly the European Union, where public deliberation may represent an important political resource.[39] If deliberative assemblies can foster the emergence of shared identities and a stronger conception of the common good, they offer an effective way to draw together constituencies of diverse people.

NOTES

1. Zoe Melantha and Helen Anderson, "At the Borders of Belonging: Representing Cultural Citizenship in Australia, 1873–1984" (PhD diss., University of Western Australia, 2009); Catriona Elder, *Being Australian: Narratives of National Identity* (Crows Nest, NSW: Allen and Unwin, 2007).

2. Scott Brenton, "Public Confidence in Australian Democracy" (Democratic Audit Discussion Paper 8/08, Australian National University, 2008), accessed January 1, 2012, http://democratic.audit.anu.edu.au/categories/pub_optfrm.htm.

3. Using an ex post facto, largely qualitative, interpretive methodology such as this to try to re-create the steps that led to an unexpected outcome is both a common and a mindful method of inquiry. See Sally Thorne, *Interpretive Description* (Walnut Creek, Calif.: Left Coast Press, 2008).

4. This survey had an 87 percent response rate, with 130 of the 150 CPs completing it.

5. These results are based on 107 surveys, a 71 percent response rate when counted against the 150 CPs we tried to contact in the follow-up survey.

6. Anderson, "At the Borders of Belonging."

7. On deliberative democracy, see Simone Chambers, "Deliberative Democratic Theory," *Annual Review of Political Science* 6 (2003): 307–26, and John Uhr, "Review Essay: Deliberating About Democracy: Five Perspectives," *Australian Journal of Political Science* 44 (2009): 529–35.

On pluralism, see John S. Dryzek, "Deliberative Democracy in Divided Societies: Alternatives to Agonism and Analgesia," *Political Theory* 33 (2005): 218–42, and Peter Levine, Archon Fung, and John Gastil, "Future Directions for Public Deliberation," in *The Deliberative Democracy Handbook: Strategies for Effective Civic Engagement in the 21st Century*, ed. John Gastil and Peter Levine (San Francisco: Jossey-Bass, 2005), 271–88.

8. On "reasoned consensus," see Jürgen Habermas, *The Theory of Communicative Action*, vol. 2, *Lifeworld and System: A Critique of Functionalist Reason*, trans. Thomas McCarthy (Boston: Beacon Press, 1984), and Joshua Cohen, "Deliberation and Democratic Legitimacy," in *The Good Polity*, ed. Alan Hamlin and Philip Pettit (New York: Basil Blackwell, 1989), 17–34. See also Adrian Little, "Between Disagreement and Consensus: Unravelling the Democratic Paradox," *Australian Journal of Political Science* 42 (2007): 143–59.

9. In the case of Australia, see Ian McAllister, "Political Parties in Australia: Party Stability in a Utilitarian Society," in *Political Parties in Advanced Industrial Democracies*, ed. Paul Webb, David M. Farrell, and Ian Holliday (Oxford: Oxford University Press, 2002), 379–408. More generally, and with reference to the United States, see Mark D. Brewer and Jeffrey M. Stonecash, *Split: Class and Cultural Divides in American Politics* (Washington, D.C.: CQ Press, 2007).

10. Wendy M. Rahn, "The Role of Partisan Stereotypes in Information Processing About Political Candidates," *American Journal of Political Science* 37 (1993): 472–96; Diane Carole Mutz, *Hearing the Other Side: Deliberative Versus Participatory Democracy* (New York: Cambridge University Press, 2006); Dan M. Kahan, "The Cognitively Illiberal State," *Stanford Law Review* 60 (2007): 115–54.

11. Henri Tajfel, "Social Categorization, Social Identity, and Social Comparison," in *Differentiation Between Social Groups: Studies in the Social Psychology of Intergroup Relations*, ed. Henri Tajfel (London: Academic Press, 1978), 63.

12. Judith A. Howard, "Social Psychology of Identities," *Annual Review of Sociology* 26 (2000): 367–93; Michael A. Hogg, "The Social Identity Perspective," in *The Handbook of Group Research and Practice*, ed. Susan A. Wheelan (Newbury Park, Calif.: Sage, 2005), 133–58.

13. Brian Mullen and Li-Tze Hu, "Perceptions of Ingroup and Outgroup Variability: A Meta-analytic Integration," *Basic and Applied Social Psychology* 10 (1989): 233–52; Heidi Schütz and Bernd Six, "How Strong Is the Relationship Between Prejudice and Discrimination? A Meta-analytic Answer," *International Journal of Intercultural Relations* 20 (1996): 441–62.

14. Mutz, *Hearing the Other Side*; Dan M. Kahan, Donald Braman, John Gastil, Paul Slovic, and C. K. Mertz, "Culture and Identity-Protective Cognition: Explaining the White-Male Effect in Risk Perception," *Journal of Empirical Legal Studies* 4 (2007): 465–505.

15. Samuel L. Gaertner, John F. Dovidio, Jason A. Nier, Christine M. Ward, and Brenda S. Banker, "Across Cultural Divides: The Value of a Superordinate Identity," in *Cultural Divides: Understanding and Overcoming Group Conflict*, ed. Deborah A. Prentice and Dale T. Miller (New York: Russell Sage Foundation, 1999), 173–212; Sujin Lee, "Judgment of Ingroups and Outgroups in Intra- and Intercultural Negotiation: The Role of Interdependent Self-Construal in Judgment Timing," *Group Decision and Negotiation* 14 (2005): 43–62.

16. Claire M. Mason, "Exploring the Processes Underlying Within-Group Homogeneity," *Small Group Research* 37 (2006): 233–70.

17. Elder, *Being Australian*; Anderson, "At the Borders of Belonging."

18. Neville Meaney, "Britishness and Australian Identity," *Australian Historical Studies* 32, no. 116 (2001): 76–90; Judith Kapferer, *Being All Equal: Identity, Difference, and Australian Cultural Practice* (Oxford: Berg, 1996), 14–17.

19. Alastair Davidson, *From Subject to Citizen: Australian Citizenship in the Twentieth Century* (Cambridge: Cambridge University Press, 1997), 87–89; Ien Ang and Jon Stratton,

"Multiculturalism in Crisis: The New Politics of Race and National Identity in Australia," *Topia: Canadian Journal of Cultural Politics* 2 (1998): 22–41.

20. M. C. Ricklefs, "The Asian Immigration Controversies of 1984–85, 1988–89, and 1996–97: A Historical Overview," in *The Resurgence of Racism: Howard, Hanson, and the Race Debate,* ed. Geoffrey Gray and Christine Winter (Clayton, VIC: Monash University Department of History, 1997), 39–61; Suvendrini Perera, "Whiteness and Its Discontents: Notes on Politics, Gender, Sex, and Food in the Year of Hanson," *Journal of Intercultural Studies* 20 (1999): 183–98; Peter Mares, *Borderline: Australia's Response to Refugees and Asylum Seekers in the Wake of the "Tampa"* (Sydney: University of New South Wales Press, 2002).

21. Nicolas Peterson and Will Sanders, eds., *Citizenship and Indigenous Australians: Changing Conceptions and Possibilities* (Cambridge: Cambridge University Press, 1998); Anthony Moran, "The Psychodynamics of Australian Settler Nationalism: Assimilating or Reconciling with the Aborigines?," *Political Psychology* 23 (2002): 667–701; J. Koolmatrie and Ross Williams, "Unresolved Grief and the Removal of Indigenous Australian Children," *Australian Psychologist* 35 (2000): 158–66; Royal Commission into Aboriginal Deaths in Custody, *National Report, Overview and Recommendations,* vol. 2 (Canberra: Australian Government Publishing Service, 1991).

22. Anne Pedersen, Brian Griffiths, Natalie Contos, Brian Bishop, and Iain Walker, "Attitudes Toward Aboriginal Australians in City and Country Settings," *Australian Psychologist* 35 (2000): 109–17; Kevin M. Dunn, James Forrest, Ian Burnley, and Amy McDonald, "Constructing Racism in Australia," *Australian Journal of Social Issues* 39 (2004): 409–30; Anne Pedersen, Jamie Beven, Iain Walker, and Brian Griffiths, "Attitudes Toward Indigenous Australians: The Role of Empathy and Guilt," *Journal of Community and Applied Social Psychology* 14 (2004): 233–49.

23. Martha Augoustinos, Keith Tuffin, and Mark Rapley, "Genocide or a Failure to Gel? Racism, History, and Nationalism in Australian Talk," *Discourse Society* 10 (1999): 351–78.

24. Iris Marion Young, "Communication and the Other: Beyond Deliberative Democracy," in *Democracy and Difference: Contesting the Boundaries of the Political,* ed. Seyla Benhabib (Princeton: Princeton University Press, 1996), 120–36; Lynn M. Sanders, "Against Deliberation," *Political Theory* 25 (1997): 347–76.

25. Melissa S. Williams, "The Uneasy Alliance of Group Representation and Deliberative Democracy," in *Citizenship in Diverse Societies,* ed. Will Kymlicka and Wayne Norman (Oxford: Oxford University Press, 2000), 124–54, raises these concerns. More optimistic views are expressed by W. Barnett Pearce and Stephen W. Littlejohn, *Moral Conflict: When Social Worlds Collide* (Thousand Oaks, Calif.: Sage, 1997), and Lincoln Dahlberg, "The Habermasian Public Sphere: Taking Difference Seriously," *Theory and Society* 34 (2005): 111–36.

26. Evidence comes from juries (Andrea Hickerson and John Gastil, "Assessing the Difference Critique of Deliberation: Gender, Emotion, and the Jury Experience," *Communication Theory* 18 [2008]: 281–303) and Deliberative Polls (Alice Siu, "Look Who's Talking: Deliberation and Social Influence," paper presented at the annual meeting of the American Political Science Association, Toronto, Canada, September 3–6, 2009, accessed January 2, 2012, http://ssrn.com/abstract=1468078).

27. Recommendations referring specifically to Indigenous people included

(1) Recognize Aboriginal and Torres Strait Island peoples as the First People of Australia in the Constitution;

(2) Minority group representation, [recognizing that] our "we" is all Australians, [and we need] a system that gives more minority groups representation, particularly Indigenous people;

(3) The possibility of an Aboriginal reconciliation day or 21st-century treaty signed to recognize the past; and

(4) Indigenous Citizens' Parliament: possibly a CP concerning Indigenous Australians, or a regional CP representative of all Indigenous peoples, if that would fit with Indigenous culture.

28. Brian Galligan, *A Federal Republic: Australia's Constitutional System of Government* (Cambridge: Cambridge University Press, 1995).

29. The top-ranked recommendation was "Reduce duplication between levels of government by harmonizing laws across state boundaries: making laws consistent across the states to avoid duplication or differing requirements." The eleventh-ranked proposal was "Remove or reduce state level of government: having only federal and regional governments, with local government to be replaced with larger regional councils."

30. Larissa Larsen, Sharon L. Harlan, Bob Bolin, Edward J. Hackett, Diane Hope, Andrew Kirby, Amy Nelson, Tom R. Rex, and Shaphard Wolf, "Bonding and Bridging: Understanding the Relationship Between Social Capital and Civic Action," *Journal of Planning Education and Research* 24 (2004): 64–77.

31. Vicky Cattell, "Poor People, Poor Places, and Poor Health: The Mediating Role of Social Networks and Social Capital," *Social Science and Medicine* 52 (2001): 1501–16.

32. See Linzi Murrie, "Changing Masculinities: Disruption and Anxiety in Contemporary Australian Writing," *Journal of Australian Studies* 56 (1998): 169–79.

33. Lisa E. Wolf-Wendel, J. Douglas Toma, and Christopher C. Morphew, "There's No 'I' in 'Team': Lessons from Athletics on Community Building," *Review of Higher Education* 24 (2001): 369–96.

34. Pete Cruttenden, "Power to the People," *The Big Issue*, 2009, accessed October 23, 2009, http://newdemocracy.com.au/index.php?option=com_content&task;eqview&id=88&Itemid=67.

35. On small groups, see John Gastil, *The Group in Society* (Los Angeles: Sage, 2010). On team building, see Eduardo Salas, Dana E. Sims, and C. Shawn Burke, "Is There a 'Big Five' in Teamwork?," *Small Group Research* 36 (2005): 555–99.

36. Kenneth J. Gergen, *Realities and Relationships: Soundings in Social Construction* (Cambridge, Mass.: Harvard University Press, 1994).

37. Benjamin R. Barber, *Strong Democracy: Participatory Politics for a New Age* (Berkeley: University of California Press, 1984); Mark E. Warren, "What Should We Expect from More Democracy? Radical Democratic Responses to Politics," *Political Theory* 24 (1996): 241–70.

38. Jane J. Mansbridge, *Beyond Adversary Democracy* (Chicago: University of Chicago Press, 1983); Barber, *Strong Democracy*.

39. There is considerable awareness of this potential in the EU, which has sponsored many transnational deliberative events already. See, e.g., James S. Fishkin, *When the People Speak: Deliberative Democracy and Public Consultation* (New York: Oxford University Press, 2009).

19

MEDIATED META-DELIBERATION: MAKING SENSE OF THE
AUSTRALIAN CITIZENS' PARLIAMENT

Eike Mark Rinke, Katherine R. Knobloch, John Gastil, and Lyn Carson

Most of the chapters in this volume look inside the Australian Citizens' Parliament (ACP) to study the practical and political challenges of deliberating together in an assembly of ordinary citizens. However, the ACP also created the possibility for a kind of deliberation that can occur only through mass communication.[1] The news coverage of the ACP had the potential to spark a *mediated deliberation*—a process whereby newspapers, online news outlets, and other media help the wider public understand and think through issues in at least a quasi-deliberative way.

In our view, projects like the ACP succeed or fail not only based on their internal quality but also depending on how they engage the media and, ultimately, the broader public. This essay presents a particular aspect of this larger public engagement, which we call "mediated meta-deliberation." In simple terms, a meta-deliberation involves deliberation *about* deliberation, or how we talk about this special kind of talk. In the context of this chapter, we focus specifically on how the media do this, hence the term "*mediated* meta-deliberation."

In the sections that follow, we explain why organizers of deliberative initiatives should care about the mediated meta-deliberation that occurs regarding their activities. We then apply this concept to the ACP and present a comprehensive analysis of the quantity and character of news coverage generated by the ACP in Australian print media.

Mediated Meta-deliberation

Deliberative-democratic theory has helped give rise to discrete public-engagement processes, such as the ACP, but its origins lie in a broader concern about the quality of reasoning that occurs among the larger body of citizens in larger public venues and across diffuse public spaces or "public spheres." The normative ideal envisions public spheres as places of inclusive, reason-based, and civil exchanges of ideas aimed at discerning the value, legitimacy, and validity of various claims made in the public interest.[2] Robust public spheres help us understand what practices, processes, and policies best serve the collective good.

Research addressing the role that media plays in such public processes sometimes refers to itself as the study of mediated deliberation. Typically using content analysis to categorize and compare media coverage of political issues, events, and actors, mediated-deliberation research provides a relatively new paradigm for understanding the normative implications of modern, large-scale communication systems for deliberative democracy.[3]

The concept of mediated deliberation has not yet been formulated in a unified fashion, and we do not have an integrated theory available that would reconcile rival conceptions of this phenomenon. For instance, some scholars focus on how mediated deliberation emerges from a "division of labor" between media outlets that complement each other in a society-wide process of deliberation, whereas others focus more on comparisons of individual media outlets' contributions to societal deliberation (i.e., on their "internal" mediated deliberations).[4] In this chapter, we adopt the latter approach to examine the quantity and quality of ACP coverage across the Australian print media system.

Our research constitutes a case study of meta-deliberation because we study how the media deliberated about a deliberative event, namely, the ACP. To render collective judgments about the quality of ostensibly deliberative public processes and institutions, it is imperative that such meta-deliberation take place.[5] When this process of analysis and judgment takes place through the mass media, we refer to it as mediated meta-deliberation. Mediated meta-deliberation fulfills an important function by conferring legitimacy onto some processes while denying it to others. In this manner, it serves an important function by subjecting political communication to critical mediated inquiry, including the fundamental question of what place deliberation should have in it.[6]

Mediated meta-deliberation can manifest in a variety of forms and through diverse communication media, and it can concern an even wider variety of political-communication processes. One example is the mediated discussion of campaign rules and the conduct of political debate in television news coverage.[7] In that example, a mediated meta-deliberation would constitute something of a self-critique, with some elements of a larger media system scrutinizing other political media from the standpoint of deliberative democracy. In the United States, media-criticism programs such as *CounterSpin*, and even satirical offerings like *The Daily Show*, can provide a measure of mediated meta-deliberation.[8]

It is just as important to scrutinize more specific deliberative events, such as the ACP. Sometimes they constitute empowered bodies, but even when they do not, deliberative mini-publics can exert macro-level political leverage through their influence on broader public debates.[9] There are at least four potential consequences of such media coverage that suggest that inclusion in public communication should be part of the evaluation of deliberative events. Mediated meta-deliberation on such events can do at least four things:

1. Raise people's awareness of the event's outcomes (in this case, the six recommendations issued by the ACP)
2. Foster people's interest in the issues deliberated upon, as well as in participatory and deliberative politics generally
3. Persuade people of the value of deliberation as an alternative mode of politics
4. Establish deliberation in the public's mind as an available standard for the assessment of political processes (irrespective of whether a media report or its particular reader deems this standard as legitimate)

Though each of these effects on individuals exposed to mediated meta-deliberation is important, their aggregation gives the mass media the power—in contrast to a discrete event like the ACP—to enact larger-scale change. Raising awareness of the substantive outcomes of the event can exert direct discursive pressure on political decision makers (e.g., "Implement the recommendations!") or through an indirect route via a populace's heightened knowledge about or interest in the issues deliberated upon (e.g., "Do something quickly about problems A and B because of concerns X, Y, and Z").[10] Over time, fostering interest in participatory politics, along with persuading people of the merits of deliberation and establishing it as a viable standard for democratic politics, should contribute to a political discourse culture that constitutes a fertile ground for a more deliberative democracy.[11] Taken together, these potential consequences of mediated meta-deliberation are good reasons why the organizers of deliberative events must have a media-relations plan if they hope to have an impact on society and politics from the "outside."[12]

Unfortunately, there exists hardly any empirical literature that systematically analyzes the mediated discourse surrounding deliberative initiatives. In a noteworthy exception, political scientist Lawrence LeDuc focused on how three major Canadian newspapers reported on the 2006 Ontario Citizens' Assembly on electoral reform.[13] This study showed that predominantly negative coverage of the Assembly, which included vilification of both the whole initiative and Canadian citizens' ability to engage in meaningful deliberation, undercut the perceived legitimacy of the Assembly. The study was confined to a simple summary measure of public sentiment towards the event and accompanying anecdotal evidence. Nonetheless, even this single, limited case study raises the question, did the Australian media report on the ACP in a similar way? What else can we learn by looking at how the media covered the ACP?

Mediated Deliberation About the ACP

In our analysis of mediated meta-deliberation on the ACP, we break our findings into two parts, one concerning the volume and general topics of the coverage and the second concerning the tone and perspective in the coverage.[14]

The first part of our study looks at the visibility of the ACP to get a general sense of how often ACP topics, ideas, and arguments recirculated into Australian public discourse through the mass media. Here, our question is, *who* discussed *what* and *when*?[15] In this dimension, we looked into the volume of coverage the ACP received in the media as well as the prominence of different aspects of the deliberative process (analytic, social, or decision making), including the six final recommendations made by the ACP. We also looked at the sources used by journalists in their reports of the ACP.

In the second part of our study, we examined how ACP participants and ideas were treated in the mediated meta-deliberation on the event. Here our question is, *how* was the ACP discussed? In this dimension, we specifically looked at the tone with which journalists reported on the ACP and how they portrayed the competence and participation of citizens.[16] This analysis provides a better sense of the perspective from which media reported on the ACP and the judgment their coverage suggests about the quality or legitimacy of the event.

Our study began by collecting a broad sample of ACP coverage in printed newspapers and magazines. In doing so, we tried to collect as high a percentage as possible of all ACP coverage in Australian print media. This was done through a content analysis of articles retrieved from two comprehensive digital news archives, NewsBank and LexisNexis, covering 262 (NewsBank) and 70 (LexisNexis) daily and weekly Australian newspapers, respectively.[17] These include nineteen of the twenty-five most circulated newspapers in Australia, including all top ten publications.[18]

Visibility of the ACP in Australian Print Media

Our first question related to the visibility of the ACP through media coverage. How much reporting did it receive? By whom and when? And what aspects of it were discussed? Our search turned up a total of seventy-four unique published articles that made mention of the ACP.[19] A total of fifty-nine print media outlets in Australia published at least one news item or opinion piece, and thirty-nine authors (journalists or not) wrote about the event. Citizens in the many scattered parts of Australia could potentially encounter a news story mentioning the ACP in their regional or local paper, or its online equivalent. The flipside of this finding is that forty-eight (or 81.4 percent) of these papers published only a single article referring to the ACP, and most articles took the form of short announcements that local citizens would be participating in the event rather than in-depth reporting and analysis of the ACP. After all, the median ACP news item was just 243 words long.

More notably, fifty-seven (or 77.0 percent) of the articles were published *before* the main Citizens' Parliament that took place in Canberra from February 6–9, 2009. Almost all of these pre-Canberra articles were published in the two months preceding the February meeting. In short, there was a heavy focus on pre-coverage of the event but significantly less coverage after the event. In the period from the main meeting at Old Parliament House in Canberra until two weeks after the event, not more than four articles were published in searched publications.

Although these pre-Canberra stories included one of the longest and most in-depth reports on the ACP, written by an invited panelist and published in the *Canberra Times,* the dramatic drop in coverage from before to during/ after the ACP is testament to the impact of the Black Saturday bushfires. These disastrous fires occurred in the state of Victoria at the same time as the main meeting in Canberra, and they dominated media coverage through the duration of the ACP.[20] Although the ACP participants themselves stayed focused on their task at hand—even while following the news closely during breaks in their deliberations—the media found itself unable to divide its attention and stayed focused on Victoria. This alone explains why the ACP was more present in the news before it had actually "happened" than during or after the Canberra meetings.

The bushfires drew away media attention that could have scrutinized more thoroughly the ACP process. Such attention, in turn, could have familiarized the public with what "having a Citizens' Parliament" actually means—a gap in understanding that would have consequences for public discussions of deliberation in Australia the following year (see chapter 20). Procedural reporting would have helped readers understand the distinct analytic, social, and decision-making aspects of the ACP.[21] Not surprisingly in light of the above findings, there was not much coverage that made reference to any of these aspects. Our coding of the ACP coverage found not a single mention of its analytic process (i.e., the substance and rigor of the Canberra deliberations). Likewise, only three articles (or 4.1 percent of all) examined the social aspects of the Canberra deliberation (e.g., the respect or listening that occurred). The aspect that received the most print coverage was the decision making that the ACP was supposed to enable. This received mention in six articles (or 8.2 percent of all). In sum, scant mediated meta-deliberation occurred with regard to the quality of the main deliberations of the ACP.

The Victoria bushfires also effectively precluded a substantive and sustained debate in the media on political issues for which the ACP could have served as a convenient peg. As we argued earlier, deliberative events have the potential to motivate media coverage that takes a step back to reflect on the state of the political system as much as on the benefits and challenges of particular deliberative initiatives. Although we did not code for this, our reading of the ACP print news coverage indicates that, in spite of external events, this happened to a limited extent, with some articles presenting the inclusive goals of deliberative politics and others referring to common criticisms of the current political system, particularly adversarial party politics.[22]

Another desirable outcome of deliberative events is providing inroads for substantive media debate of policy issues. In the case of the ACP, citizens debated issues with a procedural focus (i.e., how Australia's political system could be strengthened to serve citizens better). To what extent were the ACP's answers, available in the condensed form of a six-item list of recommendations, present in the media? In the end, the recommendations that came from the Canberra deliberations received limited coverage. About one in four articles (28.4 percent, $n = 21$) made reference to at least one ACP recommendation, but only four of those were published during or after the main event in Canberra, which means that even the substantive coverage of the ACP was largely of a prospective nature. This coverage often transpired in previews of the ACP that portrayed the Citizen Parliamentarian representing the newspaper's area of circulation. For example, one typical report stated that the regional representative would be presenting a proposal to change the system of voting used in Australian elections.[23]

Figure 19.1 shows the number of items in the printed news media making reference to and/or giving explications of the top six ACP recommendations.[24] Perhaps counterintuitively, the ranking of items on the list did not match their salience in the media. The second-ranked recommendation ("Empower citizens to participate in politics through education") was by far

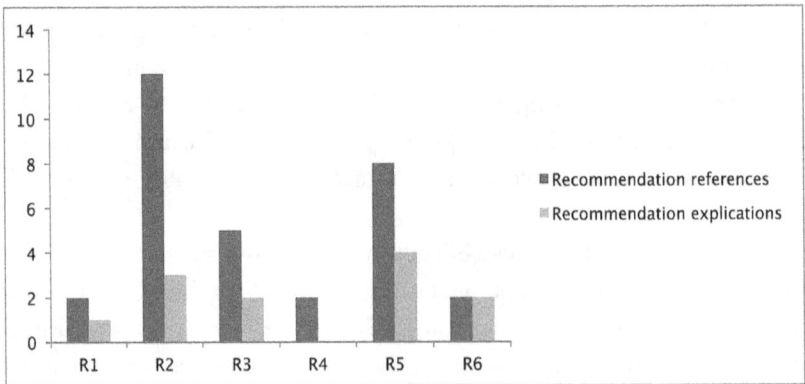

FIGURE 19.1   References to and explications of ACP recommendations in Australian print media
NOTE: Figure shows absolute number of articles that made reference to the final ACP recommendations and/or explicated them (N = 74). R1: Reduce duplication between levels of government by harmonizing laws across state boundaries; R2: Empower citizens to participate in politics through education; R3: Accountability regarding political promises and procedures for redress; R4: Empower citizens to participate in politics through community engagement; R5: Change the electoral system to Optional Preferential Voting; R6: Youth engagement in politics.

the most referenced one, though it did not receive much more explication than most others. Looking at the content of the articles, this pattern often reflects journalists' inclinations to connect this recommendation to the participatory/civic educational nature of the ACP itself. Indeed, several references to a need for educational empowerment were made in articles published before the final ACP meeting. The second most commonly referenced and most often explicated was the fifth-ranked ACP recommendation ("Change the electoral system to Optional Preferential Voting"), a much more concrete—and possibly contentious—item on the list of proposed changes. In sum, we see a tendency to report on ACP recommendations that relate to the event itself or bear a potential for conflict.

One other angle of the visibility of the ACP concerns whose voice appears as a source in the articles. Most articles mentioning the ACP cited someone other than the journalist (83.8 percent), but articles relied mostly on a single source (60.8 percent of all articles). The right-hand side of figure 19.2 shows that, distinguishing among five categories of sources (participants, organizers, politicians, experts, and nonparticipating citizens), we find almost no range of voices in individual ACP articles; only 23.0 percent of articles feature sources from more than one of our categories. Put another way, there was almost no comparison or contrast of perspectives on the ACP among sources *within* individual articles.

What did the pattern look like *between* articles? Was there considerable diversity of sources cited? Figure 19.2 shows that Citizen Parliamentarians were by far the most frequently cited group in the articles related to the ACP: nearly two-thirds of articles (63.5 percent) relied on participants as sources. One in every four articles (27.0 percent) quoted one or more orga-

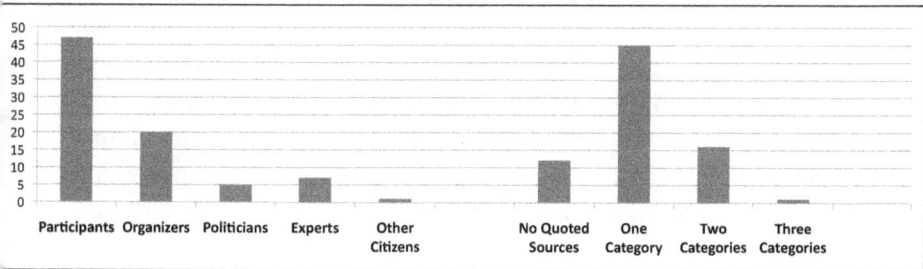

FIGURE 19.2   Types and diversity of sources in ACP articles in Australian print media

NOTE: Figure shows absolute number of articles that used at least one source from the respective category (left) and absolute number of articles using sources from no, one, or more than one source category (right) (N = 74).

nizers. By contrast, politicians, experts, and non-ACP lay citizens played marginal roles in the mediated meta-deliberation on the event. The coverage largely revolved around those who had a direct role in the ACP itself, giving them some room to articulate their views. With the exception of one article about them—Prime Minister Rudd's "Sorry Speech" that made passing reference to the ACP—citizens not involved with the ACP were not given any voice in the coverage at all.

Mediated Assessment of the ACP

Going beyond asking *what* was reported to asking *how* the ACP was represented in that reportage, we found that the overall tone of the coverage was largely positive: more than half of the articles presented a favorable picture of the ACP (54.1 percent); many remained neutral (37.8 percent); and only six articles (8.1 percent) presented an ambivalent view. There were no unambiguously negative reports on the event.

A sizable share of the articles (25.7 percent) even advocated more or less explicitly for the ACP as a process worth pursuing in the future. Most articles, however, remained silent in this regard. More notably, almost none of the articles included a prediction that the ACP would have a real impact on Australia's governing structures. (On the other hand, we found in the coverage no predictions of zero impact either.)

Finally, we looked at how the mediated deliberation represented the capabilities or intellect of ACP participants, as well as the Australian public at large. Aside from one ambivalent article,[25] none of the reporting made a reference to the Citizen Parliamentarians' competence. One in five articles (19.2 percent), however, referred positively to the capabilities of ordinary citizens in general to engage directly in policy making. Only one (1.4 percent) portrayed Australian citizens as incapable of deliberating about complex policy, and this came in relation to Prime Minister Gillard's 2010 plan to convene a similar event, a Citizens' Assembly, on climate change (see chapter 20).[26] Overall, therefore, the coverage appeared mildly favorable toward the idea of further citizen involvement in Australian policy making.

Putting these pieces together, we find a depiction of the ACP as a lovely but toothless tiger, a charming initiative that the coverage kept insulated from the real world of politics it was designed to have an impact on. Several articles (21.6 percent) went at least far enough to support the vague real-world goal of increasing the political engagement and participation of citizens. Generally, however, meta-deliberation of the ACP shied away from pondering the worth and weight of its substantive contributions.

Conclusion

Earlier, we explained why mediated meta-deliberation is an essential component of a deliberative political system.[27] Our foray into mediated meta-deliberation in the case of the ACP now puts us in a better position to speculate about the four potential impacts of this case of mediated meta-deliberation on the public and public debate.

Our first conclusion is that the scant visibility granted to the ACP probably failed to *raise awareness* of the outcomes it produced, particularly the final recommendations, simply because the event and recommendations received limited coverage. Moreover, the coverage it received was heavily skewed toward the lead-up to the Canberra meetings and was therefore unable to report on the final recommendations.

Our second conclusion, however, is that the coverage the ACP received had considerable potential to *stimulate interest* in inclusive politics and deliberative variants in particular. Given the positive overall tone of the coverage and the frequent connection to generic demands for more citizen participation in democratic processes, it is likely that foreshadowing the ACP aroused curiosity in many readers about what such an event might produce by way of outcomes.

Third, we conclude that, given the prospective character of most reporting and especially the absence of any statements about the efficacy of the process, mediated meta-deliberation on the ACP was unlikely to generate *support for deliberative politics* per se. Had favorable reporting continued at a steady clip after the ACP, it might have given curious readers a better sense of how such an event might transform Australian politics.

Finally, we conclude that coverage of the ACP worked to *promote deliberation as a common standard* for politics only insofar as democratic deliberation implicates generic demands for citizen participation. The deliberative processes and standards implemented in the ACP go well beyond mere participation, and the almost complete lack of reporting on them constituted a missed opportunity for mediated meta-deliberation to judge the soundness of this approach for addressing future Australian political conflicts.

All of this provides new beginnings for both organizers and scholars of deliberative democracy. The ACP teaches us that practitioners should consider carefully the newsworthiness of the deliberative process. Upon completion of such analysis, it might make sense to employ media strategies that capitalize on those aspects of a deliberative event that have stronger appeal to media outlets. In the case of the ACP, the experience of ordinary citizens received relative prominence in journalistic accounts of the event, indicating that what was newsworthy here was the inclusion of ordinary citizens.

An effective media strategy could also highlight the clearest political or policy conflicts at play in the issues deliberated upon at the event. But this would be a delicate task that would require close work with journalists that sensitizes them to the rationales and goals of deliberation in relation to the standard conflict-oriented frames through which we understand "normal" party politics.

This case study, however, stands as but one data point in what we hope becomes a larger body of work on mediated meta-deliberation. Any single study has the limitation of its particularities, but this case may prove unique in the degree to which external events took over the news cycle just as the ACP came to its climax. The disastrous Victoria bushfires were an immediate and compelling distraction, in addition to a global economic crisis that was already looming by the time the Citizen Parliamentarians arrived in Canberra. Generalizations to similar events in Australia or other places must be drawn with caution, given the small amount of coverage that was generated and the limited set of content categories we employed. Further, although we provided analysis of news coverage, we do not have the data necessary to understand how the public responded to that news coverage, and future research could make good use of survey data coupled with a finer-grained time series of news coverage.

More modestly, we simply hope that our case study serves as a stepping-stone toward continued research on mediated meta-deliberation in other contexts. We look forward to discovering the commonalities across cases and learning the particular circumstances under which journalists use the outcomes of deliberative events to confront the assumptions and stances of both lay citizens and political elites, thereby increasing an event's "deliberative impact."[28] We also hope that future research will show the full variety of meta-deliberation that occurs in different media outlets, in print and television as well as more interactive online settings. How might such meta-deliberation alter the public's sentiments toward policy making, deliberation, and public participation? Questions such as these—answered across different social, cultural, and situational contexts—open the way for a new research program that has only just begun.

NOTES

1. For perspectives extending the deliberation concept to mass-mediated communication, see John Gastil, *Political Communication and Deliberation* (Thousand Oaks, Calif.: Sage, 2008); Jürgen Habermas, "Political Communication in Media Society: Does Democracy Still Enjoy an Epistemic Dimension? The Impact of Normative Theory on Empirical Research," *Communication Theory* 16 (2006): 411–26.

2. Jürgen Habermas, *Between Facts and Norms: Contributions to a Discourse Theory of Law and Democracy* (Cambridge, Mass.: MIT Press, 1996); Gastil, *Political Communication and Deliberation*; Hartmut Wessler, "Investigating Deliberativeness Comparatively," *Political Communication* 25 (2008): 1–22.

3. For examples, see Benjamin I. Page, *Who Deliberates? Mass Media in Modern Democracy* (Chicago: University of Chicago Press, 1996); Dennis Pilon, "Investigating Media as a Deliberative Space: Newspaper Opinions About Voting Systems in the 2007 Ontario Provincial Referendum," *Canadian Political Science Review* 3, no. 3 (2009): 1–23; W. Lance Bennett, Victor W. Pickard, David P. Iozzi, Carl L. Schroeder, Taso Lagos, and C. Evans Caswell, "Managing the Public Sphere: Journalistic Construction of the Great Globalization Debate," *Journal of Communication* 54 (2004): 437–55; Xiang Zhou, Yuen-Ying Chan, and Zhen-Mei Peng, "Deliberativeness of Online Political Discussion: A Content Analysis of the *Guangzhou Daily* Website," *Journalism Studies* 9 (2008): 759–70; Rousiley C. M. Maia, "Mediated Deliberation: The 2005 Referendum for Banning Firearm Sales in Brazil," *International Journal of Press/Politics* 14 (2009): 313–34.

4. See the system-level perspectives introduced in Gastil, *Political Communication and Deliberation*, and Habermas, "Political Communication in Media Society." For two examples of perspectives focusing on deliberation occurring within individual media, see Wessler, "Investigating Deliberativeness Comparatively"; Todd Graham and Tamara Witschge, "In Search of Online Deliberation: Towards a New Method for Examining the Quality of Online Discussions," *Communications* 28 (2003): 173–204.

5. Dennis F. Thompson, "Deliberative Democratic Theory and Empirical Political Science," *Annual Review of Political Science* 11 (2008): 497–520; John Dryzek, "Democracy and Earth System Governance," paper presented at the Amsterdam Conference on the Human Dimensions of Global Environmental Change, "Earth System Governance: People, Places and the Planet," Amsterdam, the Netherlands, December 2–4, 2009.

6. Amy Gutmann and Dennis F. Thompson, *Why Deliberative Democracy?* (Princeton: Princeton University Press, 2004); Thompson, "Deliberative Democratic Theory."

7. Eike Mark Rinke and Hartmut Wessler, "Comparing the Deliberativeness of Television News in Germany, the U.S., and Russia," paper presented at the annual conference of the International Communication Association, Political Communication Division, Boston, Mass., May 26–30, 2011.

8. See Gastil, *Political Communication and Deliberation*, 43–46.

9. See, e.g., Mark E. Warren and Hilary Pearse, eds., *Designing Deliberative Democracy: The British Columbia Citizens' Assembly* (Cambridge: Cambridge University Press, 2008) on the Citizens' Assembly; John Gastil and Katie Knobloch, *Evaluation Report to the Oregon State Legislature on the 2010 Oregon Citizens' Initiative Review* (Salem: Oregon House Rules Committee, 2010) on the Citizens' Initiative Review; or Boaventura de Sousa Santos, "Participatory Budgeting in Porto Alegre: Toward a Redistributive Democracy," *Politics and Society* 26 (1998): 461–510 on Participatory Budgeting; Robert E. Goodin and John S. Dryzek, "Deliberative

Impacts: The Macro-political Uptake of Mini-publics," *Politics and Society* 34 (2006): 219–44; James S. Fishkin and Robert C. Luskin, "Bringing Deliberation to the Democratic Dialogue," in *The Poll with a Human Face: The National Issues Convention Experiment in Political Communication*, ed. Maxwell McCombs and Amy Reynolds (Mahwah, N.J.: Lawrence Erlbaum, 1999), 3–38.

10. For similar arguments, see James S. Fishkin, "Consulting the Public Through Deliberative Polling," *Journal of Policy Analysis and Management* 22 (2003): 128–33; Archon Fung, "Recipes for Public Spheres: Eight Institutional Design Choices and Their Consequences," *Journal of Political Philosophy* 11 (2003): 338–67.

11. For accounts of the importance of cultural foundations for public deliberation, see Andreas Hepp and Hartmut Wessler, "Politische Diskurskulturen: Überlegungen zur empirischen Erklärung segmentierter europäischer Öffentlichkeit," *Medien & Kommunikationswissenschaft* 57 (2009): 174–97; Bernhard Peters, *Public Deliberation and Public Culture: The Writings of Bernhard Peters, 1993–2005* (Basingstoke, UK: Palgrave Macmillan, 2008); also Henry E. Brady, James S. Fishkin, and Robert C. Luskin, "Informed Public Opinion About Foreign Policy: The Uses of Deliberative Polling," *Brookings Review* 21, no. 3 (2003): 16–19.

12. The distinction between "inside" and "outside" strategies in deliberative event planning is introduced in Peter Levine, Archon Fung, and John Gastil, "Future Directions for Public Deliberation," *Journal of Public Deliberation* 1, no. 1 (2005): art. 3, accessed January 16, 2012, http://services.bepress.com/jpd/vol1/iss1/art3.

13. See Lawrence LeDuc, "Electoral Reform and Direct Democracy in Canada: When Citizens Become Involved," *West European Politics* 34 (2011): 551–67.

14. Wessler calls these "input" and "throughput," respectively; he also identifies a third dimension (the "outcome") that is not part of our analysis. Wessler, "Investigating Deliberativeness Comparatively." For an account of one specific outcome of the ACP, its consequences for public discourse in subsequent Australian elections, see chapter 20.

15. There are contrary views about whether deliberation scholarship should focus on questions of who deliberates (e.g., Page, *Who Deliberates?*) or what ideas and topics are deliberated upon in public. See ibid.; Wessler, "Investigating Deliberativeness Comparatively." We elude this dichotomy altogether and prefer a more comprehensive approach that takes both aspects of mediated deliberation into account.

16. Generally, throughput analyses in the mediated-deliberation framework focus on justification, rebuttal, and civility as assessment criteria, since these are particularly important from a deliberative point of view. While this is reflected in our other work, we focused here on the more substantive question of tone in coverage, given our aim to contribute to a broader ex post assessment of the ACP.

17. There are some downsides to relying on digital news archives for research. In particular, they can present an incomplete account of the actual printed news coverage since they are often stripped off newswire articles. See J. H. Snider and Kenneth Janda, "Newspapers in Bytes and Bits: Limitations of Electronic Databases for Content Analysis," paper presented at the annual meeting of the American Political Science Association, Boston, Mass., September 3–7, 1998; David A. Weaver and Bruce Bimber, "Finding News Stories: A Comparison of Searches Using LexisNexis and Google News," *Journalism and Mass Communication Quarterly* 85 (2008): 515–30. However, this is less of a problem for us as articles reporting the ACP are unlikely to have come primarily from wire services, due to the characteristics of the event. The search also included items disseminated by the Australian national news agency, AAP. The query used to search the databases was (Citizens' Parliament). The searches covered all articles published by August 31, 2011. Inspection of the resulting items and other coverage yielded that this query had good discriminatory power to capture all of the ACP coverage available.

18. Based on circulation figures for the second quarter of 2011. See Newspaper Works, "Circulation—June 2011 Quarter: Australian Printed Newspaper Circulations Decline in Worsening Retail Conditions," August 12, 2011, Newspaper Works, accessed January 16, 2012, http://www.thenewspaperworks.com.au/news/circulation-june-2011-quarter/.

19. A small number of ACP articles were published in multiple newspapers. These articles were only counted once.

20. John Dryzek, "The Australian Citizens' Parliament: A World First," *Journal of Public Deliberation* 5, no. 1 (2009): art. 9, accessed January 16, 2012, http://services.bepress.com/jpd/vol5/iss1/art9.

21. For an exposition of this analytic distinction for the evaluation of deliberative events, see John Gastil, Katie Knobloch, and Meghan B. Kelly, "Evaluating Deliberative Public Events and Projects," in *Democracy in Motion: Evaluating the Practice and Impact of Deliberative Civic Engagement,* ed. Tina Nabatchi, John Gastil, Matt Leighninger, and G. Michael Weiksner (Oxford: Oxford University Press, 2012), 205–30.

22. Two examples are Robin Brown, "Power, and Policymaking, to the People," *Canberra Times,* September 7, 2010; John Warhurst, "Power of Non-party People," *Canberra Times,* February 12, 2009.

23. Kirsten Leiminger, "Citizens to Outline Views in Canberra," *Journal* (Dandenong, VIC), January 18, 2009.

24. We counted thematic references; that is, they needed not necessarily mention the recommendation itself but had to refer to the policy goal it formulated.

25. Joanne McCarthy, "Grassroots Government," *Newcastle Herald* (Newcastle, NSW), January 29, 2009.

26. "Climate Assembly Valuable, Says Expert," *AAP News,* July 23, 2010.

27. Gutmann and Thompson, *Why Deliberative Democracy?*; Thompson, "Deliberative Democratic Theory."

28. Goodin and Dryzek, "Deliberative Impacts."

20

HOW *NOT* TO INTRODUCE DELIBERATIVE DEMOCRACY:
THE 2010 CITIZENS' ASSEMBLY ON CLIMATE CHANGE PROPOSAL

Lyn Carson

During the 2010 federal election campaign in Australia, climate change surfaced as a major issue. Prime Minister Julia Gillard announced a Citizens' Assembly on Climate Change (CACC) involving 150 randomly selected citizens.

Those of us who had worked on the Australian Citizens' Parliament (ACP) one year earlier wondered whether this could be the moment in history when Australian politics took a deliberative turn, perhaps inspired by the ACP itself.[1] That hope quickly faded. This chapter explains why and, in doing so, uses the Gillard case to illustrate seven different errors one can make when proposing a deliberative political reform.

Context of the CACC Announcement and Reaction

On June 24, 2010, the Australian Labor Party ousted its leader, Prime Minister Kevin Rudd, and replaced him with Julia Gillard, who became Australia's first female prime minister.[2] Among other problems, there had been some controversy during Rudd's tenure about his retreat from an emissions trading scheme to address climate change, especially since he had earlier described climate change as "Australia's great moral challenge."

The development of national economic policy in response to climate change had been a tortuous affair in Australia, one of the strongest economies in the world, underpinned by natural resource extraction and coal

power generation.[3] The Copenhagen Summit had passed in disappointment, with Australia committing to only a 5 percent reduction in emissions
by 2020. The industrial and political forces pitted against government
intervention with a carbon emissions trading scheme (ETS) had been
relentless.

Opinion polls showed strong public acceptance for an ETS, but a vocal
minority of individuals, motivated by climate-change skepticism and free-
market ideology, spurned any such government intervention. In spite of
this contention, even within each major party, they came close to legislative
agreement on an ETS, only to fall away for various reasons. The Greens, for
example, found the version too compromised to support.

With that failure, the government had the trigger to take the electorate to
a double-dissolution election, that is, dissolving both houses of Parliament
at the same time, but ignored that opportunity as it neared the end of its
term of office. At the time of the election, the government had deferred the
possible introduction of ETS legislation until 2013, blaming the recalci-
trance of the Opposition.

Thus, this issue remained unresolved when Gillard began the election
campaign just one month into her tenure as prime minister. Not even a
week had passed in the federal election campaign when Gillard took action,
announcing on Friday, July 23, 2010, that she wished to convene a deliberative Citizens' Assembly on Climate Change (CACC).

It would be a monumental understatement to say that the CACC announcement failed to attract an enthusiastic response. Instead, it met skepticism—
from Opposition parties, media commentators, industry, environmentalists,
and even the wider community. It is edifying to analyze the reasons for this
collective resistance, as well as the strategic errors that likely caused—or at
least contributed to the negative reception.

The most common critique was that the CACC appeared as yet another
delaying tactic. Though Gillard simultaneously announced a number of
other policy decisions related to climate change, some believed the CACC
would slow down the progress that had been made toward a comprehensive ETS policy on climate change. What happened next showed not only
that critics rejected citizen deliberation on climate change but that they also
had little interest in deliberating *about* such deliberation.

Australian political philosopher Tim Soutphommasane has written,
"The real test of a democracy is not whether it can overcome its disagreements, but how it conducts itself in light of them. The manner in which our
open, honest national conversation proceeds will say a good deal about our

democratic maturity."[4] Albeit in the pressure-cooker environment of an election campaign, the vitriolic discourse that followed Gillard's CACC announcement indicates that Australia's democracy may not be as grown up as Soutphommasane would wish. Political columnists fly with creative ridicule without regard to the facts. Involving citizens in policy making was likened to witchcraft and brainwashing. In one pundit's view, the CACC was a

> melange of bewitching hokery-pokery and beguiling flummery . . . The chosen ones will be subjected to a "rigorous process" to establish consensus, Gillard said. After 12 months of duchessing, subtle bullying and brainwashing, what kind of consensus will materialise? . . . [B]y what sinister means are we to be more "deeply" persuaded? . . . C. S. Lewis would recognise her ploy of beguiling the masses with endless supplies of Turkish delight, just as her lookalike, actress Tilda Swinton, does as the White Witch, Jadis, who froze Narnia in the Hundred Years Winter.[5]

Even some of those who wanted to see deliberative political reforms succeed in Australia took a dim view. Immediately after Gillard's first comments to the media on CACC, I received an e-mail from a public participation practitioner and colleague: "I think Julia Gillard has set back the cause of citizens' assemblies as a politically useful exercise by years, if not decades." Indeed, Gillard's announcement enhanced the cynicism in the public discourse against which advocates of Australian public engagement must now push.

Eight Errors in the Promotion of Deliberative Democracy

It is unfortunate that this high-profile effort to bring public engagement into the politically charged arena of climate change was executed so poorly. The bulk of this section will show how the adverse reaction stemmed, in part, from several key miscalculations, confusions, and errors in the CACC's introduction. Afterward, I will offer some words about the need for public engagement scholars and practitioners to gain more traction in their efforts to raise public awareness and appreciation of deliberative democracy.

Error No. 1: Divergence from Deliberative Principles

Despite the critiques contained in this book about the Australian Citizens' Parliament (ACP), this does not detract from the necessity for deliberative public participation to inform and monitor public-policy formation in contexts that are contentious and long-term. This stance is in itself contentious, as it runs contrary to the prevailing paradigm of representative democracy that conventionally grants authority to elected politicians and the public-service executive. However, designing public-engagement processes that invite statistically representative or diverse samples of people into facilitated policy deliberation has been shown to be effective.[6]

The recommendations arising from deliberative processes are thoughtful and reasonable. They attract support from the wider community if that community is aware of, and has confidence in, the robustness of the process. This means they must be procedurally fair. A public deliberation like a citizens' assembly (CA) must possess certain attributes and these have been canvassed elsewhere in this book and need not be repeated here.

During the election campaign, Julia Gillard was advised by Tom Bentley,[7] former director of the nonprofit Demos think tank in the UK. Bentley was the prime mover for this announcement. He has been an active advocate of institutionalized public engagement and grassroots participation. In 2005 he wrote, "[T]he essential lesson of democratic history is that unless the maintenance of political structures is combined with deepening cultures of democratic participation, democracy will fall apart. The solution is not simply to create more direct democracy, or to set up an ever-growing array of consultative processes divorced from the exercise of real power, but to embed both these principles—direct and deliberative—in the range of institutions through which people can express their concerns, their needs and their identities."[8]

There is ample academic literature about the theoretical benefits of *deliberative democracy*—a representative legislature and public administration that is informed by officially sanctioned processes of public deliberation (analogous to juries that determine trial verdicts in a judicial system).[9] But like most theorists, Bentley did not advance how a deliberative democracy should actually be introduced.

Error No. 2: Commentators and the Public Did Not Understand the CA Process

Aside from this fundamental theoretical flaw, the remainder of errors amounted to a series of more specific conceptual confusions and tactical errors. At the top of this list, Gillard's staff provided no information package to describe the CACC process to the media. Commentators were left to make incorrect and damaging presumptions based on poor engagement practices in the past, thus misinforming the public. So a CACC was repeatedly discounted on false premises.

Gillard inappropriately set the agenda while omitting details about how the CACC would actually work. Climate Change Minister Penny Wong added to the confusion, never explaining a CA but stating, "It's a way in which we ensure that we give a voice to ordinary Australians."[10] CAs should canvass a wide range of perspectives.[11] Wong undermined the promise of "a wide range of advocates" to inform the CA. When asked "whether the assembly would be addressed by climate skeptics," Wong said, "[I]f they're credible scientists."[12] Gillard had a view that a CA involves passive participants, being consulted.[13] At its best, it would build consensus. At its worst, Gillard positioned herself with "I will lead the debate and lead the advocacy of our approach."[14]

The CACC process was described variously as a national focus group, a committee, or a Deliberative Poll.[15] This led to knee-jerk reactions like the demand of the Food and Grocery Council that the CACC "include industry representatives."[16] The executive director of a conservative think tank suggested that "we'll be doing climate policy on Facebook next."[17] He said that it was possibly "the single worst idea that has ever been floated by an elected government in a federal election."

The media canvassed criticisms of it almost exclusively.[18] This happened through their choice of opinion pieces, news coverage, letters to the editor, television panelists, and news interviewees. Damning the CACC became a blood sport. Journalists called it "risible" and "pathetic,"[19] and tabloid slogans dominated, predicting "squabbling and seething" and that "only idiots" would dedicate a year to a CA. Another reported that people consider it "a bit of nonsense."[20] Headlines described it as a "gabfest." Gillard was accused of engaging in "gimmicks," and one columnist claimed that "the idea of consensus is the great hoax."[21] The Opposition's spokesperson, Greg Hunt, thought it "farcical," "national policy by lottery," with participants "chosen from the phone book," adding that it was "2020 Summit meets Copenhagen conference."[22]

Letters to the editor showed no more mercy. A sampling includes these reactions: "May I suggest the following makeup of the citizens' assembly: 30 coal industry executives and workers; 30 members of the finance industry; 30 people from suburbs known as 'aspirational'; 30 farmers. It would be interesting to know what the consensus would be"; "[I]f you don't have a clue, form a committee. Turn your thoughts to the 2020 summit, at which 1000 of the smartest Australians were called together by a different prime minister with much fanfare to determine our future. Pure spin and no substance. Nothing has changed"; "Julia Gillard needs to be advised that the Federal Parliament is the elected citizens' assembly of the Australian people. If she is unable to convince that group she should move on."[23]

Error No. 3: Expressing a Desire for "Deep Consensus" (Perhaps Rhetorically)

It is unclear what the Labor Party election strategists thought that a CACC could achieve. Ideally, it was to produce a policy that everyone could at least live with and that could survive successive election cycles through a process perceived as relatively nonpolitical.

Since Gillard always spoke of the CACC in the same breath as "building a community consensus," one academic noted that CAs do not educate the wider community and do not promote consensus among the general public: "Citizens' assemblies work fine—in theory" and "Worthy as a citizens' assembly might be, if the purpose of this proposal is to build consensus, then much more needs to be done."[24] This does ignore evidence from the British Columbian experience that onlookers trusted the judgment of fellow citizens and voted accordingly, so education and consensus building *can* occur.[25]

However, it is true that a CA itself is not designed to necessarily reach consensus among CA participants. It is designed to explore and establish the extent of common ground, creating space for preferences to shift but allowing for minority views to emerge and be retained. If coupled with comprehensive media coverage, it *could* stimulate a national conversation. Unfortunately, environmental activists who would benefit from a more informed public were imploring, "It's time to stop having complex conversations and start implementing some simple solutions."[26]

Error No. 4: Announcing the CACC as a "Policy" During an Election Campaign

The CACC was not a policy, and hardly a "centerpiece." It was a process issue. There could have been a broad policy announcement, for example, *institutionalized public engagement,* that would go beyond the issue of climate policy to all government activity. Announcing one process, the CA, meant that it became lost in all the electioneering.

Perhaps the government really had so little to offer after the deferment of its ETS policy that this was just a creative exercise, not expected to fly, but signaled so that it would not come as a surprise later. One journalist noted that "Labor MPs are deeply embarrassed by Julia Gillard's 150-person citizens' assembly she hopes will find a consensus for climate change. Several of them are deliberately downplaying it and instead focusing on Labor's other environmental promises. *The Australian* [newspaper] has spoken to several Labor MPs who privately concede the idea has gone down 'like a lead balloon' and has hurt, rather than helped, Labor's climate change credentials."[27]

Error No. 5: Not Recognizing the Government Itself as a Stakeholder

The Labor Party had earlier advocated an ETS, namely the Carbon Pollution Reduction Scheme, which failed to gain full legislative support. During the election, the language shifted to "putting a price on carbon," so they remained fully committed to advancing a "carbon-based economy." Rather than providing the CACC with an unbiased agenda, it was clear that the CACC's task was to consider the method of pricing, but not whether carbon should be priced at all. Participants in the CACC cannot be coercively or politically "educated" to adopt a government position.

A CA should never be convened by a stakeholder in an issue. More work should have been put into the method (and to the way this method is communicated to the public) by which the CA would be given transparent independence from the government and all other stakeholders.

Therefore, the Carbon Pollution Reduction Scheme should have been one of many proposals that the CACC could have examined, not the *basis* for its work. People should be encouraged to push any barrows they like before a CA—push them all into the room, and let participants decide.

Error No. 6: A Confused Relationship Between Political Leadership and
Public Engagement

Most of the caustic commentary was about "failure of leadership." Deconstructing the commentary, one finds an almost universal expectation that politicians should exercise power in a liberal-democratic tradition that provides them with that mandate. Gillard fell into the same trap by saying that she would "lead the CA," which is inappropriate. That the CACC would "merely" inform the politicians is derided; the expectation by those who design such processes is that a CA should directly determine, or at least genuinely influence, policy.

"We already have a citizens assembly—a democratically elected Parliament," said one journalist,[28] echoed in dozens of comments in online forums and Twitter. The Greens and a number of political commentators also ran this line. But Parliament is not descriptively representative, as the CACC would be. It does not represent the full range of social perspectives on complex issues. Parliament had also been the impediment to change, since both Coalition conservatives and Greens refused to pass the Carbon Pollution Reduction Scheme. Parliament has become so adversarial and polarized that approving climate-change mechanisms is vexing. At the time of writing (July 2011), several independent MPs (unaffiliated with a political party) hold the balance of power. Along with the Greens, they are struggling to create a carbon-pricing scheme that works to reduce pollution without significantly raising the cost of living.

Back in 2010 Ben Cubby noted about the CA that "[d]ebate has deteriorated to the point where 150 unelected, randomly selected Australians that would sit in a Gillard government 'citizens' assembly' are probably more likely to see the issue clearly and reach a consensus than Federal Parliament."[29]

It is unlikely that there will ever be a consensus on this issue. Two Australian political leaders have already fallen over it—former leader of the Opposition Malcolm Turnbull and former prime minister Kevin Rudd. Climate change has been described as a diabolical policy problem for good reason: there are political costs; the science will always be contested; economists disagree about the best way to price carbon; and there are inevitable financial costs for all. Nobody likes costs, especially when imposed by the government.

Political leaders avoid being responsible for imposing such costs, but ultimately must do so and thereby earn the ire of voters. As one journalist said, "Labor knows a carbon price is inevitable. So do many Liberals. They just aren't quite ready to unwrap this policy in front of the electorate."[30]

The Opposition was either unable to conceive of public engagement as a kind of stewardship or took glee in goading the Labor Party to try imposing costs on a resistant electorate. Thus, the Opposition spokesperson on climate change described the CACC as "a massive failure of leadership."[31] A journalist wrote that Gillard is "the archetypical professional prime ministerial procrastinator."[32] A business leader stated that, whereas Labor's commitment to building community consensus was constructive, "in this complex policy area, long-term solutions that balance Australia's economic and environment considerations will only come through strong political leadership."[33]

However, leadership is easy if everyone agrees or if the leader does what the stakeholder wants. Involving voters in difficult decisions is one way to diffuse that anger by sharing ownership of those decisions. Furthermore, experts alone will not resolve this issue. Diabolical policy problems require more than facts; they involve values, and the solution rests on the willingness of citizens to sacrifice one value for another.

Neither bureaucrats nor technocrats alone can deal with these vexing issues. Parliaments certainly cannot. This is going to require the collective intelligence of the nation, most easily organized through miniature populations or mini-publics (and certainly not via superficial polling or focus groups; it requires public judgment, not public opinion).

Error No. 7: Failure to Explain How Citizens Can Serve as Trustworthy Deliberators

It turns out that citizens do not even trust themselves, since most apparently want elected leadership to do their job. The media either influenced voters or accurately reflected their opinion. Poll respondents firmly rejected the CACC.[34] A public radio broadcaster reported that "60 percent of Australians are unimpressed by centerpiece of climate policy, the citizens' assembly," and this was consistent with the Herald/Nielsen poll that found that only 41 percent of respondents wanted the CACC.[35]

But there is a glimmer of hope for deliberative democrats in that 41 percent figure. Surely, most of those respondents did not even know what a CA was. Imagine the level of support that might have appeared had voters been given clear information about a CA by elected representatives and the media.[36]

Following an article published online by the *Age*, one blogger stated, "You ask ignorant citizens (science illiterates), you get bad policy."[37] Letters to the editor attracted comments such as this: "I do not want a citizens' assembly of 150 rank-and-file Australians to decide the fate of Labor's climate measures on my behalf."[38] With no experience or understanding of the educational aspects of a CA, it is clearly troubling for citizens to imagine themselves into a deliberative space and the insistence on *informed* choice.

Error No. 8: Introducing Public Deliberation Much Too Late

One of the few commentators with a good understanding of the CACC gave it merit in principle, yet remained critical. "The problem with a climate change jury," he explained, "is that it is far too late in the game."[39] This perception fed the suspicion that the CACC was nothing more than a distracting stunt. It may very well have been a stunt, insofar as Labor really did not have any direct policy action prepared (and they would be lambasted for changing their mind mid-election, in any case). So strategically this was probably the best solution they could come up with. Summarizing this view, one commentator observed, "The majority of Australians will see this for what it is: a feeble attempt to defuse climate change as an election issue. But the time for talking is over; it's time for action."[40]

After hearing such criticisms from the Greens, and being aware that they had a policy of supporting CAs, I contacted a Greens MP. The response was that the Greens supported community engagement for policy development, but not on this issue at this time—the CACC was being used to delay action. This was not entirely accurate, since action had been delayed *already*. Prior to announcing the CACC, the PM had already said she would not introduce her centerpiece climate-change policy until 2013. In the interim Gillard wanted to build a public consensus on climate-change action because of the polarized, divisive nature of the debate.

I have sympathy for the Greens' position. Having codesigned a number of deliberative forums on climate change (including a large one in New South Wales involving local and state government), I have witnessed how everyday citizens think about this issue. My belief is supported by a credible four-year study "targeting more than 7000 Australians" by the Centre for the Study of Choice at the University of Technology, Sydney.[41] A clear majority wanted the government to adopt a carbon-pricing policy. Citizens are already acting in their local communities and want their governments to catch up. Unfortunately, cautious politicians are lagging behind their constituents and heeding the ghettos of like-minded people with whom they usually discuss these matters. A CA could, perhaps, help to correct that.

Improving Future Announcements

As the days passed, others tried to shore up the value of the CACC and correct the errors. Academic Carolyn Hendriks wrote, "Citizens' assemblies are tools for eliciting considered policy advice from informed citizens."[42]

The CACC should have been introduced as part of a campaign that situates public participation as a central policy platform in line with the government's own *Declaration of Open Government*,[43] which states that the Labor government "is committed to open government based on a culture of engagement." The CACC was not couched in these terms. It may not be mere coincidence that the minister responsible for this *Declaration*, Lindsay Tanner, resigned from Parliament. Maybe he lacked support for this policy direction. Perhaps his colleagues prophesized the fallout.

One of this book's editors, Ron Lubensky, offered this suggestion: "The output of a citizens' assembly will be judgments that the government can apply with confidence to satisfy and respect the broadest range of public, private and institutional interests, with a greater chance of achieving support from across the political spectrum. Provided that the government implements policies that are consistent with those judgments, the citizens' assembly adds legitimacy to those policies that will stand the test of time."[44] During a video interview with *Sydney Morning Herald* on August 13, Gillard said much the same thing—too late.[45]

Conclusion

There is a clear incompatibility between perceived leadership management imperatives and the facilitative nature of participatory governance. This is nowhere more apparent than in the worldviews expressed by the initiator of the CACC, Tom Bentley, and the PM who communicated the details. Bentley sees a future in which local people make their own decisions in sustainable self-organizing communities; Gillard is a creature of elected parliaments supported by expert policy advisors, exercising strong leadership. The two are not incompatible but are often seen, or portrayed, as such. Given this divide, deliberative democrats may have a long wait until congruence emerges between the worldviews of initiators and their political champions.

Had the CACC been announced for a less pressing issue, one that had no demonstrable mandate, such as a sustainable-population policy, would it have been supported rather than derided? I believe the legitimacy issue and the misunderstandings would persist. Not until CAs become routine will these challenges abate, along with less dependence upon strong leadership and more emphasis on collaborative governance.

Those defending Parliament have criticized it, yet defend its capabilities in contrast to a deliberative innovation involving citizens. Given the democratic deficit that exists, it seems sensible to look at ways to improve public confidence in policy making. Who has an eye on the long term—an elected politician preoccupied with electioneering or an everyday citizen without any vested interest except in his/her own future? In other words, a CA could enhance legitimacy. Excluding the public can compromise legitimacy.

Timing is everything with community engagement, and every process designer will list "timeliness" as a precondition for engagement. Always stressed is the importance of engagement occurring early in the life of a policy challenge. The government could have convened a CA when it took office in 2007. Collaborative governance was a recommendation arising from the 2020 Summit, which Prime Minister Rudd commended and then ignored. The government failed to take up the opportunity when it had the chance to introduce it well, thus avoiding the humiliation wrought by announcing a CA during an election campaign.

In 2011, an academic team in Ireland conducted a national citizens' assembly,[46] which was modeled largely on the ACP, including asking participating citizens how their system of government could be improved. Though there are significant differences between the political, social, and economic contexts of Australia and Ireland, they came up with recommendations of similar range to that of the ACP. Without the distraction of an election campaign or raging bushfires, however, they were more successful in gaining support through the media and consequently in gaining positive public interest for such national deliberative conversations.

If Tim Soutphommasane is right and the test of our democracy is in the way we conduct ourselves in the light of disagreements—resolving those intractable problems—then the future could be grim if we proceed as we have begun during this recent election campaign. Clearly, there is more work to do to educate political parties and the public about the potentials of public engagement. This is the type of work being done in local governments across Australia but rarely in federal government. A shift is needed in the public perception of democratic participation from mere voting to engagement processes that have more power than focus groups or opinion polls. This transformation would see an electorate confidently embrace collaborative, deliberative governance.

NOTES

1. Citizens' assemblies had been convened by governments elsewhere, for example, in British Columbia, Canada (2004); Ontario, Canada (2006/7); and the Netherlands (2006)—each of these on the topic of electoral reform.

2. The Australian public does not elect the national leader. Political parties determine party leadership and, therefore, the position of prime minister.

3. An earlier version of this chapter was published as Lyn Carson, "Growing Up Politically: Conducting a National Conversation on Climate Change," *APO: Australian Policy Online*, September 9, 2010, accessed January 4, 2012, http://www.apo.org.au/commentary/growing -politically-conducting-national-conversation-climate-change.

4. Tim Soutphommasane, "The Way We Disagree Will Test Our Democracy," *Australian*, July 10, 2010.

5. Miranda Devine, "PM's So Sure Bob's Your Uncle," *Sydney Morning Herald*, July 24–25, 2010, weekend edition.

6. John Gastil and Peter Levine, eds., *The Deliberative Democracy Handbook: Strategies for Effective Civic Engagement in the Twenty-First Century* (San Francisco: Jossey-Bass, 2005).

7. Michelle Grattan, "Wily Wonk Devised PM Gob Starter," *Age* (Melbourne), July 28, 2010.

8. Tom Bentley, *Everyday Democracy: Why We Get the Politicians We Deserve* (London: Demos, 2005), 22, accessed January 4, 2012, http://www.demos.co.uk/files/everydaydemocracy .pdf.

9. See, e.g., Gastil and Levine, *Deliberative Democracy Handbook*, and John S. Dryzek with Simon Niemeyer, *Foundations and Frontiers of Deliberative Governance* (Oxford: Oxford University Press, 2010).

10. Australian Associated Press, "FED: Labor's Climate Policy Attacked," *AAP Newsfeed*, July 23, 2010.

11. James Bohman, "Democratising the Global Order: From Communicative Freedom to Communicative Power," *Review of International Studies* 36 (2010): 431–47.

12. Grattan, "Wily Wonk Devised PM Gob Starter."

13. Kerry O'Brien, "Gillard's Feisty New Direction," *7:30 Report*, ABC, August 3, 2010.

14. Julia Gillard (speech, University of Queensland, Brisbane, Australia, July 23, 2010), quoted in Lenore Taylor, "Gillard Seeks Citizens' Group on ETS Policy," *Age* (Melbourne), July 23, 2010.

15. George Megalogenis called it "a national focus group," then confused it with the Deliberative Poll on the republic ("Citizens, It's Up to PM to Talk the Talk—ELECTION 2010," *Weekend Australian*, July 24–25, 2010). Lenore Taylor called it a "committee" ("New Policy, Same Old Delay on Carbon Price Scheme," *Sydney Morning Herald*, July 23, 2010).

16. Chief Executive Kate Carnell's comments can be found in ABC News, "Industry Wants a Seat at Citizens' Assembly," July 24, 2010, accessed January 4, 2012, http://www.abc .net.au/news/stories/2010/07/24/2963071.htm.

17. Richard Denniss, executive director, Australia Institute, quoted in Australian Associated Press, "FED: Labor's Climate Policy Attacked."

18. To be fair, ABC Radio National's *Life Matters* program on July 30, 2010 ("Talkback: Do You Want to Be in Charge?," accessed January 4, 2012, http://www.abc.net.au/rn/life matters/stories/2010/2967459.htm), devoted sixty minutes to a balanced discussion about civic participation, culminating in the last twenty-five minutes focused on the citizens' assembly.

19. Glenn Milne, on *The Drum*, ABC News 24 (Television), July 29, 2010, 6:20 p.m.

20. Michelle Grattan, on *Breakfast Program*, ABC Radio National, July 26, 2010.

21. Paul Kelly, "Labor Can't Be Serious About Citizens Plan," *Weekend Australian*, July 24–25, 2010.

22. Greg Hunt, on *Breakfast Program*, ABC Radio National, July 27, 2010; Greg Hunt, quoted in Australian Associated Press, "FED: Labor's Climate Policy Attacked." The Australia 2020 Summit was an event convened in 2008 by Prime Minister Kevin Rudd soon after his election (in 2007). Participants, including the author, have been critical of its process and outcomes. See Lyn Carson, "2020 Summit: Meetings in the Foothills," *Australian Review of Public Affairs*, May 2008, accessed January 4, 2012, http://www.australianreview.net/ digest/2008/04/carson.html; see also chapter 2 of this book, where the 2020 Summit and the ACP are compared.

23. "Citizens' Assembly a Useless Gesture by a Gutless PM," *Sydney Morning Herald,* July 24, 2010.

24. Anne Twomey, "Citizens' Assemblies Work Fine—in Theory," *Sydney Morning Herald,* July 27, 2010.

25. Fred Cutler, Richard Johnston, R. Kenneth Carty, Andre Blais, and Patrick Fournier, "Deliberation, Information, and Trust: The British Columbia Citizens' Assembly as Agenda Setter," in *Designing Deliberative Democracy,* ed. Mark E. Warren and Hilary Pearse (Cambridge: Cambridge University Press, 2008), 166–91.

26. Richard Denniss, quoted in Australia Institute, "Delay Is Denial, It's Time to Act," news release, July 23, 2010, accessed January 4, 2012, http://www.cana.net.au/sites/default/files/AustInst_MediaRelease_230710.pdf.

27. Patricia Karvelas, "Citizens' Assembly a No-Go for MPS—ELECTION 2010," *Australian,* August 13, 2010.

28. Devine, "PM's So Sure Bob's Your Uncle."

29. Ben Cubby, "Both Parties Still Stuck in Climate Change Quagmire," *Sydney Morning Herald,* July 24–25, 2010.

30. Lenore Taylor, "New Policy, Same Old Delay on Carbon Price Scheme."

31. Greg Hunt, quoted in Australian Associated Press, "FED: Labor's Climate Policy Attacked."

32. Peter Hartcher, "Great Procrastinator Takes Reins of Inaction on Climate Change," *Sydney Morning Herald,* July 24–25, 2010, weekend edition.

33. Katie Lahey, CEO, Business Council of Australia, quoted in James Massola and Sid Maher, "Climate Change Policy Feels Heat—ELECTION 2010," *Weekend Australian,* July 24–25, 2010.

34. See, e.g., Galaxy, discussed in Simon Benson, "Voters Reject Julia Gillard's Citizens' Assembly," *Daily Telegraph* (Surry Hills, NSW), July 26, 2010, accessed January 4, 2012, http://www.news.com.au/features/federal-election/voters-reject-julia-gillards-citizens-assembly/story-e6frfllr-1225896774582.

35. Fran Kelly, on *Breakfast Program,* ABC Radio National, July 27, 2010; Phillip Coorey, "Support for ETS Dwarfs Backing for Assembly," *Sydney Morning Herald,* July 31–August 1, 2010, weekend edition.

36. Indeed, I conducted informal interviews in the marginal western Sydney seat of Lindsay and found that the support swung easily to convene a CA once the idea was properly described.

37. "Prince Planet," July 26, 2010.

38. Letter to the editor, *Sydney Morning Herald,* July 27, 2010.

39. Mark Bahnisch, "Julia Gillard's Climate Change Policy and Citizen Juries," *The Drum,* ABC Online, July 23, 2010, accessed January 4, 2012, http://blogs.abc.net.au/drumroll/2010/07/julia-gillards-climate-change-policy-and-citizen-juries.html.

40. Richard Denniss, Australia Institute, quoted in Cathy Alexander, "FED: Gillard Handballs Climate to the Public," *AAP Newsfeed,* July 23, 2010.

41. See University of Technology Sydney, "Australians Want Action on an ETS Now," news release, August 10, 2010, accessed January 4, 2012, http://www.newsroom.uts.edu.au/news/detail.cfm?ItemId=22663.

42. Carolyn Hendriks, "Citizens' Assembly on Climate May Turn Heat on Gillard," *Age* (Melbourne), July 27, 2010, accessed January 4, 2012, http://www.theage.com.au/opinion/politics/citizens-assembly-on-climate-may-turn-the-heat-on-gillard-20100725-10qej.html.

43. Lindsay Tanner, "Declaration of Open Government," *AGIMO Blog,* July 16, 2010, accessed January 4, 2012, http://agimo.govspace.gov.au/2010/07/16/declaration-of-open-government/.

44. Ron Lubensky, "A Policy By the People, For the People," *Sydney Morning Herald,* July 26, 2010.

45. Julia Gillard, "Part 2: PM Stands Firm on Mental Health," interview by political writers of *Age* (Melbourne), *Sydney Morning Herald*, August 13, 2010, accessed January 4, 2012, http://media.smh.com.au/opinion/national-times/part-2-pm-stands-firm-on-mental-health-1777309.html.

46. "We the Citizens," accessed January 4, 2012, http://www.wethecitizens.ie/.

CONCLUSION: THEORETICAL AND PRACTICAL IMPLICATIONS
OF THE CITIZENS' PARLIAMENT EXPERIENCE

Janette Hartz-Karp, Lyn Carson, John Gastil, and Ron Lubensky

It was evident from the outset that nothing would go as planned for the Australian Citizens' Parliament (ACP). When more than a third of those who received an invitation to participate rushed to their phones and computers to accept, the organizers knew the experience would be an exciting challenge for all. In the end, the ACP proved to be an important case study through which core hypotheses and accepted tenets of deliberative democracy were tested, and this book has reported the results of those tests. Its various authors have shown how deliberative exercises can lead to personal transformation and deep learning; however, many authors also have exposed the ACP's shortfalls as an instance of democratic deliberation.

In this conclusion, we review the findings of this book by addressing the central questions of this project. First, we reflect on what the ACP achieved and where it foundered. The second question asks about the character of deliberation the ACP generated. That, in turn, raises the question of what caused and resulted from the ACP's deliberation. After asking what the event means for critics of deliberation, we consider the efficacy of the methodological pluralism present in this volume. We conclude by reviewing the key practical insights the ACP has yielded regarding the design of deliberative democracy.

What Did the ACP Achieve?

In terms of intent, design, and execution, the ACP was firmly based on the principles and ideals of deliberative democracy. It was a mini-public acting on behalf of the whole community—in this instance, a whole nation. The participants had in-depth conversations on Australian politics, and they tried to speak with a coherent public voice so that the larger community and government could hear what they had to say. Given the external constraints they faced, they mostly succeeded.

Some aspects of the ACP were unique. It was initiated and run by a nongovernmental organization and a collaboration of academic researchers from multiple universities. The organizers and researchers had to do deliberative democracy in order to experiment with it. Citizens were brought into the mix at an early stage to frame the content of the proposed deliberations. Later, interested researchers from across the globe helped develop and analyze the data that were gathered. We hope that such a multifaceted collaboration becomes the norm, but it remains somewhat unusual.

Volunteers from across the nation played a variety of crucial support roles throughout the ACP. The deliberation process was innovative, involving pre-event regional meetings of participants and self-managed online deliberations involving many of those attending the face-to-face ACP in Canberra, as well as others not chosen in the final random selection. This Online Parliament developed proposals that provided the initial content for the face-to-face ACP, a four-day deliberative process that integrated a broad array of dialogic and deliberative techniques.

The goodwill and dedication to the task by both the participants and support team were outstanding, especially given the extreme difficulties of a highly oppressive heat wave, unprecedented, catastrophic bushfires that deeply affected participants, and a demanding agenda, day after day. Finally, the outcomes were more empowering than expected. As the ACP developed, an unexpected shared identity of "being Australian" evolved, unusual among Australians except at sporting events, which enabled participants to deliberate across political and cultural differences and arrive at a coherent voice. Additionally, many participants experienced transformational shifts in their political self-confidence, identity, and view of Australian politics as a result of participating in the ACP. A full year after the ACP had concluded, they still felt these changes within themselves.

At the same time, the ACP fell short of its aims. The organizers were unable to adequately sustain the commitment to participate from the first point of contact through to the main Canberra event. As with most minipublics, therefore, the recruitment effort yielded a near-random cross-section that approximated but could not quite match the target demographics. Likewise, the Online Parliament did not involve as many as initially hoped, and those who did participate tended to visit intermittently, rather than deeply engaging in the development of the proposals. In both the online and face-to-face events, the "charge," or frame of the deliberations—namely, reforming Australian politics and government—proved to be too broad to allow for in-depth deliberation on the more than fifty proposals that emerged.

There was insufficient time to unpack and reflect on the complexity of the task the participants faced. This challenge emerged in many of the chapters, which discuss the question of Aboriginal Australian identity and inclusion, the underdeveloped idea of civic education, and the vagueness of many proposals, which hinted at the public's judgment without making any firm recommendations. Thus, for example, the ACP's final list of recommendations included a small gesture toward reconciliation with Aboriginal Australians, but little more was possible given the ACP's limited space for truly open-hearted dialogue or in-depth discussion on this or any thorny aspect of Australian politics. The recognition of the complexity of their task may have contributed to the Citizen Parliamentarians' increased respect for government (chapter 9), which faces the same challenge of managing complex tasks efficiently.

The media coverage the ACP received was disappointing, but circumstance may have overwhelmed strategy. The organizers hoped to bring the event's deliberations to the attention of the broader community, and the run-up received good early coverage, particularly in local outlets. The main event, though, passed by largely unnoticed because it proved impossible to attract public attention while the bushfires dominated the media during the Canberra meetings.

In addition, the federal government did not appear directly influenced by the results of the ACP process, though they had officially opened the proceedings and formally received the findings on the last day in Canberra. Mini-publics such as the ACP—no matter how grandiose in scope and design—appear unlikely to achieve transformational change in terms of public policy making without extensive and impartial media coverage, more collaborative forms of democratic governance, and a stronger institutional foothold.[1]

What Kind of Deliberation Did the ACP Produce?

As outlined in the introduction, the ACP was designed to generate democratic deliberation by performing a series of demanding tasks, including randomly selecting participants; making them feel welcome and included; developing mutual respect and trust; then providing ample opportunities to carefully consider information from different viewpoints, bring deep values to the surface, discover a range of policy options, and collaboratively weigh them against participant-generated criteria to develop a coherent voice. Organizers put in place complex procedures to achieve these goals, particularly once the face-to-face meetings began in Canberra. Daily random seating was designed to diffuse the patterns of influence, and each small table was facilitated to improve the effectiveness of deliberation. Evening facilitator debriefs reflectively examined the process to highlight daily successes and difficulties.

However, most of the chapters were premised on the notion that the design of a deliberation is insufficient to determine deliberativeness. Understanding what should constitute ideal deliberation was addressed using diverse methodologies and different modes—social scientific, interpretive, and critical. Different ways of understanding deliberativeness included self-reports and observational data, recorded and transcribed table conversations analyzed qualitatively and quantitatively, and survey and Q-sort methodologies. These various takes on what constitutes deliberativeness are described below.

What participants and observers judged to be ideal deliberation was analyzed in chapter 7, which compared participant self-report survey data and observational approaches of third-party table observers. The analysis included the social processes of deliberation, including the spirit of equality, mutual response, and consideration of diverse views, as well as the analytic component, including comprehension of information and values, identification of solutions, weighting, and decision making. The analysis of responses highlighted discrepancies between participant self-reports of both the online and face-to-face deliberations, which were highly complimentary of both the social and analytic aspects of the ACP, and the observers' analyses, which were more skeptical, particularly of online discourse and overall discursive analytic rigor.

The kind of topic flow and influence constituting good deliberation was analyzed in chapter 11, using a computational approach to systematically measure the flow of language and ideas from the Online Parliament to the face-to-face ACP. The issues were tracked through a digital record of the thread of online discussions and the recorded and transcribed table conversations at the face-to-face ACP. Through computer-aided textual analysis, the researchers found a clear flow of deliberation from the online to the face-to-face deliberation, with the few exceptions traceable back to the influence of the expert panel.

Speaking-turn distribution, examined in chapter 9, was said to be the most basic of the principles of deliberation; that is, group deliberation cannot work if one or a few participants monopolize the conversation. The authors found the most equal participation occurred when participants discussed and rated the top policy options, described as the most important juncture of the ACP, but equality diminished before and after that day. In the end, the authors hit a note common to many chapters—that events like the ACP need to place more emphasis on participant training, in this case concerning techniques for better equalizing speaking turns.

A rich understanding of how participants appreciated good deliberation was examined in chapters 5 and 6. Chapter 5 used a storytelling approach, following one topic through the deliberative process. It found relatively few well-developed stories illustrating the exchange of reasons, with most on understanding the issues and grappling with the complexity. It suggested that participants need to unpack and reflect on what they said to each other, and for this they would need more time, more guidance from table facilitators, and an improved process design. Chapter 6 searched for stories as a way to vicariously witness the proceedings in order to understand what makes deliberation worthwhile. The researchers found stories had multiple purposes: they served a relational function, increased understanding about values, explained reasons for and against proposals, raised questions about power and inclusion, and helped articulate a shared vision—all important elements of deliberation.

Chapter 10 tested the deliberative presumption that participants really do influence one another—enabling the building of common ground. These researchers applied Q-sort methodology, administered at critical points throughout the ACP deliberative process, both online and face-to-face. The Q-sort results supported the presumption of democratic theory that people influence one another through interaction. This remained prominent even a year after the event, particularly for those who had felt most involved in the deliberations. Moreover, it found that online deliberation clearly impacted the content of the following in-person deliberation and hence acted as a powerful building block. The authors suggested that common ground—or here, convergence of judgments—bolstered by the development of a strong sense of common identity built trust, and, in this instance, resulted in increased trust in political institutions, even though the deliberation was designed to scrutinize the political status quo. The deliberative impacts were strong, both cognitively and affectively.

Chapter 12 took a different approach to investigating the presumption of peer influence. Given the daily random seating of participants at small tables, the researchers were able to use a dyadic regression analysis of pairings of participants who were assigned to the same table in order to examine how common ground was reached. The influence on policy attitudes on Day 3 of sitting together on one of those days was statistically significant, regardless of gender, age, and education level.

Finally, good deliberation needs to result in defensible outcomes. This was examined in chapter 15, which assessed whether the final recommendations were normatively defensible, practical or implementable, and well-informed and comprehensive. Though the authors noted the lack of definitive answers to these issues, they concluded that the ACP aptly displayed the potential of deliberative processes to contribute to a renewed political system, and in particular, the practice of democratic citizenship.

What Are Key Antecedents and Consequences of Deliberation?

The obvious antecedent to the ACP's deliberativeness was its design. This includes the likely influence of the deliberation, what organizers called their public "promise" as to what participants can expect from their participation. This was noted in the introduction, which described the purpose of the agenda and the repeated clarification of expectations. The importance of influence was also discussed in chapter 2, which compared an engagement on governance that was inspired and led by the prime minister, with the ACP, noting the reliance on expert knowledge and elite participants in the government's Summit. The ACP yielded less influence on public policy than the Summit. Whether or not, as described in chapter 20, the aborted climate-change deliberation proposed by the government was influenced by either of these initiatives, the errors made when proposing this deliberative political reform proved insurmountable.

Another enabler examined in the research was the role of the facilitator in face-to-face deliberation. As noted in other chapters, chapters 13 and 14, each using a different research methodology, assessed the role of the facilitator and found it was a critical enabler to effective deliberation.

It is claimed that media and broad public involvement is essential for a public deliberation to enhance its legitimacy. Those claims found support in chapter 19, where the role of the media was examined and found wanting. This was due to lack of funding and competing media attention on the unprecedented and destructive bushfires; the ACP media strategy was not as effective as hoped. Public deliberations like the ACP succeed or fail not just as a result of their internal quality, but also based on whether they have engaged the media and ultimately the broader public in helping them to think through the issues in at least a somewhat deliberative way. Examining what they termed "mediated meta-deliberation," deliberation about deliberation, the authors found that the ACP did not raise awareness about the outcomes it produced, but it had the potential to stimulate interest in inclusive, deliberative politics, though the coverage was unlikely to generate support for deliberative politics per se, nor to promote the soundness of this approach for addressing future Australian political conflicts. These issues would need to be central to a future media strategy, accompanied by research to better understand the event's deliberative impact.

In terms of consequences, the ideal outcomes of democratic deliberation include personal transformation, group learning, and social and political change. Many of the chapters referred to the group learning that occurred during the ACP, including the impact of peer influence and that of expert panels in increasing the learning of groups. With respect to transformation, one of the most surprising and oft noted outcomes of the ACP was the emergence of a common identity. Chapter 18 described this as the emergence of a superordinate identity of "being Australian," in terms of mateship, a "fair go" for all, and determination in the face of adversity—attributes traditionally linked to Australianness.

The issue of self-transformation also came to the fore. Chapter 17 described how the researchers helped participants assess the effect of the ACP and Online Parliament on their political and community lives. When surveyed a year later, participants reported changes in how they viewed themselves, politics, and public life; the results suggested that changes in attitudes were likely related to changes in behavior, though the authors noted more research is needed to pursue this.

Many of the transcribed conversations quoted throughout the chapters highlighted examples of social and political change and personal transformation. Although the ACP was unable to effect policy change or democratic change to a more deliberative mode, it impacted all those who participated in it in highly meaningful ways.

What of Deliberation's Critics?

This book has also addressed a number of key critiques of public deliberation. The first of these is the inevitability of unequal power—the "difference perspective," which expects that dominant majority interests will forever obscure or distort minority perspectives.[2] The introduction outlined how the agenda design attempted to address this, and chapter 9 analyzed the ACP's transcribed discussions to gauge the extent to which this was achieved. The introduction noted how the design of the agenda was framed to capture minority viewpoints. This included keeping the framing of the "charge" broad enough to capture all viewpoints (also described in chapters 15 and 16), the mixture of dialogic and deliberative sessions, the special facility of the 21st Century Dialogue software to capture and label minority viewpoints, and the daily facilitator debriefs to reflect on issues such as equity.

The ACP discussions analyzed in chapter 8 led to the conclusion that the agenda was more deliberative than dialogic, which inhibited the "building" function, engaging in difference to think more deeply about an issue and become more aware of its complexity.

Skepticism about public deliberation often comes from public officials and other decision makers. These critics doubt that ordinary citizens have the capacity to address complex issues, which are best dealt with by policy experts and other technocrats (see Chapter 20). The underlying task of the ACP and much of the research was to explore the capacity of ordinary citizens to consider a many-sided issue. None of the analyses, quantitative or qualitative, found that these ordinary citizens were not up to the task.

An insider critique—sometimes the anxiety of planners themselves—holds that deliberative events like the ACP have difficulty avoiding bias, which seeps into the event's issue framing and facilitation.[3] This was not found. The broad "charge," critiqued as too broad (e.g., chapter 15), was designed to avoid bias. Discourse analysis showed a clear alignment with the aims of the agenda for each day researched. Additionally, both chapters 13 and 14 highlighted that facilitator bias was not a factor, taking both analytic and social elements into account. This finding was also supported in the qualitative reporting of the lead facilitators in chapter 12.

Questions about the inevitability of bias, despite organizers' best efforts, with only some being seen to be problematic, were raised in chapter 16. The author's conclusion was that in practice, eliminating bias is extraordinarily difficult. The best practice would be to allow expressions of bias but to consistently and openly acknowledge them, and to give participants the skills of critical analysis and reflection to do so.

Was Methodological Pluralism Useful?

The ACP was the most rigorously researched public deliberation on record.[4] The myriad research techniques applied throughout the process—together with the international, multidisciplinary group of researchers analyzing the results—enabled testing several important hypotheses (sometimes for the first time) and generating many new ones. The ACP enabled some researchers to gather evidence in favor of using one research method over another, as in the case of the multiple approaches to studying deliberation herein. In other instances, different methods simply added depth to the understanding of what really went on, as in the multiple perspectives on diversity, disagreement, and the role of facilitators.

Complementary analyses provided alternative perspectives, each uncovering different nuances of the same phenomenon. Systematic statistical analyses alternately bolstered or questioned assertions made using more ethnographic approaches, which provided a thicker description than could quantitative summaries. Overall, the methodological variety yielded a textured mosaic that revealed many different facets of democratic deliberation at the ACP.

Where to Go from Here?

We conclude by emphasizing what we consider the three most important practical lessons from this study of the ACP. These concern diversity, training, and institutionalization. As to the first, the ACP achieved a level of demographic and attitudinal diversity that proved essential to its success. Too often, advocates and critics both presume deliberative processes orient toward a common public voice, but such an outcome should come as a remarkable accomplishment, not a fait accompli. It was the diversity of the ACP that led to some of its most memorable moments—a measure of reconciliation between white and Aboriginal Australians and a trans-generational affirmation of the importance of youth civic education.

Even with a diverse body of committed citizens, however, the uneven experience visible across the different discussion tables at the ACP suggests the need for more rigorous training. The role and capacity of both facilitators and participants are critical to deliberative effectiveness. Despite the half-day facilitator training session immediately prior to the ACP, earlier information sent to them regarding their role, the ACP purpose and process, and detailed written descriptions received at the training session, as well as daily facilitator debriefs during the ACP, the research highlighted such a wide range of facilitator tactics in managing their groups that it appeared their different professional experiences yielded distinct ideas about the ACP's purpose and process. More extensive and innovative facilitator training, focusing on the standards required for that critical role, would have likely normalized the participant experience. However, we have to concede that training alone might not be enough to interrupt facilitators' personal styles. More important was the training the participants received. The initial orientation through regional meetings proved invaluable, but many of those appearing at the Online Parliament or in the face-to-face Canberra meetings did not have the benefit of that preliminary workshop. In all likelihood, each participant would have benefitted from a more thorough review of the methods and purposes of public deliberation—a process that can take an entire day in comparable events.[5]

Finally, we believe that events like the ACP have an important role to play in the history of democracy by rekindling public and public officials' confidence in the ability of lay citizens to play a direct and active role in the policy-making process. That said, the time has come to build on demonstration projects like these and design firm institutional footings for future deliberations. It took the criminal jury system centuries to evolve into the taken-for-granted deliberative process it has become in many countries, and even in the accelerated time scales of the modern world, deliberative-democratic innovations will take decades to cohere.

A compelling story about the public's deliberative capacity is emerging from successes like the Participatory Budgeting rules in Brazil, the Citizens' Assemblies in Canada, the Citizens' Initiative Review in Oregon, and Citizens' Juries and Deliberative Polls across the globe.[6] One common theme in many successful projects is an effort to link deliberation with existing political institutions, community structures, and cultural norms to create fewer isolated deliberative events and more comprehensively deliberative democratic systems.[7]

Given Australia's prominent role in democratic innovation, it is time for Australia to normalize its own deliberative process. In doing so, it will hopefully become one of a growing number of nations, states, and localities to experience the transformative potential of deliberative democracy.

NOTES

1. On the importance of embeddedness, see Elena Fagotto and Archon Fung, *Sustaining Public Engagement: Embedded Deliberation in Local Communities*, Occasional Research Paper from Everyday Democracy and the Kettering Foundation (East Hartford, Conn.: Everyday Democracy and the Kettering Foundation, 2009), accessed January 21, 2012, http://kettering .org/news_room/news_listing/new-report-from-elena-fagotto-and-archon-fung-sustaining -public-engagement.

2. The most widely cited version of this critique may be Lynn M. Sanders, "Against Deliberation," *Political Theory* 25 (1997): 347–76.

3. Amy Lang, "But Is It for Real? The British Columbia Citizens' Assembly as a Model of State-Sponsored Citizen Empowerment," *Politics and Society* 35 (2007): 35–70.

4. This approach was inspired, in part, by its precursor. Maxwell McCombs and Amy Reynolds, eds., *The Poll with a Human Face: The National Issues Convention Experiment in Political Communication* (Mahwah, N.J.: Lawrence Erlbaum, 1999).

5. The five-day Oregon Citizens' Initiative Review devotes almost its entire first day to such orientation. See "Citizens' Initiative Review," accessed January 30, 2012, http://healthy democracyoregon.org/citizens-initiative-review.

6. See, respectively, Brian Wampler, *Participatory Budgeting in Brazil: Contestation, Cooperation, and Accountability* (University Park: Pennsylvania State University Press, 2009); Mark E. Warren and Hilary Pearse, eds., *Designing Deliberative Democracy: The British Columbia Citizens' Assembly* (Cambridge: Cambridge University Press, 2008); and John Gastil and Katie Knobloch, *Evaluation Report to the Oregon State Legislature on the 2010 Oregon Citizens' Initiative Review* (Salem, Ore.: Oregon House Rules Committee, 2010). For examples of numerous Citizens' Juries, Deliberative Polls, and other public engagement processes, reference the online repository http://www.participedia.net.

7. On the interplay of deliberation at different levels of society and government, see John Parkinson and Jane Mansbridge, *Deliberative Systems: Deliberative Democracy at the Large Scale* (New York: Cambridge University Press, 2012).

CONTRIBUTORS

Editors

Lyn Carson (PhD, Southern Cross University) is a professor in the Business School at the University of Sydney. Several of her chapters were written during her time with the United States Studies Centre at the University of Sydney and with the University of Western Sydney. She co-authored *Random Selection in Politics* with Brian Martin and has written dozens of chapters, journal articles, and handbooks on deliberative democracy and civic engagement. As a former elected representative she has a deep interest in experimenting with robust decision-making methods that involve the entire community. Carson is the essay editor of the *Journal of Public Deliberation* and a director of the newDemocracy Foundation.

John Gastil (PhD, University of Wisconsin–Madison) is a professor in the Department of Communication Arts and Sciences at the Pennsylvania State University. His books include *The Jury and Democracy, The Group in Society, Political Communication and Deliberation, By Popular Demand*, and *Democracy in Small Groups*. He also co-edited *The Deliberative Democracy Handbook* and *Democracy in Motion*. He studies the intersection of political communication, group behavior, and democratic theory. His current projects include an intensive study of the Oregon Citizens' Initiative Review process. Gastil lives in State College, Pennsylvania, which has reconnected him with his Quaker cultural roots.

Janette Hartz-Karp (PhD, University of California, Los Angeles) is a professor at the Curtin University Sustainability Policy (CUSP) Institute, Western Australia. She combines deliberative democracy practice (design, strategic support, and facilitation) with research and publication in articles and book chapters in a broad range of areas (e.g., sustainability, education, and digital citizenship). Deliberative democracy initiatives she has designed and stewarded have been recognized internationally, such as Geraldton 2029 and Beyond, which won a 2011 UN-sponsored LivCom Award for participation and empowerment and was a 2011 Reinhard Mohn Prize finalist.

Ron Lubensky is a doctoral candidate in the School of Humanities and Communication Arts at the University of Western Sydney. His thesis "Citizens Make Sense in Deliberative Activity," based on observation and analysis of the Australian Citizens' Parliament, explores public deliberation from a constructionist perspective, suggesting that it is time for fresh and compelling narratives about the experience of public engagement. Lubensky is the assistant editor of the *Journal of Public Deliberation*. Before awakening to the potential of deliberative democracy, he had an eclectic career in interactive media design and organizational and technology-mediated learning. He lives in Melbourne, Australia.

Authors

Patrick Anderson is a PhD candidate at Curtin University's Sustainability Policy Institute. His research focuses on "civic consciousness"—an innate sense of altruism, comradeship, wisdom, and civic responsibility that tends to emerge when citizens deliberate on matters of political significance.

Luisa Batalha (PhD, Uppsala University) is a postdoctoral research fellow at the Centre for Deliberative Democracy and Global Governance at the Australian National University. She is trained as a social psychologist and is currently investigating the links between deliberation and psychological change.

Luca Belgiorno-Nettis is the executive director of Transfield Holdings, chairman of the Biennale of Sydney, and chairman of the Arts Advisory Committees at UTS and UWS. He has a degree in architecture and a postgraduate diploma in urban estate management. He is the founder of the newDemocracy Foundation, a not-for-profit research organization focused on political reform.

Laura W. Black (PhD, University of Washington) is an associate professor in the School of Communication Studies at Ohio University. She studies public deliberation, dialogue, and conflict in small groups and is specifically interested in how personal storytelling functions in public forums.

Joseph A. Bonito (PhD, University of Illinois at Urbana-Champaign) is a professor in the Department of Communication at the University of Arizona. His research focuses on participation in small-group discussion and decision making.

John S. Dryzek (PhD, University of Maryland) is an Australian Research Council Federation fellow and professor of political science at the Centre for Deliberative Democracy and Global Governance at the Australian National University. He is the author of several books on the theory and practice of democracy, environmental politics, and climate change.

Jennifer Ervin is a doctoral student in the Department of Communication at the University of Arizona. Her primary research interests include small-group processes and decision making, with an emphasis on influence processes and participation.

Andrea Felicetti is a PhD student at the Centre for Deliberative Democracy and Global Governance at the Australian National University. His main interest is deliberative democratic theory and practice, and he is currently working on deliberative assemblies as well as on the investigation of deliberative capacities in our societies.

Kath Fisher (PhD, University of Western Sydney) is a lecturer at Southern Cross University specializing in community-engaged learning and critically reflective practice. She is also an experienced facilitator with particular expertise in deliberative democracy. Fisher has designed and facilitated a number of citizens' juries for local councils wishing to consult their communities on complex challenges such as climate action planning.

Max Hardy is a director at Twyfords, a consulting firm based in Wollongong, New South Wales, that specializes in collaborative governance and community engagement. An experienced and popular facilitator, Max enjoys designing and facilitating collaborative and deliberative processes on the most complex of issues and draws heavily on appreciative inquiry to inform his work.

Katherine R. Knobloch (PhD, University of Washington) is an assistant professor and the associate director of the Center for Public Deliberation in the Department of Communication Studies at Colorado State University. Her work focuses on evaluating the quality of deliberative public projects as well as on how deliberative events affect the attitudes and actions of participants and the wider public.

Li Li (PhD, Ohio University) is an assistant professor in the Department of Communication and Journalism at the University of Wyoming. She studies instructional communication and mainly focuses on the influences of culture, persuasion, and technology on student learning.

Ian Marsh (PhD, Harvard University) is a visiting professor at the ANZSOG-ANU Institute for Policy and an adjunct professor at the Australian Innovation Research Centre at the University of Tasmania. His most recent study, *Democratic Decline and Democratic Renewal: Political Change in Britain, Australia, and New Zealand* (co-authored with Raymond Miller), was recently published by Cambridge University Press.

Renee A. Meyers (PhD, University of Illinois) was a professor in the Department of Communication at the University of Wisconsin–Milwaukee. She passed away in March 2012 after having contributed to this volume. Her research focused on small-group decision making and argumentation, and she authored more than seventy published works in her lifetime.

Simon Niemeyer (PhD, Australian National University) is an Australian Research Council future fellow based at the Centre for Deliberative Democracy and Global Governance at the Australian National University. In addition to his research on preference change during deliberation, he has published in environmental politics, climate change governance, and political theory.

Eike Mark Rinke is a doctoral candidate and research associate in the Department of Media and Communication Studies and the Mannheim Centre for European Social Research (MZES) at the University of Mannheim in Germany. He studies normative aspects of political communication with a particular interest in mediated public deliberation and comparative research.

Brian Sullivan is the founder of Practical Evolution, LLC, where he designs web, mobile, and face-to-face applications and activities that help groups think together so that they can act together. CivicEvolution is his project to bring these capabilities to civic engagement.

Luc Tucker is a PhD candidate in economics at the University of Warwick. His main areas of study are peer effects in networks and the economic impact of elected representatives.

Anna Wiederhold (PhD, Ohio University) is an assistant professor in the Department of Communication Studies at the University of Nevada, Reno. Her interests in organizational communication and public policy have focused her studies around deliberation, conflict, and interorganizational network building.

John Wilkerson (PhD, University of Washington) is a professor of political science at the University of Washington and director of the Center for American Politics and Public Policy. He specializes in legislative institutions and behavior and computational approaches to the study of politics.

Fletcher Ziwoya (PhD, Ohio University) is an adjunct professor at Ohio University. He previously worked as a journalist in Malawi, and he studies grassroots participation in democratic processes.

INDEX

Page numbers in italics signify tables and figures.

RDD
RHETORIC AND DEMOCRATIC DELIBERATION

EDITED BY CHERYL GLENN AND J. MICHAEL HOGAN

THE PENNSYLVANIA STATE UNIVERSITY

Books in the series:

www.ingramcontent.com/pod-product-compliance
Lightning Source LLC
Chambersburg PA
CBHW021850020426
42334CB00013B/269